JOHN HILLER
Pitcher

TIGERS

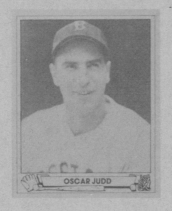

OSCAR JUDD

CUBS

OF

Astros

TERRY PUHL

GIANTS

KEN MacKENZIE   pitcher

★ AAGBL ★

MARGARET CALLAGHAN
Infield

Astros

PITCHER
ASTROS   TOPPS

★ AAGBL ★

HELEN CALLAGHAN
Outfield

PAUL HODGSON   1B

SS-OF

Blue Jays   BOB BAILOR

TED BOWSFIELD
Pitcher   Los Angeles Angels

AL

8 JIM McKEAN

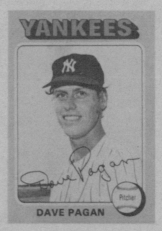

YANKEES

Dave Pagan   Pitcher

DAVE PAGAN

DAVE McKAY

Goodwin Rosen

THE GOODY ROSEN EDITION

NO. *52* OF *200*

—DOUBLE DUSTJACKET—
FIRST BOOKS OFF THE PRESS

HEROES, BUMS AND ORDINARY MEN

Best wishes.

DAN TURNER

HEROES, BUMS AND ORDINARY MEN

PROFILES IN CANADIAN BASEBALL

Dan Turner

DOUBLEDAY CANADA LIMITED, TORONTO

Design: Don Fernley
Typesetting: Compeer Typographic Services Limited
Baseball cards courtesy of Randall Scott Echlin

Canadian Cataloguing in Publication Data

Turner, Dan
   Heroes, bums and ordinary men

ISBN 0-385-25189-0

1. Baseball players – Canada – Biography.
2. Baseball players – Biography.   I. Title.

GV865.A1T87 1988   796.357′092′2   C88-094185-5

Printed and bound in Canada

Published by Doubleday Canada Limited,
105 Bond Street, Toronto, Ontario, M5B 1Y3

Pages 143–145 from *Ten Lost Years 1929–1939*, by Barry Broadfoot. Copyright © 1973, by Barry Broadfoot. Published by Doubleday Canada Ltd. Reprinted by permission of Doubleday Canada Ltd.

Page 149–50 from *100% Cracked Wheat*, by Denis Gruending. Copyright © 1983 by Denis Gruending. Published by Coteau Books. Reprinted by permission.

CONTENTS

APPRECIATION

Whether you drink beer or not and how much you drink is your own business, as long as you're old enough to be legal. So let's get this straight: I'm not asking you to go through a couple of cases of beer a night. Beer, like an alcoholic beverage, should be handled with care.

Having said that, if you are thoughtfully contemplating a cold one anytime in the next little while, I'd appreciate it if you'd consider something brewed by Labatt's: Blue, 50, John Labatt Classic, whatever.

What? The author as a beer huckster? Let me explain. The chances of me criss-crossing North America to talk to the people I had to connect with to write a book centered around Canadian ballplayers — and to get some decent pictures of those players — was zilch until Labatt's came along. If the company hadn't agreed to help finance this book it either wouldn't have gotten off the ground or you'd have been asked to shell out $40 for it instead of $24.95.

There are a lot of kids and adults I know who couldn't have afforded $40, and I am deeply appreciative to Labatt's for coming through. The company took it on as a project because it will do almost anything to help revitalize baseball in Canada. Baseball fans have some awareness of this because of the company's ownership of the Toronto Blue Jays and sponsorship of the Montreal Expos. But if you take a closer look you'll find that Labatt's was instrumental in getting the National Baseball Institute — Canada's first major college baseball program for Canadian players — underway. And that it is heavily involved in sponsoring amateur baseball teams in Canada.

It behooves me to say thank you.

Dan Turner

Labatt Breweries of Canada appreciates the contribution Dan Turner has made to Canadian Baseball through the writing of this book.

We hope you enjoy its contents and we are pleased to have been able to contribute in part to its existence.

Labatt's

Pat Borders pays homage to the sponsor. (Terry Vollum)

ACKNOWLEDGMENTS

During the late winter of 1987 I joined Alje Kamminga, *Ottawa Citizen* sports editor, and Nelson Skuce, then the *Citizen's* managing editor, for lunch at the Silk Roads Restaurant on Sparks Street in Ottawa. (Yes, the same Nelson Skuce who went to spring training with the Toronto Maple Leafs in 1957, where manager Dixie Walker raved publicly that the Ottawa kid had the best curveball of any pitcher in camp.) Skuce and Kamminga not only paid for lunch, but agreed to kick off this book with a series of *Citizen* features that allowed me to research the first eleven chapters. I am deeply grateful.

Terry Vollum, of Mid-Town Sounds in Toronto, steered me toward help with production costs and boosted me every step of the way, even using his camera when he had to. Paul Beeston, the Blue Jays' VP, offered good advice and let me drop his name around town. He also pointed to Labatt's, without whose help I couldn't have traveled beyond Nepean. Don (Ditch) Dickerson, Terry Vollum's partner at Mid-Town Sounds, hooked me up with Barry Snetsinger at Labatt's. Snetsinger gave an enthusiastic yes to my proposal that the company help out with the book, then departed. John Millar kept Labatt's behind us.

John Neale at Doubleday Canada tied everything together, shook his head and said, "Sure, I bet you can pull this off, maybe. Hell, yes." Michael Rafelson signed on as chief photographer for a stipend much smaller than that to which he has become accustomed. Most of the color photos were taken by me; all of the superb color photos were taken by Michael.

Randall Echlin, secretary of the Canadian Baseball Hall of Fame, pitched in with his goodwill and extensive baseball-card collection. Kelly McBride, who keeps the Hall ticking over at its temporary Ontario Place location, fielded my queries and came back with helpful replies. Deborah Smith and Suzanne Loninger of Ottawa, experts in retouching and restoration, saved several photos. Steve Proulx, the kindly sex god at the *Ottawa Citizen* library, bailed me out on several occasions, asking only that the title be changed to *The Steve Proulx Baseball Book*.

I needed help finding photos and got it from Paul Godfrey and Bob Carroll at the *Toronto Sun*, Jean Bradshaw and John Honderich at the Toronto *Star* and Brian Kappler at the Montreal *Gazette*. Pat Gillick said "Anything you want, call me," and I did.

Hugh Riopelle of Air Canada got me out to see Dave Shury. My wife

Gayle Turner stole from her hope chest to send me to California to see Helen St. Aubin. Neil MacCarl, Trent Frayne and Earl McRae helped prep me for interviews. Joanne Sunstrum spent weekends battling with my computer, punching in several chapters when I was on the road. Ottawa restaurateur Joe Ross, who knows more about the history of the minor leagues than most people do about the majors, did research.

Canada's most stimulating baseball family, John and Angela Wing and Co., of Sarnia, made me keep going. Beyond their interests in the law, theater, comedy, music and academe, they wanted to know more about Canadian ballplayers than they were finding on gravestones. Dunc Macintyre, who directs the Detroit Tigers from his Windsor law office, gave tips on titling. Ron Girard and Ellen Wright, to whom I had commitments, kindly waited. Sharon Roepke (PO Box 3675, Flint, Mich.) sent me two sets of her copyrighted baseball cards and her book *Diamond Gals* to fill me in on the All-American Girls Professional Baseball League.

Speaking of baseball cards, my thanks to the people at Topps, O-Pee-Chee (London, Ontario), Donruss, Star and TCMA for producing the fine cards which adorn the inside endpapers.

Charis Wahl edited the book, saving it on several occasions from death by excess. Finally I have to thank Wendy, Kate and Jody Vollum, my second family, for providing advice, love, a bed and sustenance as I made my way around the continent huntin' up all them guys and the lady. I hope I did you all proud.

Dan Turner
Ottawa
October 4, 1988

INTRODUCTION

Heroes: These folks weren't war heroes. They weren't even baseball super-heroes in the order of Babe Ruth, Ted Williams and Stan Musial. But there is something heroic about heading south to dance the high wire, especially when you've never had your feet more than a few inches off the ground.

Bums: We're all bums some of the time. Was Doug Frobel a bum because he didn't live up to expectations? Was Reggie Cleveland a bum because he pickled the latter part of his career in malt and hops? Was Oscar Judd a bum because he threw at Jackie Robinson? You choose. You may decide that Goody Rosen is the only bum in the book — Goody played for the sacred Bums of Brooklyn. And then you may not.

Ordinary Men: When I was five years old my mother took me to the circus, and from a distance the clowns looked like magical creatures from another world. After it was over she took me up close to see one, and the clown shook my hand. He had hair on his arms, like my father. He was . . . one of us. So are these people, and it's kind of nice.

Warning: There is a woman in here. Which screws up the title, all right. The title should have been *Heroes, Bums, Ordinary Men and Helen Callaghan*. We didn't have room.

Further Warning: There are Americans in here: Bill Lee, Woodie Fryman, Bob Bailor, Mack Jones, Rocky Nelson. They're here because Canadians liked them. They're as much North as South.

The book is primarily about Canadian ballplayers. Don't let that scare you. It may be true that there has never been a Canadian ballplayer worth more to the record keepers than a couple of Babe Ruth's pinstripes. But that doesn't mean our northern brigade has lacked fiber. They fought their way through snow and clumsy coaching to get where they got.

Most of the people inside have been off the playing field for a while, meaning they've been able to regain some sense of humanity. They've had a chance to roll life over their tongues a bit and ponder the aftertaste.

Most of the guys still out there on the playing field tend to be a bit one-dimensional. They lead a difficult existence when they're there, constantly threatened by failure. They live out other people's fantasies. Mobs can get cruel when you undermine their fantasies. Boys get hardened young in the dugout. It was a pleasure to see how much ballplayers grow when they get away from the field.

10

The final product is the culmination of an odyssey that was completed over two years. I made my way from Moncton to Vancouver, North Battleford to Dunedin, turning over rocks, looking for baseballers who've been special to us. Some players I visited will be familiar even to younger fans: Fergie Jenkins, Terry Puhl, Rob Ducey. Some were well known back before the Second World War: Phil Marchildon, Goody Rosen. And some others, including people you may never have heard of before, will, I hope, be worth meeting.

It's not your patriotic duty to be interested. But when it comes to baseball, a little Canadiana can be fun. Bill Humber made the history fun in *Cheering for the Home Team*. W. P. Kinsella made the fantasy fun in *Shoeless Joe, The Iowa Baseball Confederacy* and *The Further Adventures of Slugger McBatt*. Mordecai Richler even made the underlying nastiness of a friendly softball game fun in *St. Urbain's Horsemen*. So I hope this is fun.

It's about making your way south, standing on the edge of a ball diamond filled with ballplayers who have been nurtured in the game for years, and saying: "Can I play?" We've all done something like that, eh? It's scary. Sometimes they say no.

Dan Turner

1

TEASING THE GODS

Toronto, Ontario
July 1, 1987

"It breaks your heart. It was designed to break your heart. The game begins in the spring, when everything else begins again, and it blossoms in the summer, filling in the afternoons and evenings, and then as soon as the chill rain comes, it stops and leaves you to face the fall alone."

A. Bartlett Giamatti

The Expos in 1981, the Blue Jays in 1985: RIP. Each of these ghostly squadrons needed to win only one final game to put a Canadian-based team into the World Series for the first time. In both cases their opponents had to scrape their backs from the wall. The 1981 Dodgers and then the 1985 Royals needed to fight back and win two straight games to vanquish the northern hordes. Both did and both did it cruelly, on Canadian soil.

In Montreal, the first time, it felt like a kick in the stomach. But in that one, at least, the players appeared to have some control over their own destiny. In Toronto it was more soul-destroying because the spirits got involved. If you didn't know this, you may as well know it now: that Toronto game was over before it began.

On October 16, 1985, your reporter awoke with a terrible sense of foreboding and spent much of the afternoon staring out his hotel window at a sky filled with bruised clouds. Surely, he thought, his mind should open wide to the Blue Jays' ever-so-giddy prospects and relegate the long-dead Expos to the scrapbook of the heart.

But the mind couldn't help drifting back to the autumn of 1981. Autumn belongs to Canada. There's a red maple leaf in the middle of our flag, which makes this clear. Strange, then, that for many of us the annual death ritual lying at the very core of autumn is best evoked by the mention of two more southerly names: Steve Rogers and Rick Monday.

Cynics will say that the names Steve Rogers and Rick Monday are foreign, which is rubbish. Steve Rogers may have had some tenuous connection with Jefferson City, Missouri, and Rick Monday with Batesville, Arkansas, but anyone with a passing interest in the earth's crust or free trade knows how closely these places are linked to the Canadian Shield.

The same scoffing fools will pooh-pooh baseball itself (as though it were not greater than music, the theater and literature combined) and turn to the poetry of Baudelaire for their annual dose of autumn ennui. Well, Baudelaire lived in Paris and couldn't bunt, so you can have him.

Steve Rogers, on the other hand, was both a jock and an artiste who possessed a number of pitches Rick Monday couldn't hit for distance. But Rogers chose to throw him one he could, which Monday, in turn, chose to crush. And there is the nub of all that is sad about a Canadian autumn.

The clouds were just as bruised back on October 19, 1981, as they would be on October 16, 1985. The National League Championship Series was even at two games apiece. The Expos had taken a 2-1 lead in games over the Dodgers in the three-out-of-five series. But just as the Jays would do four years later, the Expos proceeded to lose the fourth game at home to force a deciding encounter. The final game was rained out on the Sunday and delayed for twenty-six minutes on the Monday because of rain again; there were forecasts of snow.

Ray Burris started for the Expos, and was superb. Fernando Valenzuela started for the Dodgers, and had four pitches working so well that he was just short of unhittable.

The score was 1-1 at the end of eight, and Burris was exhausted. Expos manager Jim Fanning brought in Rogers. Rogers was not a reliever. He was a starter used to four days of rest between outings. In this case he had had three, having won a splendid five-hitter to give the Expos their second win of the series.

Rogers, a demonstrative, often fretful man on the mound, looked frazzled and ineffective. The second batter of the inning, Ron Cey, took him deep to the track in left, which should have served as a warning that something was terribly wrong. Rogers grimaced. Woodie Fryman, the left-handed veteran, and Jeff Reardon, the right-handed strikeout artist, were warming up in the bull pen. But Fanning stuck with Rogers against Monday, who had, after all, struck out in four of his five Series at-bats.

Rogers got two strikes on the left-hander. Then Monday drove a fastball deep to right center field into a spot in the stands that to this day remains the focal point of Olympic Stadium.

Rogers later snarled in the clubhouse that at Monday's advanced age of

13

thirty-five, his bat speed was so slow that a fastball was the only pitch he could have put out of the park. He never explained why, if that were the case, he had thrown one.

What did this have to do with the Jays on October 19, 1985? Why would this memory engender such an overwhelming sense of foreboding?

Well, only two days earlier, Dave Stieb, ace of the Blue Jays pitching staff, had sat in the dugout and confided to your reporter that not only was Steve Rogers a good friend, but that Stieb shared Rogers' way of thinking and liked his style on the mound. Stieb has changed in the last couple of years, but in 1985 he was the American League's most devoted adherent to the Rogers style.

The style in question has always been the bane of those who deem it their duty to guard . . . what? To guard the stillness of the soul at the core of the baseball universe. There is a modicum of whirling and dancing and whapping in baseball, but when you get by all that it is more like yoga than football.

Stieb and Rogers, while both master craftsmen, had nevertheless betrayed a fretfulness when anything went wrong that in professional baseball players is seen as self-indulgence—a betrayal of the fragile team sense struggling to get a grip on a largely individualistic game. There are egos all over the field, and they must be gathered together for battle. The pitcher must pay a price for enjoying center stage—he is not allowed to be precious: he must wear the team mask. The mask either can be blank or can glare at the batter. It cannot glare at teammates or at itself. It must reflect strength, resolution and invulnerability, and continues to do so even when base hits are stinging the field like arrows, and the battle is surely lost.

Stieb and Rogers had always given the impression they would prefer stage paint to the team mask. From the beginning of their careers they had dared to show their emotions on the mound—to the point, one suspects, that they would bay at the moon between batters if they felt like it. But the team mask does not bay. Nor grin, writhe or sigh. Nor otherwise show signs it can be distracted from the team goal, to vanquish. Blue Jays general manager Pat Gillick, the Blue Jays' vice-president for baseball, once told Stieb that as talented as he was, he was not pleasant for a baseball man to watch: "You're either mad at yourself, a teammate or an umpire." Not enough stillness of soul.

Just as the very establishment of the Expos and Jays on foreign soil had once been troubling to the baseball universe, so in the first half of the eighties was the deportment of these teams' number-one starters. There-

Dave fought the umpires, his nature and the gods. (Toronto Star)

Steve knew there was only one pitch Rick Monday could hit out. (Ottawa *Citizen*)

fore, seeing these two men tied together at the soul, pitching under the same brooding cloud conditions four years apart—keeping in mind what had happened the first time—made one apprehensive enough.

But having both of them throwing with three days' rest in the critical final games of a series that had once appeared won only to become tied was . . . crying out for lightning bolts. Baseball's soul was rumbling. The lesson had not sunk in north of the border. The punishment would come again.

Shaken by the inevitability of it all, your reporter put in a call to Richard Griffin, the Expos publicist, and told him exactly what was going to happen and why. Griffin was quick to pick up the vibrations and said he'd call his bookie and get a bet down on the Royals.

"But who," he wondered, "will play the role of Rick Monday?" After some pondering, he came up with a name. "Pat Sheridan."

Like Monday before him, Sheridan had been overmatched throughout the championship series, having gone 1-for-16. In the fourth inning that night Stieb chose to throw Sheridan a fastball that Sheridan chose to hit over the right center-field fence. Where else? The blow gave the Royals a lead they'd never relinquish.

Others will offer more clinical reasons for the desolate ending to such a fine season — that the Jays left twenty-five runners stranded in their final twenty-seven innings of play, for instance. That's the mathematics of it.

But that's not what unites baseballers in English and French Canada in a mystical understanding of the death ritual at the core of autumn — an understanding that all the pretty leaves can't camouflage. Rogers and the Dodgers, now Stieb and the Royals.

Baudelaire be damned. Baseball is a mystical game.

2

THE SPACEMAN

Moncton, New Brunswick
July 12, 1987

He's the freest man in the world, Bill Lee: ballplayer, politician and, most of all, the Spaceman.

And what a guy is Bill.

He's a pug-nosed eccentric who passionately loves baseball, but he's given the finger to the major leagues and plays sandlot ball for the Moncton Mets.

He's a man of outspoken social and political beliefs. But he's kissed off the mainline political parties, both American and Canadian. He's running for president of the United States on behalf of that tiny gang of spoofers, the Rhinoceros Party. He eschews money, rules and the punching of clocks. He's got a gorgeous, easy-going second wife, lightly freckled and rich. Not to mention three kids, who live with his first wife during the runny-nosed gloom of winter before gloriously reappearing to play with him when the sun shines.

Oh, free rhymes with Lee, as in Bill.

Abbie Hoffman, Bob Dylan, Margaret Trudeau, John Lennon—all revolutionaries or flower children of the sixties, all gone now. Disappeared, tired, neutered or mute.

Not the Spaceman, who, when asked why he lives mostly in Canada now, came out with the rationale that has eluded Canadian nationalists for decades: "I've got a lot of plaid shirts."

Not the Spaceman, muffler of bats and perennial nettle to the Establishment, forty years old and still running free.

Oh, please Lord, not Bill Lee.

The enemy, of course, is age. If Bill Lee stays young, we all stay young. If he can't do it — jogging, eating health food, avoiding all forms of stress,

Some ballplayers play between the white lines. Bill prefers the Cartesian coordinates. (Dan Turner)

seeing the silly side of everything—what hope is there for anyone on life's main assembly line?

But Moncton's Kiwanis Park, an hour before the start of a doubleheader, presents a scene so pure, so innocent, that you wonder why you ever doubted that Peter Pan could stay young forever.

There's Bill, out in center field by the fence. You can see he's as gray as your banker now, and even—my goodness—a bit stooped. As all the young men around him swat and shag, swat and shag, sweating and grunting earnestly in preparation for the game, Bill plays catch with a little girl.

It is his ten-year-old daughter, Katy, and he is teaching her how not to throw like a . . . well, how to throw like a player should. He is showing her the grip for the sinker, explaining the effect of the seams on the rotation.

He will do this not just for his own children. People in Moncton will tell you he's a Pied Piper with young ballplayers, teaching and encouraging the weak-of-arm and strong with equal enthusiasm. He likes working with kids, and he'd like to open a baseball camp some day, he says, suggesting his charges would flourish under a patented Bill Lee mix of stoicism and hedonism.

"These kids would have to get up in the morning, make their beds just like in the Marines, have nothing but fruit and juices during their morning routine, then have their big meal and rest up in the afternoon, then play games until nine or ten at night . . . " An impish smile sweeps across his face. "Then they gotta drink beer until we tuck them in."

For a few seconds he revels in the idea of what a Bill Lee baseball camp would be like, then impatiently tosses it away. "I'm not ready to quit playing yet—I'm just not ready to stop. Playing baseball keeps you young, you know," he says with a frown. "You don't age if you keep playing. Look at Pete Rose. He quit, and now he looks like a turnip."

Well, maybe Bill's right. Maybe you don't age. After all, the people who run major-league baseball didn't turn their backs on Bill Lee in 1982 when he was thirty-five because he was too old. Quite the opposite — they thought he was too immature. He'd said that he liked to sprinkle marijuana on his pancakes. In 1981, he'd injured himself at a crucial point in the season by supposedly falling over a cat.

That wasn't the whole story, he admits now. "My first wife and I hadn't been getting along. I went out at six in the morning, bent on reconciliation. So I jogged over to the apartment of this girl I'd been seeing to tell her it was over.

"Sure there was a cat involved—a black cat. I nearly fell when it came out from under a parked car just as I turned the corner to her house. But

I kept my feet. Except then the girl was asleep upstairs in the triplex she lived in, and I tried to scale the wall, but with the black cat and all, I fell on the wrought-iron fence underneath and banged up my iliac crescent."

The reconciliation failed, he says, because his wife left town before he could get out of the hospital and get his message to her. So he remarried. But not to the girl in the apartment.

The Montreal Expos endured this incident, categorizing it, perhaps, as a "dangerous but permissible hobby," the way the Kansas City Royals did in 1987 with left fielder Bo Jackson's craving to be hugged by middle linebackers.

But the year after the cat incident the Expos dismissed second baseman Rodney Scott for a variety of reasons: he was often irascible, he couldn't hit right handers, and all too often he had an illegal smile.

The release of his friend infuriated Lee, causing him to rip up what he could of his double-knit uniform (you can look silly wrestling with polyester) and stomping off to a bar instead of to the bull pen, and . . . well, after that John McHale had had enough.

Baseball is run mostly by people who worked very hard to make it but still hit .222. They aren't amused by talented folks who don't think they have to salute. McHale, the Expos general manager who hit .193 for Detroit over a five-year career, told Lee he would never play major-league baseball again.

And despite several nibbles—all of which fell curiously silent after the nibblers reflected further—it turned out McHale was right. After thirteen years entertaining the good folks of Boston and Montreal, after having racked up 119 wins against 90 losses with a commendable 3.62 ERA, the vegetarian — um, the near-vegetarian, non-eater of red meat, who only likes a hamburger every now and then, and well, sure, occasionally a steak, was dead meat.

It has been four years since Lee joined the Moncton Mets, an amateur team that plays on a par with lower-level minor-league teams, more or less, some of the time. One of Lee's conditions of employment is that he bat for himself.

He should put a banner on his bat when he goes to the plate—he is like an old-fashioned knight-errant battling on behalf of the smoldering hordes of baseball purists who loathe the designated hitter. His contempt for the DH is legend. When he was trying to get back into the majors he wrote only to National League teams, which continue to insist that their pitchers at least pretend to be athletes by sending them trembling to the plate. He has a bumper sticker on the back of his 1979 Volkswagen van: DUMP THE DH.

He rails against the DH all the way from the ballpark to his borrowed, needlepoint-decorated bungalow, where he will grab a bite to eat before the doubleheader. His wife, Pam, is there. She is beautiful, sensual and funny—everything a cult figure deserves. And young! Whew, is she young—twenty-eight. That damned Bill . . . .

He isn't in the house for two minutes before he pulls out his thumb-worn copy of Buckminster Fuller's *Operating Manual for Spaceship Earth.* The book falls open to the chapter that explains how specialization will destroy humanity. Which is exactly what the DH is doing to baseball, says Lee indignantly. "The designated hitter is overspecialization. It will eventually cause the extinction of baseball. It's happening. All the home runs that they're giving up now—the pitchers of today don't know how to hit. Therefore, they don't know the game in totality and they don't know how to pitch."

Pitching hasn't been a problem for Lee this year. He is still the prince of guile on the mound, mixing an assortment of sinkers and change-ups to keep most of Atlantic Canada's amateur batters off stride most of the time.

And batting has never been a problem, either. Just like reading without glasses isn't a problem for a lot of people. *Right up until they turn forty.*

Bill Lee looks up something else for you. There it is, in one of the Wildcats' yearbooks. In 1986 he led the league in pitching with a 7-0 record and hit .382 during the season, with five home runs in the Atlantic championships. *All, of course, when he was thirty-nine.*

This year's stats show a fine 4-1 pitching record with a 2.86 ERA and a batting average of—whoops—.226. "Not seeing the ball," he says. A cornea infection, contacts, his glasses—something's wrong. He bounces out of his chair over to the refrigerator, looking for the yogurt. "It's simply a hand-eye problem," says the voice from the kitchen.

His own hand-eye breakdown had not deterred him, back at the ballpark, from doling out advice at the batting cage: "Let your arms go to sleep and keep your mind alert . . . Hold your bat like a baby—the tighter you grip it, the slower your swing."

For Lee, every thought that attempts to skip past can be caught and turned into a theory. "The essence of Rhinoism is to lighten up," he says.

"Like you can't swing hard if you grip the bat too tight."

He would like to just "stay here and play ball and be nice to people and fish, but that's kind of the ostrich theory of life, of hiding my head in New Brunswick while everyone else has to suffer under Reagan."

So he will stand as a candidate for the president of the United States. Will people actually be able to vote for him? He thinks so, although a sudden look of doubt crosses his face. "We're registered as a nontaxable organization.

"We're really going to screw up the banking system, because our maximum contribution will be a quarter. And it will cost the banks a dollar fifty each to process those checks. So they'll go broke."

Does Pam think . . . "Hey, Pam, you think you're gonna be first lady?"

"Well, I haven't picked out my china," she says with a patient smile.

Some of Lee's life-style still seems to sit well with her—after all, she married him when he looked like a mountain man with his long, frizzled beard, so she knew what she was getting. She talks with enthusiasm about having picked up five good pieces of clothing at the flea market for $4.85, including a Black Watch cotton bathrobe for $1.50.

But she shakes her head when he starts to drone on about organic foods. "First you were heavy into no dairy products. Now, because the neighbor brings them over, you're into raw milk and raw eggs and cheese. You wouldn't touch that stuff a month ago."

"Well, tell me," he counters lamely, "when's the last time I've been sick?"

He goes on to argue the advantages of marijuana over tobacco, with total disregard for every unkind word the cancer people have had to say about both. "How many ball players have died of brain tumors induced by marijuana? There have been a lot of them die because of tobacco chewing. Dick Howser's condition, I believe, was brought on by nicotine."

Marijuana, on the other hand, is not habit forming, he says. "Indian tribes did it long ago. They used to smoke it as a way of conjuring up spirits, to eliminate hostilities between the tribes. I see it that way as not bad.

"Everything I do or say my brain computes it and asks, 'Is it logical? Does it work between the Cartesian coordinates based on the foundation of Buckminster Fuller and Einstein?'"

The doubleheader commences. In the first game, Moncton wins 14-4, banging out thirteen hits, including three home runs. Lee, hitting eighth and playing first base, is 0-for-3, striking out limply on a curve, grounding weakly to first and reaching base on a dropped pop-up between the mound and first. In the second game, it is 5-1 for the visiting Kentville Wildcats in the bottom of the eighth. Lee has been dropped to ninth in the batting order. He has struck out after failing to lay down a bunt, then gets thrown out by two steps on another attempt to reach first on a bunt.

Then the Kentville manager makes a mistake, removing his Lee-like junk-ball pitcher and replacing him with a second baseman who throws faster, but straight down the middle.

The Mets rise up, slamming the ball around and out of the park to tie the score 5-5. With two out, Bill Lee—*goodness, he looks stooped*—walks to the plate.

His stance is strange, his elbow down in a seeming half-bunt position. But he is swinging away, sort of, yes, like a gate, and his first feeble effort brings groans.

"Hey, Bill, ya wanna borrow my glasses?' heckles a Moncton fan from ten feet behind the screen.

"He's too anxious," moans fourteen-year-old Andrew Steeves, who Lee has helped with both pitching and batting. "He's got to get his elbow up."

The count goes to 3-2.

At home Pam Lee—plucked eight years ago by the Spaceman from the heart of upper-crust Westmount society—is watching the game on cable. Pam's mother wasn't in favor of the plucking until one of her friends—another matron of Montreal society—told her that Lee was the man she always thought of when she asked herself who she would like to join her on a water mattress with a bottle of Dom Perignon.

At this 3-2 moment Pamela Lee, finishing-school graduate, leaps up and begins to grind out a frenzied dance, whooping out what she claims are voodoo chants. She is joined by Dominique Langevin, a Rhino disorganizer from Montreal who is not as young as her hostess but who can still grind. Seconds earlier Langevin had been moping about Lee's occasional public wipeouts, when he momentarily loses all zaniness and takes on an earnest, pedantic and even boring semimaturity. This is not the Rhino way.

"It's not always so funny living with him, you know," Dominique had observed. But right now all is forgiven in a frantic effort to transmit youth, grace and vigor through the TV set and out to the ball park.

Where erstwhile second baseman Robbie Mann succumbs to the voodoo by telegraphing a big, fast change-up that floats to the plate like a harvest moon. Bill Lee swings and rips the ball down the right-field line. Fair ball. The runner on second scores.

Bill's question is this: How many ballplayers have died of brain tumors induced by marijuana? (Ottawa *Citizen*)

The next thing anybody knows Lee is flat on his stomach, beached between second and third—tagged out by a Wildcat while trying to stretch a double into a triple. No matter. The lead run has scored and Moncton goes on to win.

Five minutes later a weary Spaceman, caked with sweat and infield dirt, sits smiling and vindicated in the Mets' dressing room, changing from his spikes into his well-worn sandals.

At the bungalow, Pam Lee has thrown herself on the couch, her voodoo completed. A winning hit will mean a cheerier mood.

She would like to do something different next year, she says determinedly, sheltering her head with her forearms lest the gods strike her down. Get out of the bungalow, for sure. Maybe not even come back to Moncton. Maybe not even play baseball. There are other things to do with summers. Herself, she fondly remembers the summers she spent in Europe when she was growing up, visiting her parents' friends in various countries.

"Who knows what will happen next year?" She laughs giddily. She never quite says, "I'm not doing this again, that's for sure." Not in those words, just like that.

Later, at the pub, Bill Lee is smoking a cigarette. Nicotine. "Left handers are addictive." He shrugs with that crazy little smile. He looks weary, standing there, swaying slightly with his beer in one hand and his cigarette in the other. Ah, no need to worry about Bill Lee growing old, says the Spaceman. "Do you know I've got an aunt — Annabelle Lee. She played ball with Casey Candaele's mother during the war. She's eighty-two and she still mows the lawn in a rubber suit."

He pulls from his bottle of lager, then laughs that elfin laugh. Yeah, that's nice. Two fine things to run through his mind. Annabelle Lee and a game-winning hit. He shakes his head, and for a second the weariness seems to go away. He still has that little boy's smile.

Oh, please Lord, not Bill Lee.

3

NATIONAL TEAM

Waterloo, Ontario
July 4, 1987

It is hot, and the kid is throwing, and after he throws the ball hits the catcher's mitt with a thud. Now a thud is an honorable enough sound in the baseball world, way up on a ping (ball off the fists of an aluminum bat) or a splat (tobacco juice in the dirt).

In fact, a thud is all you're going to get when a breaking ball hits the catcher's mitt, so what's the problem here?

The problem here is that it is 1987, the Canadian national baseball team is holding tryouts, and the young man is not throwing his breaking ball, he is throwing his fastball. He desperately wants it to make a pop that will echo through the sticky air and into the empty stands.

Thirty-nine other prospects listen absently, some cracking sunflower seeds with their teeth, some wiping sweat off their foreheads, some in the outfield waiting for the ball in the scorching sun.

When the wait out there ends it ends with a clang that tilts the outfielders' necks back. The ball soars high over the center field fence — a cruel and unnecessary exclamation mark. The thud had really said, in its unobtrusive way, all that needed to be said: Not this year. Not in the summer of 1987, not for this young pitcher, the best to come out of his province in a while. Not with the Canadian national baseball team building up to the 1988 Summer Olympics in Seoul.

Not after all these years of finishing in the middle of the pack. Not after all the work that has been put into trying to disprove what seems so evident — that despite the occasional Fergie Jenkins or Terry Puhl, coming from Canada usually means you don't have a snowball's chance in San Pedro de Macoris of developing into a first-rate ballplayer.

If that gloomy condition has changed, the evidence isn't in yet. The Toronto Blue Jays may eventually — even soon — have a major leaguer in Rob Ducey, of Cambridge, Ontario, but bringing him up before his time didn't prove much. And as this national team holds its tryouts in preparation for the Pan-Am games in Indianapolis, he is paying his dues in Syracuse.

The Montreal Expos' latest Canadian hope is Larry Walker, of Maple Ridge, British Columbia, who has hit clusters of home runs at Jacksonville, Florida, in Double A, and is a genuine down-the-road prospect.

It's hard to be sure how many others share Ducey's and Walker's potential. But if northern tundra has yet to yield fields full of big-league prospects, the soil is being better cultivated. The national tryouts underway here in Waterloo are winnowing much of this year's crop.

Rod Heisler, a thirty-year-old left-handed pitcher from Moose Jaw, Saskatchewan, is taking a shot at beating out some of the promising youngsters that surround him. He wants to make the team for the tenth straight year. He remembers when it was an easier go.

"When I was nineteen, our club made it to the Canadian senior championships in Manitoba. The national team coaches went there, picked out what they thought were the best twenty players and sent us air tickets to Toronto. We flew in, had supper together, waited for everyone's flight to come in, went to the airport again, flew over to Italy, worked out together for three or four days and went into the world championships."

In those years the Canadian team usually finished around eighth or ninth in the world. "We had guys with talent and not much training," remembers Heisler. "Sometimes the talent made it through and we won. Sometimes the lack of opportunity to learn anything about baseball in Canada came out on top, and we lost."

Canada's first national team was pasted together in 1967 for the Pan-American Games in Winnipeg. A well-meaning band of souls led by Dave Shury of North Battleford, then secretary of the Canadian Federation of Amateur Baseball, couldn't stand the humiliating prospect of Canada not fielding a Pan-Am baseball team on the country's hundredth birthday, especially when the games were being played on Canadian soil.

So Shury pulled $5,000 out of his own wallet and scrambled to get organized. But in desperation the Canadian team tried to sneak outside the rules by fielding four players with pro experience, including John Elias, who now runs the Grand Slam Baseball School in Montreal. Elias came on to get the save by pitching the last inning of a 3-2 second-game victory over Puerto Rico. But the win was taken away when the background of the four players was revealed.

The tournament turned into something of a triumph for Canada in one sense: what was left of the team after the four were purged beat the always-powerful Cubans 10-9 on home runs by Larry Wilson from Ontario and

Maurice Oakes from Manitoba. The previously undefeated Cubans had been rubbing it in after every victory with bongo drums and conga lines, but they were quiet after this one. Oakes filled in for them by playing taps on a trumpet, and the Cubans fell to the Americans the next day to lose the tournament.

The win over Cuba was a treasure for the memory bank, but the forfeit resulting from the panic involved in putting together a last-minute team should have galvanized some kind of effort to get organized. Canada simply doesn't have enough baseball talent to put together a contending team unless someone knows (a) where that talent is; and (b) how to bring it together in time to forge a team for top international competitions.

The imperative is greater now that baseball has become an Olympic sport, on a demonstration basis at Seoul and for medal competition thereafter. Two decades after the Winnipeg embarrassment, things are starting to change.

Bernie Beckman, Baseball Canada's high-performance director, is one of the very few federal civil servants paid to hang around ballparks as

Thud is an honorable enough sound,
but sometimes it's not enough.
(Dan Turner)

*To compete with the Americans and the Cubans, you need every
Denis Boucher you've got.* (Dan Turner)

part of his job. Beckman sent out letters to a thousand American colleges this year in search of quality Canadian players to play at Seoul. A lot of the American schools cooperate because they're enthused about getting their players top international competition. Some of them wouldn't be so cooperative if they knew Beckman would dearly love to attract some of these players to the National Baseball Institute in Vancouver.

The NBI will probably provide most of Canada's national team players within a few years. It has been set up as a partnership between the private sector (Labatt's, the Toronto Blue Jays), the semiprivate sector (Petro-Canada) and the federal and British Columbia governments to deal with the problems caused by the lack of college baseball in Canada. The institute subsidizes twenty-six ball players attending universities and junior colleges in the Vancouver area, while giving them skills training and competition against good American schools. Most of these schools are in the northwest United States, but there are occasional deeper forays into good baseball country.

"In the past," says national team coach John Harr, "most of the guys we were choosing from had played thirty or forty games in Canadian summer leagues, and we were lucky if they'd seen good pitching every fourth game. Now nearly all of our kids are playing ninety to a hundred games against good American competition."

The veteran Heisler is worried that the national team will lose access to older, fully developed players. "The team has gotten a lot better from the point of view that young guys are developing both quicker and better. But at the same time they become prospects a lot sooner, and the team stands a better chance of losing them to professional clubs."

He wonders whether nineteen-year-old Denis Boucher, a promising left-handed pitcher from Lachine, Quebec, will still be around for the Olympics. Boucher has an eighty-five-mile-an-hour fastball and began to learn control of his breaking pitches while learning English with NBI funding at a Vancouver junior college last year.

The Expos have worked Boucher out at Olympic Stadium and offered him $5,000 to sign. That's a pittance, and Boucher turned it down. But would he turn down a decent offer?

At this tryout camp, Boucher says yes, unequivocally. "I've told both the Jays and the Expos that I want to go to the Olympics. Then we can talk."

The quality of competition in Seoul will be breathtaking. The 1984 U.S. Olympic team featured the likes of Mark McGwire, Will Clark, Cory Snyder, Scott Bankhead, B.J. Surhoff, Oddibe McDowell and Bobby Witt.

Many now star in the majors. And the Cubans always field a team good enough to play, and probably even win, in the big leagues.

To beat those teams you need every Denis Boucher you can get. So as you sit in the hot Waterloo sun, sucking the salt off a handful of borrowed sunflower seeds, you have to hope all the extra energy being expended in this program is going to result in kids like him ending up in Seoul.

Nothing can mess this up, can it? Stay tuned.

4

RENO BERTOIA

Windsor, Ontario
July 6, 1987

"Where ya goin?"
"Windsor."
"Whaddaya gonna do there?"
"Visit Reno Bertoia."
"He a friend of yours?"
"No, a ball player."
"Ah, I remember him. Boy, sure never thought I'd hear that
name again."

(Conversation with a U.S. immigration officer,
Bluewater Bridge.)

You can take Reno Bertoia's name and put it right next to Al Kaline's, and believe it or not, it fits.

You can try to recall the guy who elbowed Harmon Killebrew all the way across the infield, and at the back of your noggin you will find a long-lost name: Reno Bertoia.

Who was that fellow who was once compared to the great Grover Cleveland Alexander? Exactly. Reno Bertoia. Right in *Time* magazine.

And Ted Williams? Not to forget the Splendid Splinter. Not many people remember Williams' dark period in 1957, when he shut himself up in his Detroit hotel room so he wouldn't have to go *mano-a-mano* with Reno Bertoia.

Kaline, Killebrew, Alexander and Williams have all been ensconced in the Baseball Hall of Fame in Cooperstown, New York. And Bertoia? It wasn't until 1987 that the Canadian Baseball Hall of Fame at Ontario Place finally announced that a plaque was being readied for Bertoia.

And about time. It was one thing not being allowed to eat filet mignon with Kaline and Williams in the dining room at Cooperstown. It was another being denied a cheeseburger with Twinkletoes Selkirk in Toronto.

Reno Bertoia stunned the North American sports world in 1957 with one of the most remarkable performances any Canadian has ever contributed to big-league baseball. That it didn't last forever is inconsequential. Magic is measured in moments. In fact, Bertoia's magic lasted much longer —nearly one whole enchanted spring.

By rights, Reno Bertoia should have ended up a farmer in the north of Italy. When his father first came to Canada in 1920 it was to make a few bucks as a shingler and then go home and grow grapes again. But after several back and forths across the ocean, Libero and Rina Bertoia put down roots in Windsor in 1937, with eighteen-month-old Reno in tow.

The family knew nothing about baseball, other than what was important —that young Reno seemed to be able to spend most of his time with a leather left hand without inflicting undue damage upon his report cards. To the teenage girls of Windsor, the bashful, athletic boy with the green eyes and long lashes was a tragic waste of good hormones.

This was not a wild-time guy. Bertoia neither smoked nor drank, nor did he socialize much. Instead he followed the instructions of a teacher he revered. Father Cullen, his coach at Assumption High School, had a rule about "the three Ss—school, sports and social." The rule was simple —you could pay attention to only two of these three things if you wanted to do them right.

For quiet, introverted Reno, it was easy to choose: books and baseball. "All the time playing ball, ball, ball," remembers his father. "He played for sandlot teams in Detroit, going over the bridge by bus. And when the bus doesn't come because they are striking, he walks. One time he came home walking at one o'clock in the morning, and I say, 'Reno, you make me crazy, I am worried.' But he is so happy, because he won."

"In the summertime, after the baseball," says his mother, "he never went out. He would go and study in his room. Even when he was with the Tigers, he studied day and night."

Later Bertoia would look back and wonder whether confining himself to sports and study didn't smother the development of his social skills— skills he'd need badly when the pressure came.

But by the time he was nineteen it seemed he had built himself a dream life. Not only was he accepted at a good school—Assumption University in Windsor—but the Detroit Tigers came calling.

"We got the shock, you know," says his mother. "One night he comes home and says, 'Mama—somebody is coming to buy me tomorrow.' I say —God help me. I got to sell my boy?"

The Tigers leaked the news that the bonus was $25,000. In fact, it was

Reno walked right across the bridge and into the land of big league baseball. (Michael Rafelson)

$11,000 and change — $10,000 for the ball player, $1,000 for Nina Bertoia to visit her family in Italy, plus tuition fees at Assumption.

Bonus regulations required the Tigers to keep Bertoia on their major-league roster for two years. During both those years he sat on the bench most of the time. His greatest distinction was being Al Kaline's roommate — 1953 was also Kaline's first year up.

Bertoia had nothing but sandlot ball behind him, but he did get into one game, batting against the immortal Satchel Paige. He remembers the terror. "You talk about trauma. Everything seemed so far away. I was playing second and the first thing that happened was I got spiked on a double-play ball and threw the ball into the dugout. I was bleeding, but they asked me if I wanted to bat. I said yes, took three cuts against Paige, and that was it for my first year."

Over the next three years he was used infrequently as a pinch hitter and occasional third baseman. In 1954 he hit .162; in 1955 he climbed to .206. In 1956 he dropped back to .182 before being sent to the minors. He'd continued his studies throughout his major-league apprenticeship. It was starting to look like he'd need that education sooner than he'd thought.

To Ted Williams, just back from combat duty in Korea, Bertoia must not have seemed like much of a threat — some shy little bookworm who'd crawled out of Canada and looked ready to crawl back again.

But that kind of false security was endemic at the time. It was in the spring of 1957 that Prime Minister Louis St. Laurent confidently put twenty-two years of Liberal rule on the line, indifferent to the brash challenge of a fiery prairie lawyer. The same year Cuban dictator Fulgericio Batista stated flatly: "There exists no motive for revolution in Cuba." That was Bertoia: John Diefenbaker and Fidel Castro wrapped into one.

Ted Williams was usually a slow starter. But in 1957 he broke from the gate with unaccustomed ferocity, hanging around the .400 mark right from opening day.

Bertoia, then twenty-two, had stuck with the Tigers. But the club showed so little excitement about his prospects that it made a trade for third baseman Jim Finigan, a veteran, light-hitting journeyman. But Finigan got injured early, and Bertoia filled in.

On April 20, he got his first hit, a single, and went 1-for-4. The next day he was 2-for-3, but manager Jack Tighe had yet to smell the magic, and pinch hit for him in the eighth.

The Tigers were losing a lot — Kaline and Harvey Kuenn were slumping

—but nobody could blame Bertoia. There was a 1-for-3, then a 2-for-3, then a 3-for-4 and—hey!—Williams was leading the league among those with enough at-bats to qualify, at .455, but who is this hiding in the shadows, at 9-for-17 for .529?

Right. It was Reno. But this happens to somebody every spring. A few at-bats, a few hits, a high average. There are always these freaky little spurts, and nobody takes them very seriously. So Bertoia continued to bat eighth.

But the beat went on: 1-for-4, 1-for-3, 0-for-4 (rest easy, Joe DiMaggio, there goes the streak), 1-for-4, 2-for-4, 1-for-3, 2-for-4 . . . On and on and on, with not one error in the field.

It was early May. The thirty-seven-year-old Williams was still leading the league in batting, but seemed to sense what was happening. The Red Sox swung into Detroit for a two-game series. But Williams stayed in his hotel room, bothered with what the Beantowners insisted was "a heavy cold." Ha.

Bertoia went 2-for-4 and 1-for-4 as the Tigers swept the Red Sox. Tighe still wasn't sure. "I don't want to put the kid, or myself, on the spot by saying our infield problems are over, because he could start going sour tomorrow."

Bertoia rose to the challenge: 2-for-4, 2-for-4, 2-for-2, 1-for-4, 2-for-3, and 2-for-3 with a homer.

There was still a smattering of rookie-of-the-year support for Roger Maris, hitting .315. But the action was in Detroit, where Bertoia, now batting in the fifth slot, was on a rampage. On May 16 he awoke—at home, where he was living and studying for exams — batting a league-leading .383. Williams, struggling through a 3-for-23 slump, was fourth at .375.

Carefully avoiding the mention of Bertoia's name as the likely source of his frustrations, Terrible Ted lashed out. He tossed his bat in disgust after failing to get a hit. He cursed the writers.

"Watch out what you say to those guys," he yelled at a teammate being interviewed in the dressing room. "They'll twist it around somehow and make you look bad."

Petulant, petulant Ted. Still, now that he was sharing Ted's company in the headlines, Bertoia might have taken a few seconds to ponder Williams' message concerning reporters. But then what could a writer twist about a shy young guy making his mark with such a splash? "Windsor's gift to the major leagues," as the *Windsor Star* was now calling Bertoia, went blithely about his business. His bat sang a merry tune.

The Tigers and the Red Sox squared off again. This time Williams acted like the courageous fighter pilot he had been during two wars: he came to the ballpark. But he couldn't rise to the challenge, striking out three times against Jim Bunning. Bertoia went 2-for-3, lifting his league-leading average to .398.

A man named Howard Paillefer, head of Windsor's Chamber of Commerce, suggested the city throw a Reno Bertoia Day at Briggs Stadium. Twenty thousand Windsorites would cross the river for the celebration.

Bertoia was young but not foolhardy. He urged caution. He said it would be "premature." Still, it was May 17, more than five weeks into the season, and young Bertoia was still on a roll. "I feel more relaxed and confident," said Bertoia. "Maybe it's a diet of steady work."

On that very day the Associated Press ran a national wire story with the lead: "Reno Bertoia says 'happiness pills' may have lifted him atop the major league batting standings."

The great Mel Ott, who helped out with Tiger broadcasts, was fond of Bertoia. He had worried about the young man's anxious intensity. Tranquilizers were new on the market, and Ott suggested to Tiger trainer Jack Homel that Bertoia try an Equanil before every game. Bertoia did, but earnestly argues to this day that the pills had little or no effect.

Bertoia was so happy about the way things were going he was more than pleased to open himself up to the press. For whom the pills were a good news story, cheap and easy.

Time compared him to the alcoholic Grover Cleveland Alexander, sipping from a gin bottle before coming in to strike out Tony Lazerri to save the 1926 World Series. Before the tranquilizers, said *Time*, Bertoia had "sometimes performed like a cross-foot clown in the field and was too tense at bat to hit his hat size."

Bertoia, who had been so innocently open about the pills, was devastated. At first Tighe defended him, saying Bertoia's confidence had come "from knowing he is going to play tomorrow, whether he is good or bad today."

But nobody wanted a scandal, artificial or not. A new team doctor was named. He recommended that the pills be stopped, suggesting that their effect could be serious. He also pronounced that it would take from five to ten years to "establish a true line on the after-effects" that the drugs would have on Bertoia.

That weekend Bertoia went 1-for-11 and hurt his arm in warm-ups on a cold, clammy night in Washington. The following Tuesday he spent nearly the whole game in a hot shower, trying to make the water stop the pain. In the fourteenth inning, he entered the game as a pinch hitter, striking out for the pitcher. As a last gasp he singled in the sixteenth to give the Tigers a 2-1 win.

But the dream was over; the bubble had burst. Bertoia was hurting, and in and out of the lineup because of the sore arm. Tighe began to treat him like a sissy, leaving the impression he was stuck with a guy who couldn't play hurt and who couldn't hit without pills.

Reno was kind of Canada's Ted Williams, for what seemed like a long, long time. (*The Detroit News*)

At twenty-two, after leading Ted Williams five weeks into the batting race Bertoia was scared again. "I was really a very introverted kid," he remembers. "I think my main problem as a ball player, having come right from the sandlots to the big leagues, was that I was always in awe of everybody. And I was too intense. I wanted to do so well.

"The school was part of it — I guess I should have done it differently. There was too much pressure. I'd bat against Early Wynn in the afternoon and then come back at night to Assumption to write an exam. I remember one day playing a doubleheader, then going home and studying and writing an exam the next day."

Bertoia ended the year at .275. Williams, having survived the scare, regained his self-confidence in time to finish at .388. It was his fifth of six batting titles.

The next year Bertoia graduated from Assumption and was traded to Washington, where he hit .233. Despite a good year in 1960 — he hit .265 and forced the mighty Harmon Killebrew off third and over to first — Bertoia was out of major-league baseball at twenty-seven, finishing up at .244 over six years, with twenty-seven homers and sixteen stolen bases.

He is now the head of the history department at the high school he attended when he played sandlot ball. "The kids love him," says his mother.

He's turned into something of an extrovert—he's in charge of the teaching staff's golf association, organizing games, trophies and the social events.

But . . . the Tigers held an old-timers' game last year, and Bertoia practised diligently for three weeks to get ready. He got to bat once, popping out to the first baseman. "I was nervous as hell up there."

Not wildly nervous like Jim Eisenreich, he says. "Just normal nervous, like everybody gets." Eisenreich is the Kansas City outfielder who in the mid-80s twitched uncontrollably in front of large crowds. He was forced out of baseball because of the problem, but at twenty-eight fought his way back in because he found the right drug to bring his nerve endings under control.

Nobody writes stories comparing Eisenreich to Grover Cleveland Alexander. Although recreational drugs have largely been driven out of professional baseball, plenty of players take tranquilizers and other prescription drugs.

But Bertoia came along at a time when being a man in the dugout meant being a bit like a man in a cave. Players and managers took pride in showing the hair on their chests. Doubts were weaknesses, and weaknesses weren't tolerated.

"I wish I had done better. I wish I had the temperament I have today. I was going so well, and then the story hit and I hurt my arm. I couldn't play, but Tighe got on me as though I should be able to. Earl Torgenson was my good friend on that team. I should have done what he told me to. I should have walked up to Tighe and told him where to go. But I was a quiet and unassuming kid, and I was in awe."

Except for one fine spring—the year the population of Windsor came close to invading Detroit. And the year that chicken Ted Williams ran for cover.

5

PHIL MARCHILDON

Toronto, Ontario
August 3, 1987

The would-be thief of baseball's finest historical jewel hides out in a modest Etobicoke bungalow. He paces. He fidgets. His wife harangues him:

"You always were a fidgeter. In Philadelphia you used to pull at your socks and hitch at your pants and look at the sky all the time. It was awful."

Her name is Irene, but the would-be thief of baseball's finest historical jewel calls her "mother." She calls him "father," and they are obviously deeply fond of each other after forty-two years of marriage. Which does not stop her from haranguing him.

"Now leave that alone," she scolds, as he rubs up a fresh white baseball she has been saving to get Blue Jay autographs for nieces and nephews. But he is a pitcher, and pitchers must rub up fresh baseballs — it's as simple as that.

"One stupid pitch." He sighs, setting the ball down and running his fingers through his wavy, silver hair, feeling instinctively, you imagine, for the seams on his skull.

Phil Marchildon — "Fidgety Phil they called him," says Irene — is unrepentant about what he tried to do on that hot July day back in 1941.

Joe DiMaggio was forty-five games into his fifty-eight-game hitting streak, generally regarded as the greatest baseball achievement ever. The previous day the Yankee Clipper had broken Wee Willie Keeler's major-league record, set in 1896, and now he was working on putting his new mark out of reach of the likes of Pete Rose and Paul Molitor forever.

Marchildon, from Penetanguishene, Ontario, was a twenty-seven-year-old rookie who'd been playing for Creighton Mines up in the Nickel Belt League only three years earlier. He had one of those magical fastballs that appears to hop like a toad just as it reaches the batter. "He has a fastball that is so alive," wrote J.G. Taylor Spink in *The Sporting News*. "The

Had World War II not wasted him, Phil might have outshone Fergie. (Michael Rafelson)

players call it by name — 'Johnny Jumpup,' and his curve breaks like a ball falling off a roof."

Johnny Jump-Up was not going to be enough to shut down Joltin' Joe, Marchildon knew. Nobody's fastball was going to get by DiMaggio throughout the entire course of an afternoon. So Marchildon decided to concentrate on his curve, a hissing demon he remembers with great affection. "On a good day —" he smiles " — I swear I could hear the ball snapping up there."

Three times DiMaggio came to the plate, and three times Marchildon made him ground out weakly to the shortstop, all on curveballs. "I really had a sharp-breaking curve that day — down and out a little, away from the end of the bat. I can remember pretty well every pitch I ever threw, except there are some you don't want to remember."

The fourth time up Marchildon got two strikes on Joe — again, both on curves. "It was unbelievably quiet at Yankee Stadium. The place was packed, but everything was hushed — nobody was saying a thing. I called my catcher out and asked him if he didn't think we should waste a fastball and come back with another curve.

He said "Okay, but *waste* the fastball."

I said, "Fine, I'll throw it over his head."

"So I threw it, and the ball must have been a foot over his head, because I sure didn't want to get it anywhere near him.

"And he hit it out of the park."

Well . . . no harm done. Surely baseball is better for Joe getting fifty-six straight hits instead of a piddly forty-five. And think how much more furious Pete Rose would have been in 1978 to have been shut down at forty-four, just one game short of the record.

Besides, Marchildon deserves more than the footnote the curveball would have won him in Cooperstown. Indeed, had factors not conspired against him, Marchildon might have given Fergie Jenkins a run for the title of Canada's finest all-time starting pitcher.

Certainly the talent was there. Marchildon won 68 games for one of the worst teams in major-league history, Connie Mack's Philadelphia Athletics of the 1940s. Granted, that's nothing close to the 286 games Jenkins won. But by the time he was twenty-five Jenkins had already come up through the relatively sophisticated baseball world of southwestern Ontario and put in three full years in the major leagues. It may seem hard to believe, but it wasn't until he was twenty-five years old that Marchildon even learned there was such a thing as a National or American League.

That was when he came down from the wilds of northern Ontario to play for the Toronto Maple Leafs in the International League, after having been dragged to a tryout camp in Barrie. Marchildon had been recommended to Leaf general manager Dan Howley by a fishing buddy up in Port McNicoll.

He had pitched for Penetanguishene in the fierce North Simcoe League, where competition was as heated and fan abuse as vicious as anything he would ever run into in the majors—even in Philadelphia, fan-abuse capital of the U.S.A.

When they called him "Froggy" in Philadelphia, they did it in an affectionate way. Not so in Northern Ontario, he says. "I hate to say it, but the fans didn't mind bringing religion and other stuff into it — 'You goddamned mick' and so on. They tried to get on you with all those slurs." Which, of course, couldn't have been better training for Philadelphia, where they even curse Mike Schmidt if he has a bad day.

Marchildon had more or less taught himself to pitch by throwing to Penetang's barber, who doubled as the town's catcher. When there was nobody in the chair they'd shoo the dogs from the alleyway behind the barbershop and young Marchildon would wind and fire.

He quit the hometown side when nobody would give him an off-field job. He went off to Creighton Mines, where he worked underground until game time, then continued his duties on behalf of the mining company on the playing field. There was no extra money for playing, but it got him above ground early.

What Maple Leafs' general manager Howley first laid eyes on in Barrie was a twenty-four-year-old with primitive mechanics, a small (five feet eleven inches) but powerful build and the gift of all baseball gifts — a marvelous, explosive arm.

Marchildon had been reluctant to come down to Barrie to try out. And when nothing was said after he had struck out most of the batters he'd faced, he and his buddies shrugged, hopped into the Dodge coupe they'd borrowed and headed back to the mines. A few days later Howley tracked him down and Marchildon agreed to give the Leafs a try in the spring.

When he finally arrived in Toronto one of his new teammates told him the farther south a player went, the better the money got. There were, he was surprised to learn, what were called "the major leagues." Marchildon had thought Toronto was it.

Which for awhile appeared to be the case for him. He pitched for two years for the Leafs, with only limited success. Although he had a blistering fastball and a good breaking ball, nobody had ever taught him the essentials of how to throw from the mound. "In the two years I spent in Toronto I never really knew how to throw or pitch or anything. And they had nobody who could teach you."

Nevertheless, the Philadelphia Athletics, a pathetic team glued to the basement in the American League, came calling, desperate for any kind of help. They looked at Marchildon — then twenty-seven and still raw — and decided there was hope of polishing him. "I went down there and pitched in a game. [In 1940 Marchildon pitched ten innings for the A's, giving up twelve hits and eight walks, with an 0-2 record and a 7.20 ERA.] And one of the coaches, Irv Rucker, said, 'Look, kid' — he called me kid even though I was twenty-seven—he said, 'Look, kid, I know what's wrong with your delivery, and in the spring we'll straighten it out.' That's the first time anybody had ever told me I was throwing wrong. I was getting batters out on the sheer power of my arm—that's all."

What the backwoods boy from the Canadian Shield had been doing was throwing across his body, an affliction that burns out young arms more than any other. Instead of keeping the body closed until the last possible second and flinging the shoulder toward the batter, the pitcher opens up too soon and flings the shoulder sideways. With no body weight behind the pitch, the arm does all the work, unravelling as the years go on.

He reported to spring training in 1941. He was wild in the beginning, but Rucker drew a line through the middle of the pitching mound and told him to make his right foot cross over it on his follow-through. He worked on it for a month.

The results were gratifying. Marchildon won ten games in 1941, and was the only Athletics starter to give up fewer hits than innings pitched, a herculean feat considering the quality of his infielders. When he first saw that infield, he yearned for the Nickel Belt. "We didn't have an infielder on the team who could field the ball properly. Our double-play combination was the worst in the league."

Nor was the outfield always perfectly prepared. In 1941 Cornelius McGillicuddy, better known as Connie Mack, turned seventy-nine. Manager of the Athletics since 1901, Mack had invented overhand pitching and had been the first to put the catcher directly behind the plate. Previously the catcher had taken the ball on one bounce.

But genius as he was, Mack's vision was failing. Famous for waving his scorecard to move his fielders around, the truth was that he was no longer sure exactly where they were.

"He just waved them and waved them and there'd be mistakes," Marchildon remembers. "But anyway he was a fine man, except for the salaries. He was a skinflint, that's for sure." The man in the starched high collar had been financially strapped since early in the Depression, and had sold off a succession of stars, including Jimmy Foxx, Lefty Grove and Rube Walberg. Between 1934 and 1947 the Athletics never once finished in the American League's first division.

Nevertheless, in the 1940s Mack had been able to accumulate quite a good pitching staff, which included Marchildon and Dick Fowler, also of Toronto. Fowler pitched a no-hitter against the St. Louis Browns in 1945; he was 15-8 in 1948 and 15-11 in 1949.

Mack had an interesting way of calling Fowler out of the bullpen. He would have a coach pantomime a man shoveling coal when he wanted pitcher Joe Coleman; he would make the coach stoop as though he were picking flowers when he wanted Fowler. In fact he always addressed Fowler, whom he liked greatly, as "Mr. Flowers."

Mack liked Marchildon, too, if for no other reason than as soon as he was shown how to pitch the wild man from the north became the Athletics' best moundsman. In his second year, in 1942, Marchildon won seventeen games for a team that won only fifty-five all season. He made only $4,800 for his efforts, and Mack didn't even offer him a bonus. But it was a remarkable one-man performance, and Marchildon was gaining recognition as one of the premier pitchers in the American League. The newspapers had started to call him "the strong man from Penetang."

"What a pitcher that kid Marchildon is," said slugger Jimmy Foxx. "Marchildon's got the darnedest fastball I ever saw. None of the other fastball pitchers can make that ball twitch the way Phil does."

Then came the war. Marchildon was called up to the RCAF in 1943 and would miss three years of his prime. He was handed the most dangerous job in the sky—tail gunner on a Halifax bomber. "If they fired on the plane from behind, you were their first target. Well, they fired a lot. It just happened that they missed me." But his plane was shot down while dumping mines in the Skagerrak north of Denmark.

"It was probably an ME110 that got us. It hit the engine and the pilot couldn't pull it out. We landed in water, and of the seven of us the navigator

It was dead quiet at Yankee Stadium until Fidgety Phil threw Johnny Jumpup to Joltin' Joe. (Toronto Star)

and myself were the only ones to come out of it. The others landed farther out at sea, I guess, and they must have drowned.

"The navigator's name was George Gill. We were shot down at midnight, and the Skagerrak is a big body of water. We swam and swam and swam for three hours, until we couldn't swim any farther. We were getting close to land, but the current was pushing us off.

"The Danish underground was looking for us, disguised as fishermen, and were going to try to put us in a car and get us to Sweden. But after they pulled us out and we got to the dock there were German soldiers there, and that was that."

Marchildon ended up spending a year in Stalag Luft III, the infamous German prison camp. The rations took their physical toll and the whole experience would prove traumatic.

Which didn't deter Mr. Mack.

Marchildon arrived back in 1945. "I didn't get a chance to exercise when I got back, because the old man wanted me to play right away. All he wanted was the attendance. They had been getting an average of around three thousand people for a game, so he advertised me as a returning war

48

hero, and they pulled in thirty-four thousand — that was the entire ball park.

"I ripped a big muscle in my leg right away, and ended up being out for the year. I came back too soon, that's all." His line in 1945 was: nine innings, five hits, eleven walks, two strikeouts, four runs, no wins — a disaster.

There were better years to come. In 1946 he won thirteen games and in 1947 he was 19-9 with a week to go when Mack sat him down, afraid, apparently, that he would ask for a raise if he won twenty. "I can't tell you why he did it — I don't know what went on in his mind. You didn't dare ask him. He got awfully mad."

In one game that year against Washington, Marchildon set down seventeen batters in succession. Later in a Cleveland game he made it twenty-three in a row: he had a perfect game with two out in the eighth inning when the umpire called ball four on a 3-2 pitch at the knees.

Marchildon was so furious he threw his glove at home plate, which cost him a twenty-five-dollar fine from American League president Will Harridge the next day. He lost the no-hitter with one out in the ninth, but finally won the game in the twelfth by doubling home the winning run.

In 1948, he won nine games. During one of them his nerves caught up with him. "After the war the doctors told me it might be years before it happened, and they were right. It happened in Washington, and I had great stuff warming up. But when I got into the game it was like a breakdown . . . I couldn't throw the ball to the plate."

Marchildon bounced back, but his problems shifted from his head to his shoulder. "One day I was pitching against Boston in Philadelphia. We had an 0-0 game until the ninth. I was getting tired, and I started forcing myself a little bit. I didn't have the strength I had in '42 when I could pitch all day and all night. I never had that kind of strength after the war.

"For some reason I couldn't understand I started walking guys — two or three guys — and that seemed to mark what had happened. I must have torn ligaments in my shoulder. The next day I couldn't move my arm. I couldn't do any more after that. It wouldn't come around."

The strong man from Penetang was finished. He came back to Toronto — there were no jobs in Penetanguishene — and worked for Avro, the aircraft manufacturers, before moving on to another job with a friend who manufactured hospital beds.

It wasn't a glamorous ending to a big-league career, but Marchildon never picked up a lot of glamour north of the border even when he was pitching. He'd go back to his hometown every winter, and people would act as though he'd been working as a barber in Toronto.

"Nobody ever said anything to me, and I never said anything to them. People never thought anything of being a major-league ball player. It's funny — they must have known, but they didn't say anything. Then one year they gave me a dinner and a set of silverware. And then we didn't talk about it again."

But if folks didn't make a big fuss about Phil Marchildon at the time, he wasn't forgotten. In 1983 he was honored as one of the first five inductees to the Canadian Baseball Hall of Fame. And the Penetanguishene Sports Hall of Fame embraced him in 1987.

Marchildon was late beginning his career, war snatched him away in the middle and he left it before his time. But not before giving Joltin' Joe one hell of a scare.

"I threw well over ninety miles an hour, you know. And then the other day I went over to the Baseball Hall of Fame — they have a machine there to test you. And I threw forty-eight. Just goes to show, you slow down."

He shakes his head, sucks on his pipe and shakes his head again. "That damned pitch. I could have been in the record books for sure." And shakes his head once more.

6

THE DREAM

Ottawa, Ontario
July 29, 1987

These are young bodies. And as the sun beats down and small planes drone overhead and the cicadas sing, they gather at the place where young bodies are judged.

Sitting around under a high blue sky, peering at the diamond, pulling on their spikes and sneakers, practising their spitting, there's not much to chose among them. Unless, of course, you're one of those scouts who pretends he can spot "the good face" that marks a winner.

As far as bodies go, though, most of them look to be in pretty good shape, even if one, a third baseman, is a Bob Horner clone. There are a few early hints of what's here, of course. There are seventy-two of them and it's hot enough for sure. So a few wear shorts. The real thing doesn't go near a ball field in shorts — how can you slide in shorts?

And some of those with leg showing have tans like Libby's baked beans. Strike two: too much time on the beach instead of the ball field. There is a rule of thumb that baseball people don't like to look at prospects until they're sixteen. That's when they can drive a car. "If they drive it to the beach," goes the adage, "you don't want them. If they drive it to the ball-park, they're worth taking a look at."

One young man wears an earring. Relax. Dave Parker wears an earring. One has no socks on. A surfer who's strayed inland, perhaps. A couple of them look nineteen, twenty. If they had a chance to be professional ball players, someone would know by now.

Some sit and chat with their buddies, rib one another and make jokes. Good. That's ninety percent of what their lives will be about if they ever get signed. Some sit alone, looking furtive and out of place. These are the dreamers. They've goofed around with baseballs a bit, in the driveway, at the park. They know every Expo batting average. They also know they probably shouldn't be here but . . . What if, by accident, they make a beaut of a play, right here at a major-league tryout camp? How long would they remember that? For life, right? So they come.

Most of those waiting are labeled. There are the traditional brands — Glebe, Renfrew Lions Club, Canadians, Pinecrest, Elmvale, Cochrane Electric, Alta Vista, Mrs. Gee's Egg Rolls. Mrs. Gee's Egg Rolls? Well, it may not seem all that traditional, but Mrs. Gee buys bats and balls for the Pembroke team up the valley. Her name is worn proudly.

One boy has a tattoo on one arm that says "Mom and Dad" and a tattoo on the other arm that says "Bill." One tattoo might just mean stupidity, but two means he doesn't mind pain.

Oh, look, damn it, would you believe that? A good-looking kid at a big league tryout camp. And what's he wearing? A T-shirt with a big red lipstick impression on it saying: *With Love From the Red Light District in Amsterdam*. Of course there's not much you can tell when they're all just sitting there waiting. But a T-shirt like that . . . cripes.

Soon the air is filled with the sound of popcorn popping, but there's no delicious smell. What you're hearing is 72 guys playing catch, waking up their arms — pop-poppa-pop-poppa-poppa-pop — lazily at first if they're smart, harder now — who's got the better arm? — dinking around with curves when they're bored. So far, so good — how stupid can you look playing catch?

But here's Bill MacKenzie, the Expos' chief of scouting for Canada, former catcher in the Detroit Tigers organization, a man committed to uncovering every legitimate baseball prospect in the Dominion, out of the clubhouse in his white double-knit Montreal uniform, onto the field, standing there barrel-chested, and what he seems to be saying is the jig is up. It's show time.

"This is not a clinic. We're not here to teach you. This is a tryout camp. We're here to evaluate you. Running. Throwing. Fielding. Hitting. Hitting with power. If you can do two or three of these things pretty good, you've got a chance.

"But pretty good means pretty good at a major league level. What we're asking of you today is to work hard and hustle. Good luck."

What he doesn't say is that, of the five gifts, running and throwing are the most crucial. Assuming some basic athletic hand-eye coordination, the other things can be taught. If you can run like the wind and throw like a gun some old man will make it his life work to teach you the rest.

Mackenzie told them he wasn't there to teach them, but to judge them.
(Dan Turner)

So. Sixty-yard dashes for a start. Seven seconds and under, says MacKenzie, is "a pretty good time" consistent with "an average major-league runner." They run in pairs. There are slow pairs, some quicker pairs and one terribly cruel pair, in which the slowest runner in camp somehow gets thrown in with the fastest, eighteen-year-old Bruce McGregor of the Pinecrest club in Nepean, who stops the watch at 6.79.

McGregor is one of just two in the group to clock under seven seconds. The coaches hadn't had a chance to see McGregor before, although they'd heard a few good things. The camp, scheduled to last five hours, is less than an hour old, but already something has happened. There are four coaches on the field, with eight eyes in their heads. From now on—outside of the time set aside for looking at pitchers —about seven of those eyes will find some sleepy, unobtrusive way to watch McGregor.

He may turn out to be nothing to get excited about: out of 222 candidates MacKenzie has looked at in Eastern Canada in recent months he's only thinking about signing two for the Expos. *Thinking about two.* Still, to use the baseball word Joaquin Andujar loves best, you-never-know.

When throwing drills come along—from center field through the cutoff man to third base — MacKenzie wills McGregor to throw well, to put an arm on his legs. The ball has to be alive and hissing like a snake when it arrives. Most get there like groundhogs dropped from airplanes.

Matt Wheatley, who has been throwing batting practice for the Expos in Montreal all summer and has established himself as a fine all-around ball player with the Ottawa-Nepean Canadians, leads off the throwing drill by whistling three long snakes right on the money — smack! smack! smack! The sound you hear afterward involves gasping and despair from the assembled, most of whom are praying that God will, just this one time, run some magical elixir through their throwing arms.

Half a dozen players throw well, including McGregor — "Attaboy, atta-boy," enthuses MacKenzie—and Terry O'Reilly, a sixteen-year-old pitcher from Glebe, who puts a sting on the ball from the outfield that most of the pitching prospects won't show from the mound.

But there is a lot of hippety-hop, as little dead baseballs stutter toward their destination, looking for a place to hide. MacKenzie and his coaches don't mind hippety-hop. Their eyes are ruthless, but their hearts are warm enough. Tryout camps are as much about goodwill as they are about looking for prospects, anyway. For the most part the network has its own way of coughing up what's useful to the organization.

"I know a lot of organizations," says MacKenzie, "where if you don't show right off that you can run well and throw well you don't get to pick up a bat. We don't do that. I went to a bunch of tryout camps myself, and I want everyone who walks away from here to say, 'They gave me a good shot.'"

So David Gray—"I've always loved ball, but I've never been a standout in any league I've been in"—gets to bat and does okay. And eighteen-year-old Max Theriault, with the soft brown eyes of a poet, gets to bat. "I wanted to play ball in Hull, but we pay taxes in Chelsea—so where do you play? My friends and I throw the ball, but we can't have games. There are only four of us." He strikes out with dignity.

And seventeen-year-old Kombo Hassen, of Alta Vista, gets to bat, and to make a nice catch in left field. "In a way, it's like your head's in a vise. You're shaking and your knees feel rubbery. In the end, it's kind of like you're not here at all . . . but the ball is coming at you."

But McGregor is here, knows where he is and definitely gets to bat. "If you hit it," two coaches yell out, shouting over each other to make sure he hears, "run hard through the bag at first."

If you ran under seven seconds, you could still dream The Dream.
(Paul LaTour, Ottawa *Citizen*)

The stopwatch is on him. He nods, then stings the ball for a base hit to right. But he slows to round the bag, his instincts telling him to look for the chance to turn it into a double.

Damn, damn, damn. They had wanted to time him to the bag, to have another exclamation mark for his card — a little something to whistle about over beers later on. Still, McGregor has looked good and maybe he's a prospect. Except for that shirt. Jeez, what did it say? *With Love From the Red Light District of Amsterdam?*

7

DOUG FROBEL

Buffalo, New York
August 5, 1987

On midsummer evenings it usually happens during the first inning, just after Doug Frobel trots out to his position in center field.

From there he can see the stands behind the plate at Buffalo War Memorial Stadium begin to glow, just the way they did in *The Natural.* You probably remember the scene. Robert Redford—playing Roy Hobbs, the most gifted player of all time—is at the plate, his bat slowed by sin.

He turns to the stands, sees his childhood sweetheart bathed in the soft light of a Buffalo sunset—her wide-brimmed hat as radiant as a halo—and immediately smites a home run deep to right, shattering the stadium clock.

Similarities linger, long after the film crews have disappeared. Barbara Ambrose, the love of Doug Frobel's life, often sits close to that enchanted spot behind home plate, and she's just as nice and pretty as Roy Hobbs' childhood sweetheart ever was.

And say, just the other night, in a game against Omaha, the Pride of Nepean, Ont., slammed one right up there where the clock was temporarily installed for the movie so Redford could drive one off it. Frobel's 420-foot smash hit the stadium roof, then bounced up toward the moon hanging over the ballpark. The cameras should have been there.

But if there are similarities, well, there are differences, too. The first spoken words in *The Natural* set the theme: Hobbs's father tells him, out by the barn, "You've got a gift, Roy, but that's not enough—you've got to develop your talent."

Doug Frobel has talent, and nobody has ever worked harder developing it. But it's not what you'd call a gift.

"There's ability there, all right," Frobel says softly. "But there's always been one problem. Nothing I do comes natural."

Doug Frobel was supposed to be the second Canadian since the war years to wield an exciting bat in the major leagues, the other being Terry

Puhl. Puhl's career has been literally hamstrung. But before injuries relegated him to a pinch-hitting role, the native of Melville, Saskatchewan, had some outstanding years at the plate with Houston.

Things haven't worked out quite that way for Frobel. His career has been tantalizing, but so far, with the clock ticking ominously, it's boiled down to one word: almost . . .

He first attracted the baseball world's attention in 1981 when Howie Hack, the Pittsburgh Pirates' venerable head scout, proclaimed that the Pittsburgh organization had become too black-faced for the fans' liking. He isolated Frobel as the single outstanding white prospect on all the club's minor-league teams. As embarrassing as Hack's comments were for the Pirates, Canadian baseball fans pricked up their ears. One of the game's most respected judges of talent was saying the kid was good.

It had begun at a tryout camp in Utica, New York, in 1977. The stars of the camp were supposed to be a high-school shortstop named Andy Van Slyke, who has since become one of the best outfielders in the National League, and a pitcher name Andy Madden, who became a first-round major-league draft pick for the Boston Red Sox. Despite his youth, Madden threw ninety miles an hour with good movement on the ball. But Frobel wasn't intimidated.

"It stands out very vividly in my mind," recalls Branch Rickey III, then with the Pirates and now with the Cincinnati Reds. "The day before, Doug had tried out as a pitcher, because it had been raining and all we could look at were pitchers. We were impressed with his arm, but he didn't have a pitcher's mechanics, so we said thank you.

"But you could see he was hungry, and he and his sister Bernice and a friend who played hockey decided to stay over at a motel so Doug could try out as a player the next day. And the next day we ran some of the kids, and he and Van Slyke both ran under 6.8 on a lumpy field, which was good.

"Then we did some batting. Madden had a great delivery, and about the third pitch he threw to Doug was an above-average fastball with the kind of life on it you rarely see in a tryout camp.

"Lord almighty — Doug crushed it! He hit it over the right-field fence into the end-zone grass of the football field beyond. It must have gone four hundred feet. It was startling." After Frobel also laced a double down the right-field line, Rickey suggested he sign a contract — right away.

Bernice, who now lives in Toronto and listens to Buffalo Bisons games on her radio, remembers how excited Rickey was. "His eyes lit up and he said, 'I think you've got a future ball player there.'"

"Everything about Doug Frobel," says Branch Rickey III,
"is remarkable." (Dan Turner)

59

Which they did, for sure, because Frobel, twenty-eight now, has been a professional ball player for a decade and isn't looking for work outside baseball. But he is now at the age, he admits, that used to prompt him to stare at other, older, minor-league players and ask himself, What's this old fart still doing in the game?

"But I just want to play until somebody tears the uniform off me," he says. His mouth sets and his green eyes flash. "When you think about it, how many Canadians — or Americans, for that matter — wouldn't give their left testicle to be playing professional baseball?"

Left and right, perhaps, to play at the major-league level. Which Doug Frobel was doing when he was only twenty-three. He came up in 1982, after hitting twenty-three home runs in Portland, and hit two more for Pittsburgh. He went down and smacked twenty-four more for Hawaii in 1983, hitting .304, before coming up and tacking on three more homers in sixty at-bats with the big club, hitting .283.

Finally, in 1984, he got his big chance, kind of. He went north with the Pirates and got into 126 games, which is a lot, with 276 at bats, which isn't many for that many games.

He was in and out of the lineup, inserted as a defensive replacement in late innings more often than he started, and in the end he hit .203 with twelve home runs—not good enough.

Deep down Frobel feels he should have been given a full shot that year, the way Darryl Strawberry and Corey Snyder were when they foundered in the early going. But he thinks self-pity is counterproductive, so he asserts—once, twice and again—that no, he didn't get cheated.

Not when Chuck Tanner, then manager of the Pirates, quit on him so early, when he was working his butt off and members of the drug-crazed Pittsburg "family" were allowed to continue to play.

Not when the Expos signed him in 1985, then dropped him without embarrassment after giving him only twenty-three major-league at-bats. Not when Cleveland called him up from Buffalo this year, and after he hit a pinch-hit homer to win a game in his second at-bat, left him to rot on the bench long enough to send him back down with the excuse that he wasn't "fresh" anymore.

That robbed him of his pride, he says simply. But his retaliation is the same as it has always been: work harder, figure out how to get better — never, never quit.

Rickey III has done business with thousands of ball players. Once they've left the Pittsburgh organization, most of them are nothing but memories to him. But Frobel is different. Rickey keeps in touch.

60

With the clock ticking ominously, Doug's career has boiled down to one word: almost. (Dan Turner)

"Everything about Doug Frobel," he says, "is remarkable. Doug Frobel amazes me. I can't remember anyone who ever tried so hard." Frobel doesn't find himself remarkable. But he thinks he might be crazy. He made it to the big leagues, and intends to return to the big leagues, on a modicum of talent he's never figured out how to polish, and a lot of hard work.

"Everything I've done in the game of baseball has been learned. Say five out of a hundred kids who sign pro contracts actually make it to the major leagues. Well, out of the ninety-five who didn't, at least fifty-five had more talent than me.

"There's no way to take a kid out of Ottawa and have him make it in the big leagues on the basis of the talent I have without that kid being a little kooky—a little crazy to prove something. And that's me."

So crazy is Frobel that although he failed to make the grade when his skills were at their peak, he intends to do it by harmonizing what he's got left. His arm is now "about average," he says—not the gun it was. Nor, he concedes, is he as fast as he used to be. "But who is?"

And finally, he says, "I wish to heck I had the [batting] stroke I had five years ago." If he could recapture this stroke—"the ball used to jump off my bat," he recalls fondly — he would revamp it to combine power with consistency.

All last winter he worked on consistency at an indoor batting cage in Ottawa, five mornings a week, turning himself into a line-drive hitter — only to decide later that if he is going to get called up again, it will probably be as a power hitter. If this confuses the issue, it only gets worse.

Frobel thinks his major problem has been a lack of the kind of "natural" rhythm Roy Hobbs and Darryl Strawberry were blessed with. "I don't have balance — kids who want to play ball should dance and do gymnastics when they're young." But at twenty-eight, he still figures he can acquire it.

Which sounds a bit like what the Wright Brothers thought they could come up with in their workshop when they first saw a bird fly. But who is to crap on the Wright Brothers? What they put together may not have had feathers, but it flew. And if you figure Doug Frobel can't learn to fly, let him tell you this:

"The answer is yes I can, and this is why I'm proud. Because look how far I've gotten, without knowing what the hell I'm doing." It has been a nonstop learning process, a fixation with figuring it out.

He was not even the best hitter in his family — his brother was. He was not a very good hitter when he played for the Ottawa Canadians baseball team. He was a lousy defensive outfielder when he signed his pro contract.

But he practised and practised his hitting, and he hit more than twenty home runs in the high minors three times, and more than .300 at Triple A. And he practised and practised his fielding, until he was being inserted as a defensive outfielder at the major-league level.

Rickey III says Doug Frobel stories abound in Pittsburgh. There is a late-night story: Rickey stumbles across the legendary baseball coach Billy Scripture long after a night game is finished.

Scripture, a fanatical creature, is throwing and hitting to Frobel, another fanatical creature. They go through bucket after bucket of base-balls, retrieving them time after time. It is long after midnight when Rickey finally breaks the spell and convinces them to stop.

There is an early-morning story: "At spring training Pittsburgh's ground crew really gets up early," says Rickey. "They pull up to the field with their headlights on. One morning I got up really early and went for a jog. I met one of the ground crew guys, and he said, 'Geez, one of your kids really scared me this morning.'

"He'd gotten to the field and couldn't see anything, but then this guy came running out of the black and said hello.

"I couldn't imagine it being one of our guys, unless he was just getting in from a night on the town, so I asked him whether he was sure. 'Yeah,' he says. 'It was the Canadian kid. He was doing wind sprints on the field.' "

Part of what drives Doug Frobel is named Doug, and part is named Tim. Tim was his older brother. Tim died of a heart attack at sixteen.

"I've always been trying to be better than I thought Timmy would be. He meant a great deal to my father, so I was trying to replace in my father's eyes what he had lost." Their father, Frank, remembers Doug as the best ball player in the family. No, says Doug. "Timmy was the athletic one. He played football for the Nepean Rams when they went to the Little Grey Cup, played baseball and hit three home runs in the championship game."

For ten years Doug Frobel has been coming early to the ballpark. "I always thought that if people saw someone that wasn't going to quit, who would give it everything he had, they'd say, hey, this is the kind of guy I want on my ball club."

If there is a little bit of bitterness, he says, it comes from watching the Expos expending so much energy on bringing Pascual Perez back, after having dumped Frobel following a short trial. "And I'd have done anything for them."

But that's history, not to be dwelled on. For now, he's busy figuring out how to combine power with consistency in that perfect, natural way. The one he hit toward the moon, the night before, has been encouraging.

He's hit home runs to all fields this year, he points out. His average has been decent (.303) and he's hit fifteen balls over the wall in fifty-four games, and he's been better at waiting for his pitch. All this, he says, means, "We're moving up to a different level."

And if nobody wants him to play winter ball this year, there's a hitting clinic in Boston that some major leaguers have gone to . . .

"And sooner or later—if I can learn the rhythm part—my strength will take over."

And the stands will glow behind home plate, as *The Natural* smites the ball.

8

LARRY WALKER AND COMPANY

Jacksonville, Florida
August 20, 1987

When Joe Kerrigan's red head hit the roof, the Prospect woke up. And none too soon, according to Peter Bragan, Sr., who owns both the Jacksonville Expos and a voice as voluminous as his cigar.

"Now don't get me wrong, son," intones Bragan, in his most resonant Foghorn Leghorn drawl. "I like Larry Walker. He is not just a Canadian, or the finest prospect on our baseball club. He is a thoroughbred."

Bragan hesitates, stabs a smoldering acre and a half of Cuba's 1986 tobacco crop at the ceiling, and proceeds with furrowed brow: "But when I see a young man throw his helmet, or get nipped by an eyelash at first base because he stood in the box and watched the ball after he had hit it, I see things I do not like.

"I do not want to be unfair — the young man is only twenty years old, and off the field he is more than polite. But anybody who is twenty years old must grow up and apply himself. And this is what Larry Walker must do."

There is a system of fines in the clubhouse of the Double A Jacksonville Expos: a dollar here and a dollar there for misdemeanors, like missing signs, overthrowing the cutoff man and losing your temper. The last time the bills went out there were a few players — more than you'd like — up there over the ten-dollar mark.

But if you peek over Larry Walker's tattooed shoulder into his cubicle in the clubhouse, just across from the Dr. Pepper machine, you will see a bill for $44.50. A lot of it is temper money.

"He's got terrific athletic ability, great natural instincts in the outfield and a hockey mentality," says redheaded Joe Kerrigan, a former major leaguer and the team's pitching coach.

"He doesn't think anybody should ever get him out, and he gets mad when they do. Which is okay up to a point, but . . . "

It seems only fair that Larry Walker should have a hockey mentality. He grew up as a goalie in Maple Ridge, British Columbia, and had a tryout with the Regina Pats. But hockey made Walker nervous, in the classic Glenn Hall upchuck-before-the-game tradition.

"I'd get butterflies really bad," he remembers, stroking the pathetic wisp of a mustache he's been encouraging for weeks.

But like any kid, he'd play a little baseball now and then, no more than fifteen or twenty games a year until he was seventeen. And he always felt deliciously calm with a bat or glove attached to him.

"Playing ball just seemed to come naturally. It just seems like something I was born to do."

As soon as he saw Larry Walker, Jim Fanning agreed.

Fanning, former director of scouting for the Montreal Expos and now an Expos broadcaster, repeatedly celebrates Walker on air while listing the latest achievements of the three-man "Canadian Connection" playing in Jacksonville.

There are three members of "the Connection" at Jacksonville for this 1987 season: Walker, twenty, Andy Lawrence, twenty-six, and Scott Mann, twenty-five. Their clubhouse cubicles, which hold their uniforms, equipment, family mementoes and shaving lather, are gathered together under a large Canadian flag. "Welcome to Canada," says the sign below the flag.

Together they've provided much of the thrust that's boosted Jacksonville into the Southern League playoffs. Walker, the baby, will hit .289 with twenty-six home runs; Mann, who played hockey against Wayne Gretzky when he was a kid, will finish at .276 with ten homers; and Lawrence, who spent his childhood playing cricket in Trinidad, will end up at .291 with twelve home runs.

The organist at Jacksonville's Wolfson Stadium often plays a few bars of "O Canada!" when one of them comes to bat, and in Montreal, Fanning and other broadcasters treat them as a trio when they talk about "the Connection." But that's like saying Diana Ross was just another member of the Supremes.

Mann is an outfielder who, according to the scouts, has good but limited defensive skills and does a commendable job of hitting fastballs when pitchers put them in the wrong place.

Lawrence is a first baseman who, again according to a scout, "gets

everything out of what he's got." The scouts may be wrong in limiting their enthusiasm about Mann and Lawrence as prospects. Baseball experts make mistakes. But they don't make many.

Neither Mann nor Lawrence say he's ready to throw in the towel. But they both have educations to fall back on. Mann earned a B-plus average during four years at Indiana State, and has already taught some physical education in the winter. Lawrence is a graduate of the three-year business program at Seneca College in Toronto.

Mann is buoyant, at least on the surface. "I think I'm in a good spot," he says. Lawrence is realistic. "I have to put up some pretty good numbers over the next couple of years. I'll give it my best shot."

Walker has no education to fall back on — he didn't get out of grade twelve in Maple Ridge. But if he doesn't get seriously injured, he probably won't need one for awhile. It is Walker they call The Prospect.

It was Fanning himself who assessed Walker for the Expos when five members of the Coquitlam Reds were invited to an international tournament in Kindersley, Saskatchewan.

"I liked everything about him — his size, his strength, everything. He was seventeen and he hit a prodigious home run — a man's home run. I said, 'Sign him — whatever you do, sign him.' "

There was no cordon of irate teachers standing between the seventeen-year-old and the $1,500 signing bonus the Expos agreed to. Walker was the fourth of four boys from a determinedly working-class family, and is the first to admit that his is not a story about a potential nuclear physicist being sacrificed on the altar of sport.

At high school, he recalls faintly, he spent as many periods as he could in the cafeteria kitchen, avoiding books and baking desserts for fellow students."I just couldn't stand sitting down and trying to put my mind to something."

The alternative to making it in sports would have been working full time at Maple Ridge Bowling Lanes. Father Gary manages the local building-supply company, mother Mary works at the bowling alley, brother Cary sells cars, second brother Gary works at the rubber plant and third brother Barry is a carpenter.

Yes, that is correct — Gary, Mary, Cary, Gary, Barry and Larry. Sometimes, during the early days of his pro career, Walker almost wished he had stayed back in Maple Ridge as part of the rhyme scheme. There were fond thoughts of home on nine-hour Southern League bus trips, wending

Peter Bragan thought Larry was a thoroughbred who needed a little more schooling. (Dan Turner)

their way through sun-belt humidity the texture of soup, living life exhausted for $1,200 a month.

On the other hand, sweat can be exciting when you're twenty years old and two steps away from the majors. That someone of Walker's scant experience is playing at the Double A level would be remarkable even if he weren't playing particularly well.

But Walker has played particularly well. His 1987 numbers, in addition to the twenty-six homers, included eigthy-three RBIs and twenty-four stolen bases in twenty-seven attempts.

"This is a tough league," says Jacksonville manager Tommy Thompson. "There are a lot of twenty-five- and twenty-six-year-olds with good skills and lots of experience playing here. We've got some of the better ones right here on this team. But for everyday players, Walker is head and shoulders above anything I've got. I see Larry Walker playing in the big leagues for a long time if he continues to improve the way he has."

Thompson hesitates, looks around as if to make sure Walker isn't within hearing distance, then speaks softly and almost reverently: "Larry Walker's got it all."

Walker "is one of Montreal's big hopes in that he's a good prospect and a native of Canada," says the Jacksonville souvenir program.

There's no doubt that the native part is important. A first-rate French Canadian would be everything the Expos have ever dreamed of, but, in a pinch, a top-notch Anglo will do.

Marginal players needn't apply. Doug Frobel and Billy Atkinson were discarded as though Youppi was holding his nose at the very thought of them. In marketing terms, they wouldn't draw flies, and neither the Jays nor the Expos want to set any precedents about hiring fringe Canadians and then being nagged to play them. Walker is another matter.

Spring-training fans got a brief peek last spring when he was brought over to the major-league camp for a day, going 2-for-3 with a double, a triple and a game-winning RBI.

Fanning says flatly that Walker "may be the best offensive player we've ever developed," and he's not just talking about Canadians. Ralph Rowe, the Expos' minor-league hitting instructor, laid down an ultimatum after watching Walker hit his first two professional home runs: if anybody in the organization made the slightest move to alter Walker's batting stance, Rowe would resign. Nobody has.

Thompson predicts Walker will hit between twenty and thirty home runs a season in the majors, drive in between seventy and a hundred runs, hit .290, steal bases and play fine defensive outfield. The Jacksonville

Larry (right) *was to become part of the Canadian Connection, which is like saying Diana Ross was one of the Supremes.* (Larry Walker, Sr)

manager speaks glowingly of Walker's speed, outstanding instinctive base running, powerful batting stroke and quick reaction to balls hit to the outfield. "He glides to the ball as though he were on skates."

These are skills that bring people to the ballpark. These are skills that would turn the Blue Jays green. But it's delicate—anything short of stardom causes problems. Hitting .188, as Rob Ducey did when the Jays called him up for a month, is fine for the first little bit. But .188 for very long can lead to fan frustration and jealousy among other players who mutter about favoritism.

It's a needle-in-a-haystack kind of business. First you look for a Canadian kid with the potential to be both productive and appealing. Then try to get him ready for the pressures of the majors.

Enter Joe Kerrigan, briefly a reliever with the Expos and the Orioles. A pitching coach, to be sure, but at this level, one helps out wherever one can. Which is why he blew his stack during July after Walker struck out during a game against Columbus. The whiff wasn't the problem; Walker's reaction was. Again.

In the three years since the Expos signed him, Walker had developed the double-barreled reputation of being a hothead whenever things didn't go his way and of dogging it occasionally when he didn't think the game was on the line.

The Strawberry Syndrome. Young, gifted . . . spoiled.

On this day in July, Walker flung his bat and his helmet after striking out. The helmet hit Kerrigan, who was taking a drink at the water cooler. The bat just missed.

Kerrigan is six foot five and, at thirty-two, still in fine shape. Details are sketchy, and witnesses are careful about the kind of language that was used.

"I just said, hey, you do that again and you'll be eating your, uh, helmet," recalls Kerrigan. He probably said "plastic helmet" or some such, but is worried the listener might find the word "plastic" offensive. Whatever he said, it made quite an impression on Larry Walker.

"He kind of blew up at me, and you can see why," says Walker earnestly. "Here's an ex-major leaguer getting a drink of water and some kid whips his helmet at him. Since then, he and Tommy have taken me aside, and talked to me about how to look at things. And I've really changed my whole attitude toward the game. They've made me realize that the pitcher is getting paid, and I'm getting paid, and we're all out there being professionals. And when he gets me out he's done his job, and I owe him some respect.

"They also made me realize that Buck Rodgers isn't going to take that crap. He's going to say, hey, send Walker down, get him out of here. If he's going to pull that crap, we don't need him." Walker seems delighted to have seen the light, and somewhat astonished that maturity was always so close at hand.

"There are a couple of other guys on the team who've got a bad attitude—who throw their bats—and I see them do that, and say, 'Geez, that was me. I did that, and that's how I looked. Like some real jerk.' It's like there's a new me—that some new person crawled out from inside and started looking at the game from a whole new perspective.

"And sometimes, before, I wouldn't actually overexert myself, really. Now I do. Just the other day Tommy took me aside and told me how much they like my hustle now."

Behold The Prospect, growing up.

9

MACK JONES

Atlanta, Georgia
August 22, 1987

The first player ever to hit a major-league home run on Canadian soil was Mack Jones, who immediately became as Canadian a hero as Billy Bishop and Laura Secord.

This is not writer's hyperbole. Fans of the first-year Montreal Expos not only went spinny over Mack the Knife, they went gaga, loony, wonky and nuts.

Jones could not slip his humble red Cadillac El Dorado out onto St. Catherine Street without being mobbed. They named the cheap seats at Jarry Park "Jonesville" after him, because the kids who crammed into them so adored him.

The usually staid CBC took to tilting the letters in his name back and forth, making them dance on the TV screen whenever he put a ball over the wall. Hysterical fans stood and screamed Mack! Mack! Mack! *Mon Dieu*, Mack! And the greatest tribute of all—certainly in Jones's mind—was . . .

Well, after he hit that first big dinger—a three-run shot off Nelson Briles of the Cardinals on a snow-rimmed opening day, April 14, 1969—he went back to his hotel room. "I got 150 calls between 11 P.M. and 3 A.M. They were all from women." He recalls that with a wistful little smile.

The true measure of a hero, right there—something for the guys in the bull pen to reflect upon while pondering glory. Oh, there's no denying Jones' hallowed stature that first giddy year. How sad, then, to hear that the first Expo hero has fallen victim to a smear campaign.

It was underway as long ago as 1982, when, if one asked the Expos' public-relations people what had happened to Mack Jones, they'd say without flinching that he'd become an attendant on an assembly line that packed insulation into boxes at Owens-Corning Fiberglass Company, in Atlanta.

A directory of major leaguers who played in the sixties, called *Aaron to*

Zipfel, listed him as a "salesman for the R.N. Corning Co., of Atlanta, Ga." The distinct impression being propagated was that while the Corning people were fine-tuning their corporate name, Jones was climbing the ladder in a Horatio Alger struggle that would take him from assembly line to leading salesman and inexorably to company president.

"It sounded like they had me involved with a roofing-materials factory or something," says Jones with a shake of his head. "Number one, I don't know anything about roofs. And number two"—his puffy eyelids rise and his face lights up at the joy of it " — I never worked a day in my life. I'm not bragging," he insists. "I've just been lucky." His wife, he says, runs a car lot, and he drops in to help out a bit when he pleases.

On this day, Jones wears a red silk shirt hanging out and a straw fedora and carries a purse. He's forty-eight now, and weighs about 230 pounds. For as many of those forty-eight years as he can remember, Jones has lived a personal code that might best be described as indignant sloth.

Point no fingers. This is not some mindless stereotype of the black athletic life-style. It has nothing to do with the fierce, proud discipline of an Andre Dawson, the tireless self-improvement of an Ozzie Smith or the competitive intensity of a Bob Gibson.

It doesn't even emanate from the Jones family. Mack's father churned the streets of Atlanta as a hard-working trucker. When his son graduated from high school at sixteen and showed no inclination to do anything vaguely productive, he suggested that Mack consider the army. Jones recoiled — if one can recoil languidly. "I just wanted to hang out," he remembers. "I played a little ball, but it was just something to do to waste time."

While unstricken by ambition, Jones was riddled with talent. He could run, hit and throw—effortlessly, of course. The Indianapolis Clowns, the famous and talented black comedy baseball team, asked him to try out, then attempted to sign him. He turned them down, unimpressed by the thought of dragging himself around the country. His father was furious. Finally, a scout for the Milwaukee Braves came to the house and quietly gave his father $5,000 to borrow his son.

Before he knew it, Jones was in Waycross, Georgia, about a hundred miles from Atlanta. Atlanta was a big, predominantly black city and, while segregation was still the rule, it was easy to avoid.

Waycross was a small white town. Jones arrived at the train station at six in the morning, but didn't get to camp for another four hours because he and seven other blacks had to wait to pile into a black taxi while several white taxis sat idle.

A certain indignation began to creep in with the sloth.

When he moved up the line to Reno, Nevada, he thought things might be different. But he was the only black player on the team, and when the bus came to restaurants, he was forced to stay on board. "I could see the other guys through the window, eating steaks. And then they'd bring me a balogna sandwich and a Coca-Cola. I can't digest either of those things to this day."

Mack the Knife hit the majors in 1961, when he was twenty-two. The Braves were excited about his talent and wanted him to bat leadoff, — to get on base and use his speed in front of power hitters like Hank Aaron, Joe Adcock and Eddie Matthews.

As soon as he arrived the team went into decline. The Braves had twice finished first and twice finished second in the previous four years, but in the seven years he was with the team it never got higher than fourth, finishing fifth four times, sixth once and seventh in his final year.

Mack was the first player to hit a major league homer on Canadian soil, and the girls phoned in appreciation. (Montreal Gazette)

There were moments, right from the start. He tied a National League record, held jointly by the great Casey Stengel and the great Willie McCovey, by rapping out four hits in his first major-league game — off the great Bob Gibson. As he made his way back to the clubhouse he heard manager Charlie Dressen talking to reporters, who had asked what he thought of Jones' performance. "And I heard him say, 'Mack Jones will play this game for thirty years.' I shouldn't have heard that."

In fact, there would be only two decent years with the Braves — 1965, when he hit .262 with thirty-one home runs, and 1966, when he hit .264 with twenty-three homers. In 1968, he was traded to Cincinnati, where he hit .252 with ten homers in a part-time role.

Early on with the Braves, Dressen accused Jones of dogging it. Jones thought that was unfair, suspecting that as a black riding the first wave of black indignation in the sixties he was being judged more on style than substance. So he sulked. And he even, he acknowledges, developed "an attitude."

"That was the attitude that Charlie Dressen already said I had — that I was hard to handle." Ah, Mack the Knife. A grumbly exit from Atlanta, one mediocre year with Cincinnati . . . but wait, is that a pedestal waiting in some Alice-in-Wonderland metropolis far off to the north?

He was the Expos' second draft pick, right after Manny Mota.

"I met Mike Wegener, the pitcher, on the plane. And when we flew in to Montreal and were circling around, and I witnessed all this snow, I said, no, Mike, there ain't no way I can play up here." And when they cleared the snow from the field for the opening game he remembers thinking, "I'm going to have to talk to [Expos president John] McHale. I can't handle this thing — I'm a Georgia boy. My hands won't work when they're frozen."

But two things happened. "Right from the start I hit the ball good — the ball looked like this," he says, pointing to an enormous bowl of pretzels. "I think the weather rejuvenated me, by being so icy cool, and all of a sudden I was thinking I kind of liked this. And then I got back to the hotel, and I got all those phone calls, and I said, cancel that call to McHale — I *know* I'm going to like this."

Just when Montreal fans were desperate to believe that major-league baseball hadn't foisted off a bunch of humpties on them, Jones came through. By the time the All-Star break came along, he was hitting better than .300 and looking like he'd finish with thirty home runs and a hundred RBI.

When Mack first arrived in the big leagues he looked like another Hank Aaron. But he ended up an Expo. (Dan Turner)

75

Staub had lesser numbers, but got chosen as the token Expo to go to the All-Star Game. "It didn't bother me at all," says Jones. "In fact, it gave me three great days and nights in Montreal." There were nights with the girls —"She had long black hair, spoke French and English"—and nights with the guys—"Bob Bailey and Ron Fairly and I would start talking baseball at the hotel bar, and before you knew it, it was daylight."

By the end of the year, his average had slipped to .270 with twenty-two home runs and seventy-nine RBI, but Jones feels that had more to do with the first Expos manager, Gene Mauch, than it did with the girl with the long black hair.

"A black dude messing with a white girl in baseball is taboo. Mauch called me into his office and told me if I was going to play for the Expos any more the black-haired girl would have to go. So I told him, 'Look, Gene, I'm grown up, I'm a man and I'm not going to go fifteen or twenty miles out of the city and try to find a black chick. If you want to get rid of me, that's your prerogative.' "

Jones claims Mauch began to platoon him and use him in clever ways so that his productivity would decline. "One time I hadn't played in a month and I had been out all night. And Mauch knew that, but he put me in there. But hey—I can play along good—I hit two home runs off Milt Pappas. I know it annoyed Mauch—he took me out in the seventh inning."

In his second year with the Expos Jones hit .240. In his third year he was mired at .165 when he was released. "I had lost my incentive. I wasn't preparing myself for games."

He had been a strange sort of hero, finishing up at .252 lifetime, out of shape, his arm shot, a malingerer and a journeyman. But a hero he was.

Mack, Mack, Mack . . . *Mon Dieu*, Mack. *Mais merci.*

10

WOODIE FRYMAN

Ewing, Kentucky
August 24, 1987

The arm that has been around the world in a briefcase is chopping tobacco in a hot field. It is a left arm, a burned-out piston of an arm, and its owner grunts and puffs as he whips it back and forth.

You do not picture this man and this arm in a hot tobacco field. You remember huddling under a blanket at Jarry Park a little over a decade ago, protecting your child from whirling gusts of ice. And watching, numb and dazed, as the gimpy-winged fat man threw strike after strike after strike, straight into the teeth of a sleet storm.

The game was eventually called. The batters—thinner men than Woodie Fryman — were being blown off course as they struggled to the plate, puffing at their hands for warmth. But Fryman never flinched.

And still doesn't, under the hot sun, his forty-seven-year-old back aching from the most punishing field job there is, his eighty-year-old briefcase arm whacking away relentlessly.

The arm is baseball mythology. Dr. Larry Coughlin, the Expos' orthopedic surgeon, carries X-rays of it to medical conferences around the world to show why professional athletes can't be treated like ordinary mortals. "We treat the man, not the X-ray," says Coughlin. "And Fryman is an extraordinary man with an extraordinary pain threshold. If you looked at an X-ray of his arm, you would never, ever, think a man could throw a baseball with it. But Fryman did, for a long time."

Fryman holds both arms up, and one is three inches shorter because it won't straighten out. "I've got the arm of an arthritic 80-year-old woman." He points to the joint in his elbow. "All this in here, the bone is all wore off—it's like dust, like there's dirt lying right down the middle. It's locked up—that's why it won't straighten up.

"Then there's bone spurs all over. It just don't look like an elbow, that's all. I was in pain for the last six years I pitched. Every doctor on every team I used to play for would say, 'Woodie, you're going to throw a ball

some day soon and that will be it—you won't throw another.' And it happened. But I was forty-three when it did."

It's funny, mention Woodie Fryman's name and baseball people who can hardly recall their own hometowns will simply smile and say "Ewing, Kentucky," as though there were some magical charm to Old Goat's birthplace. And indeed, while not one of eight ordinary human beings asked for directions at the Louisville airport has ever heard of Ewing, it is the capital of charm.

The main street, which Ben Johnson could cover in six seconds flat, offers up Patsy's Beauty Salon (ten visits, twenty-five dollars), Crump's Fix-It, Biddle's Grocery, a house with a barber's pole and three dogs. Two side streets lead to fields. The Fryman home is on the edge of town, and the Goat can point over the corn field at the back to the home in which he was born. He points the other way and there it is—the five-acre bass pond.

It seems a long and heavenly way from big cities, retractable domes and even Cracker Jacks, but none of it means Fryman has left baseball—or Montreal—forever. He is here, he says, repaying his two sons, now in their twenties, for keeping the place going when he was away playing ball.

He never meant to go away. But when he finally did, baseball was good to him. It taught a taciturn young bumpkin with a grade-eight education that he could express himself as well as anyone, and more frankly than most. Baseball paid well and provided good company.

"Doing this for a living—"*chop, chop* "—makes me want to be back in Montreal—" *puff, grunt* "—right now. If they'd called me a little earlier about that broadcasting job . . . . But then I'd rather get a chance to be down in uniform with the guys."

Even more significant than the hard work is the blunt fact that tobacco prices are down and unlikely to rebound. That annoys Old Goat. He argues that the government shouldn't bend to the health lobby and should keep the price up, but he looks uncomfortable making his argument, and admits he wouldn't want his boys to smoke.

"Yeah, I'm sure the stuff is bad for you. I never drank or smoked or chewed—none of our family did. Never got the habit—all that stuff is habit. But if they're gonna kill the tobacco, they should kill the booze."

So Ewing is an idyllic place to work flat out—the Protestant ethic is burned deep in every Fryman's soul—but for what? To produce a crop that's no longer lucrative and makes you a tiny bit edgy to talk about? Is the bass pond more enjoyable than the bullpen? Doesn't he miss baseball?

"Too much work to do right now to even think about it." *Huff, puff.* There is an old-timers' game coming up in Detroit and Fryman is scheduled

Old Goat grew up and lives in Ewing, Kentucky, but he longs for Montreal. (Dan Turner)

to fly in for it, but there's a crop to take off before the rains and he's had to turn the cows into the alfalfa because there's no time to cut it and . . . No time for Detroit, no time to swap lies with those guys who won it all in '72 when he came in late in the season, shook off a sore arm and won and won and won.

Anyway, it is Montreal, a sophisticated city, you'd think, for a down-home country boy, that holds Fryman's heart. "I liked Montreal because I like people, and the people were good there — they'd stop you on the street and talk to you about the team and what to do. It was the biggest present in my life to get traded to Montreal."

It happened twice. Fryman didn't even get started in pro ball until he was twenty-five, although he had been offered a contract when he was eighteen. He'd been pitching more or less since he was a dirt-poor seven, and had control right from the start."I'd want to throw every night, but my dad would come home from the fields tired. So he'd sit in a chair under the old tree in the yard, and I'd throw to him, and if I'd miss I had to go get the ball."

He played with the men and pitched doubleheaders, and since his grand-father had been a good Kentucky ball player and his father had been a good Kentucky ball player, he didn't see any reason to leave home. Unless they were about to offer him $20,000, which they weren't. Which made him suspicious that either he didn't have the talent they said he did, or they were trying to cheat a country boy out of about half the money they were giving to a lot of city kids.

Finally, at the advanced age of twenty-five, he gave in, signing with Pittsburgh for less than he wanted and making it to the majors one year later. He might have shown up late (when the other players learned his age they started calling him Old Goat) but he made it last for seventeen years. His final record wasn't Hall of Fame stuff — 141 wins, 155 losses — but a lot of the losses came either when his arm was acting up or when he played for lousy teams, including the early Expos.

When he was hot and humping the ball with his characteristic grunt, he was one of the most formidable left-handers around. In his first year with Pittsburgh he was 12-9, pitching three straight shutouts. The third was a game in which Ron Hunt led off with an infield hit and got thrown out attempting to steal. At which point Fryman proceeded to retire twenty-six straight batters.

In 1973, the year the Tigers won the World Series, Fryman arrived late and went 10-3 in sixteen games. He got traded to Montreal in 1975, and in 1976 was named the team's player of the year for going 13-13 for a team

Other Expos dabbled in drugs,
but the milkman brought
Woodie all the kicks he needed.
(Michael Dugas)

that was 55-107. With a credible team, it would have been a twenty-win year.

In 1981, the strike-shortened year in which Montreal won its only pennant, Fryman was 5-3 with a breathtaking 1.88 ERA. He signed a $500,000 contract for 1983 but never got started — his arm was finished. People moaned that the club had been fleeced, but better baseball people knew Fryman had never cheated anybody.

Driven by the certainty that mental toughness was the measure of a man, Fryman took the ball when it was handed to him, often pitching with his elbow the size of a grapefruit. There is a hole on the inside of the elbow, where they operated when the tendon fell off. He didn't make a lot of money while he was pitching well. When he got his grand contract and couldn't produce, Fryman offered to go to the minors and at least make a contribution by helping younger pitchers.

John McHale, the Expos general manager with a reputation for knowing how to hold on to a dollar, told Fryman he had long since earned his money and sent him home to Ewing, where Fryman bought land for his kids. He is a loving man — his cattle, his pug bull terriers, his boys, his dad, his wife, his work, old ball players (Tony Taylor, Ray Burris)—those he loves he loves well.

But he is not a patient man. And the memory of the Expos he played for his second time around, from 1979 to 1983, leaves him vexed. "I thought in '79, '80, '81, '82, we shoulda won it every year. I think at one time John McHale made the statement that dope probably cost him a pennant. Well, after you came home and sat down and looked at the people he was talking about, it probably did. When you'd think about little things that happened in particular situations, you could see that was what one of the problems really was."

The smell of burning marijuana was one he came to recognize from the team bus in 1980, after Ron LeFlore had come over from Detroit and manager Dick Williams had installed Rodney Scott at second base. He commends coach Vern Rapp for standing up and telling the boys at the back to have some respect for the other people on the bus. He adds, "Williams just sat there and did nothing."

He liked Ellis Valentine and tried to talk him off drugs—without success. "They talk about the talent of Raines and Dawson. I'd have taken Ellis over either one of them when he first came up. I talked to Ellis when he had his problem, and I'd say, 'Ellis, if you'd just straighten up you could fill my metal corncrib with money.' He laughed. I'd always try to play with him and be serious at the same time, but Ellis couldn't get his act together."

There were difficulties besides drugs. Gary Carter, he thinks, may have taken an undue share of the blame for the problems of the talented team that could never win it all. "Yes, Gary Carter was a Gary Carter man. But he had super ability—he'd give you a good effort on the field, even if it was for Gary Carter. And he didn't hurt you—he threw people out, he could catch. They were all jealous of Carter, but you have jealousies on any ball club."

He is less generous about Steve Rogers. "Steve Rogers used to make me want to throw up, with the ability he had and trying to nibble at the plate all the time. He could have been one of the all-time greats in the major leagues, but when you talked to people on other teams, they knew he didn't want to be in there after the sixth inning if things hadn't gone just right."

Fryman is pleased to see Tim Raines playing well. "I'm going to tell you the truth—it didn't hurt Raines when [Andre] Dawson got out of there. Dawson had an inner racial problem. He didn't talk about it in public, but he always talked behind closed doors about it with the other blacks. That hurt Raines, because Raines idolized Dawson."

There were others — Larry Parrish, Al Oliver, Tim Wallach — whom he admired for doing their jobs as thoroughly as they could. "But we should have won — I'm sure if we'd won in '79 we'd have won for the next three years."

He will have to decide soon, he knows, whether to go back to the game or keep struggling with the land. The biggest cash crop in Kentucky now, he says with a laugh, is marijuana. Wiping the sweat out of his eyes, he ponders how he'd feel growing it.

"You can see why they do it — you've got to make a living for your family" — he's chopping tobacco again, *grunt, wheeze* — "and the government's not paying anything for this stuff." Two whacks later he ponders going back to Montreal, perhaps as a coach. "Oh, I think someday I'll probably end up back there. I don't think I'm going to grow this stuff for a living too much longer."

If marijuana and baseball are the only alternatives, Fryman may end up in uniform soon. Given his heartbreaks with the so-called Team of the '80s, you're not likely to see Old Goat weaving through a dope field.

11

FERGIE JENKINS

Blenheim, Ontario
September 25, 1987

Some of what he'd need on the mound she handed down to him genetically
—her family's height and grace. In passing on good eyesight she was more
painfully generous. When she gave birth to him—her only child—she lost
her own sight during the delivery.

But Dolores Jenkins never showed the least regret about the price she'd
paid, because she had produced Ferguson Jenkins, whom she would scold
into greatness. He took the family height and grew to six feet five inches.
He took the family grace—no pitcher threw as smoothly.

And he took the fine eyesight, which blended perfectly with his rhythm
and strength. To Fergie Jenkins' eyes, home plate was never more than an
arm's length away, just the right distance to place the ball where he wanted
it.

Jenkins could throw hard—more than ninety miles per hour in his early
years, and in the high eighties after that. And he could throw slippery—
sharp-breaking curves and sharper-breaking sliders. But what made him
great was William Tell accuracy. Up and in, low and away, not nibbling
exactly, but challenging just off the sweet spot.

In assessing the 1965 rookie crop, the editors of *Baseball Digest* managed to contain their excitement for the big Canadian:

"**JENKINS, FERGUSON**: Top fastball, control only fair . . . might be a prospect
later on . . . " In truth, his control was uncanny. When Jenkins finished
his career nineteen years later, he had compiled the best walk-to-strikeout
ratio in the history of baseball: 3.2 strikeouts for every base on balls issued,
with an astoundingly low average of fewer than two walks a game.

Baseball pitching lore is filled with the heroics of strikeouts, to which
Jenkins indeed contributed. When he retired he had struck out more batters during his career than all but seven other pitchers in the history of
the game. But lightning doesn't win ball games unless it hits the target.

As of September 25, 1987, the overpowering Nolan Ryan had, in nineteen

84

years, walked 2,354 batters, struck out 4,537 and accumulated a 261-241 won-lost record. Jenkins walked 997 batters, struck out 3,192 and finished at 284-226.

Ryan's advantage in more strikeouts — 1,345 — was almost identical to Jenkins' advantage in fewer walks — 1,357. They played for comparable teams. In approximately the same number of games, Jenkins compiled a much better won-lost record.

Statistics put together by United Press International during the 1987 season prove the point. Teams that gave up three walks a game had a winning percentage of .487. For two walks, the percentage improved to .582. And for fewer than two walks, it was .659. Pinpoint control is a ho-hum kind of subject. But Jenkins was a marksman. His control gave him a silenced, deadly weapon, more lethal than breathtaking speed. His affection for being around the plate did cost him some home runs—seven times he led the league in serving up gopher balls. Most, however, came with the bases empty. He liked a neat diamond. These kinds of things are important to know when you're measuring a ballplayer for greatness.

Because when twenty-six writers sit down in the late fall of 1988 to decide who should enter the Baseball Hall of Fame in Cooperstown, New York, in 1989, Fergie Jenkins will for the first time be on the list of eligible players in front of them. Statistically, Jenkins will be up against some pretty tough classmates: Carl Yastrzemski, Johnny Bench and Gaylord Perry, among others.

Furthermore, once they've dealt with numbers, some judges like to look at character. Power hitter Hack Wilson had to wait forty-five years to be posthumously inducted into the Hall, despite some awe-inspiring numbers. He was a notorious boozer, and the writers — not all of them teetotalers themselves — made him pay for that.

Character was important to Dolores Jenkins, as well. She wanted her son to strive for perfection — not just as an athlete, but as a person. "My dad says I got my precise pitching from her," says Jenkins softly, seventeen years after her death. "Because she was so exacting. She had great pride. Pride in accomplishment and pride in our heritage. When I started doing well in my athletic career, she was the proudest woman in Canada."

If she had lived longer, he guesses, she might have been terribly disappointed.

Right from the start, when Dolores Jenkins was disappointed, she showed it with vigor. The family lived in Chatham, Ontario, fifteen minutes from tiny Blenheim, where Fergie's Circle J farm now grows corn. His father's

ancestors emigrated from Barbados; his mother's had escaped the American south, some of them through the Underground Railroad, which brought runaway slaves to Canada.

Young Fergie sang high soprano in the school choir and even entered competitions — "It helped me gain the poise you need on the pitching mound." He was a Boy Scout and an avid earner of badges. For three summers, he bagged potatoes, cleaned cabbages and washed down carrots for a produce company from 8 A.M. until 10 P.M.—a job nobody else wanted. Later, he hoed sugar beets and detassled corn, working through lunch hours so he could get out of the fields in time to play ball. A model boy.

If there was the occasional non-angelic moment it was the usual small-town mischief. Terry's Coal and Ice Yard was three doors from his home. The Jenkinses, like most black families in Chatham, lived near the coal yard and railway tracks. When they weren't throwing stones through the open doors of passing railway cars, neighborhood kids fired at a more stable strike zone — the ice chute at Terry's Coal and Ice. The icehouse employees, committed to the concept of clean ice, finally turned him in to his mother.

"Ferguson Jenkins, what have you done now?" she would say. Which led her to the ironing closet, the cord to the iron and Ferguson Jenkins's backside. Mischief, right from the beginning, had a price.

Ferguson Jenkins, Sr., or "Big" Ferguson, as he was called, despite his diminutive size, was a cook at local hotels. He had come to Chatham during the Depression as a visiting ballplayer in one of the sandlot leagues. When he found work there he stayed on, and after finishing his career with the Chatham Black Panthers he turned over his baseball time to "Little" Ferguson, who outgrew his father early on.

The tall, stringy first baseman turned into a pitcher one day when nobody else was available, and from the beginning he threw strikes, sometimes knocking his catchers over backward.

Chatham in the fifties had the reputation of being a conservative, often narrow-minded little place. But the racism was muted. "I heard it once, when I was growing up," Jenkins remembers. "Nigger."

"When I went to the States, I heard it all the time, usually from the stands, when you were out shagging flies. And when you heard it, you'd just walk in toward the infield. If I'd been a hothead about it, I don't think I would have lasted long."

He swallowed his pride. He even got used to eating in the kitchens at restaurants while playing in the south as an eighteen- and nineteen-year-old. "You could get a cheaper meal there." He grins.

"Ferguson Jenkins, what have you done now?" Dolores Jenkins
would demand to know. (Dan Turner)

And he made it, at the age of twenty-one—four or five years earlier than most major-league pitchers do. He signed with the Philadelphia Phillies and was almost immediately traded to the Chicago Cubs.

In his first year with the Cubs, he won six games. Then came glory. Over the next six years, Jenkins won twenty or more games every year: twenty, twenty, twenty-one, twenty-two, twenty-four, twenty — one hundred and twenty-seven wins and eighty-four losses. In 1971, the year he won twenty-four games, he beat out Tom Seaver for the Cy Young Award; he was the top pitcher in the National League.

This was with a club whose cozy home was the toughest park in the majors for pitchers, and a club all too often bereft of top relief pitchers. Later Jenkins would look at Cub reliever Lee Smith—an invaluable crutch to tiring starters—with envy. "I might have won thirty games." He shrugs.

After one mediocre year (14-16), Jenkins was traded to the Texas Rangers, where he went 25-12 with a 2.83 ERA and was named American League Comeback Player of the Year by *The Sporting News*.

There were more good years in Boston, in Texas again (18-8 in 1978) and finally back with the Cubs, where he went 14-15 with an excellent 3.15 ERA for a team that went 73-89 in 1982. By the end of that year, Jenkins had 278 major-league wins, and his fans—especially his Canadian fans—had begun to strain with him when he went to the mound, in quest of the magic three hundred.

But there were only six more to come: he finished at 284-226 at the end of 1983, was losing some of his zip and was released at spring training in 1984. The Indians nibbled and demurred. The Blue Jays, unwilling to tamper with Pat Gillick's master plan for youth-fed greatness, said a cold, flat no.

Jenkins, ever easygoing, didn't complain. He played a breezy year for the London Majors in the Inter-County League, showing himself around his home turf in a final curtain call, having a little fun before packing it in.

He donated his earnings for the year to the Canadian National Institute for the Blind and the Canadian Cancer Society. His mother had died of cancer. She had reason to be proud. It was evident before she died that she had given birth to the finest Canadian baseball player of all time, and a nice young man at that. When the ballplayers invaded a whorehouse in winter ball one year, the bashful Fergie stayed at the bar drinking Cokes. When he had himself tattooed, he passed on the snakes and naked women and chose "Trust in God" instead.

He was the all-Canadian boy.

*Fergie won 60 more games than Catfish Hunter, who was inducted into the Hall of Fame on the first ballot. Fergie won't be. (*Toronto Star*)*

It's not the mysterious cloud in Jenkins' back that bothers him — it's the one over his head. He is forty-three now. Whatever his problems, his face is still sunny. He is the most handsome forty-three-year-old in Blenheim — perhaps in all of Kent County — and he has the same lithe, easygoing gait and friendly smile he always had.

Two years ago, he was in agony. The doctors found a smudge on his X-ray, between two vertebrae. At first, they thought it might be a tumor. They still haven't told him it isn't, he says, but they think it's more likely an irritation caused by disk deterioration, in turn caused by heavy athletic punishment.

"If it doesn't bother them, it doesn't bother me," he says blithely. Severe back stiffness and numbness in his limbs has eased, and he looks lean and healthy.

His father, Big Ferguson, lives at the farm with his wife, Kathy, and three daughters, Kelly, Dolores and Kimberley. Fergie does't live there. He has an apartment in town, five minutes down the highway.

Jenkins's mind is often on his various business pursuits. Right now he's trying to market souvenir baseballs adorned with color portraits of major leaguers. In the summer he'll take a minor-league post as a pitching instructor with the Texas Rangers. But he also thinks about the Hall of Fame in Cooperstown, and the possibility of becoming the first Canadian to get there as a player.

Baseball guru Bill James, writing in his 1986 *Baseball Abstract*, suggested the judges should think about passing over pitchers who haven't won three hundred games:

"Maybe the line needs to move so far as to exclude Ferguson Jenkins (284-226)," says James. "Maybe." Since James wrote those words Jim (Catfish) Hunter has been inducted, with a 224-166 record.

"Jim got into a lot of post-season play, which helps," says Jenkins, assessing the question calmly with his father at the kitchen table at the farm. "You create an image of being a winning pitcher."

On his way through, Jenkins created another image. Boston management once accused him of being asleep in the bullpen when he was needed to warm up. He shakes his head at that one. "It was early in the game, and the bunch of us were lying back, listening to the game. I had my spikes untied—that was it. When they asked me to warm up, I warmed up.

"Don Zimmer was manager then, and anybody who had been a friend of Bill Lee, like me and Reggie Cleveland, was in his doghouse." (Lee had publicly compared the fat-cheeked Zimmer to a gerbil.) But a more serious incident was to follow.

In 1980, Jenkins was caught with small quantities of cocaine and marijuana in his baggage on a team flight into Toronto. He still claims it wasn't his, that he was carrying it for a teammate. But he doesn't deny he used drugs during this period.

He was convicted and given an absolute discharge, with no criminal record. He was subsequently suspended by baseball commissioner Bowie Kuhn for refusing to appear before the commissioner to discuss the matter.

The timing was terrible—he was the first public evidence that players were caught up in something the owners felt was eroding the foundations of the game. After his conviction, Jenkins gave $10,000 to drug programs for young people.

Still, an impression lingered. He ran for David Peterson's Liberals in the 1985 Ontario election, when the Liberals made big gains. He lost by a sizable margin.

Since then, he has devoted a lot of time to talking to young people about the dangers of getting hooked on drugs. And in the summer of 1987 he served as a coach with the Canadian National Team, trying to boost the quality of its pitching staff so the team would qualify for the Seoul Olympics.

He doesn't smoke. He doesn't drink—give or take the odd beer. He may even be, in middle age, the man Dolores Jenkins so fervently prayed for. At the Hall of Fame, in Cooperstown, librarian Bill Deane ponders whether Jenkins will be admitted in his first year of eligibility. It is the most prestigious way. It is the way Catfish Hunter got in, with lesser qualifications.

"I really don't expect Jenkins to get in in his first year," says the voice at the other end of the phone. "There's all that competition—Yastrzemski, Bench, Perry . . . plus there's his police record. But he's bound to have an easy year sooner or later, and down the road somewhere I think some of the bad press is probably going to get swept under the rug. I'm sure he'll get in eventually. I think somewhere around the 1990s we can expect to see Fergie come through the door."

And so Fergie waits. But then mischief, right from the beginning, had a price.

12

GOODY ROSEN

Toronto, Ontario
January 8, 1988

Goody Rosen's first life memory is of a tough little shrimp of a kid battling to hang on to a ball, howling in protest when it was snatched away from him. He was the kid. His big brothers got the ball.

"That's my very first memory—that I wanted to be a ball player. I must have been four or five. I can see me throwing that India rubber ball up against the house and catching it, and my two brothers coming along and taking it away from me, and me running in the house screaming like crazy."

People were always trying to take the ball away from Goody Rosen. Part of the problem was that he was always a shrimp. He was also stubborn and ferocious. If you crossed him you fought with him. Sometimes the ball got lost in the scuffle.

But there's not much point in guessing how things might have gone if Goody Rosen hadn't been stubborn and ferocious. First, he was. Second, it's hard to imagine him getting where he got if he hadn't been. And third, he was probably right to be.

Life was fun, and he has stories to prove it. But life was also tough. After beating all the odds involved in being five foot nine and weighing between 135 and 150 pounds, Rosen finally made it to the Brooklyn Dodgers of the National League in 1937. He hit .312 as a rookie and .281 as a sophomore. It was a promising beginning. In his third year he got off to a scorching start at the plate before he injured his leg sliding back into first.

Which meant he couldn't drive off his back leg in the batter's box. The team doctor advised him to stay off the leg for at least a couple of weeks. But Leo Durocher, the Dodgers' hard-nosed manager, begged him to play: "Just field, never mind the hitting." Rosen played and his batting average plunged. Just as his leg was finally coming around, Durocher and team president Larry MacPhail called him in and told him to report to the minors. Rosen didn't go meekly.

"I was a little runt, but I was never scared. I lit into them. I told them they were giving me a raw deal, which was fine thanks for playing hurt. I was so mad when they sent me down I didn't ever want to come back up. I was so bitter."

But he did come back. Rosen could be wounded and Rosen could cry, but underlying everything was the ferocious drive to fight back and prove himself. It was only three years after his brothers snatched his ball away from him that he had to fight another, bigger neighborhood kid for the right to be mascot on a local amateur ball club. He won. And he got to take the equipment home and practice with it, which gave him his start.

In 1945, five years after MacPhail and Durocher had pushed him down the ladder to the minors, there was a war on. There were openings at Ebbets Field. Branch Rickey had taken over from MacPhail. He offered Rosen, then thirty-two, a final shot at the big leagues. Rosen, still indignant, thought hard about telling the Dodgers to go to hell.

But there was money involved. And beyond that there was a chance to prove something. The result was a year of glory: for one long, overdue summer, Rosen was big in Brooklyn. During the forties, right fielder Dixie Walker was adoringly known as "the pipple's cherce" in Brooklyn. Except for Goody Rosen's year: 1945.

When you're short, nicknames come easy. Casey Stengel called Rosen "Charlie McCarthy," after Edgar Bergen's famous puppet. "The Toronto Tidbit" was popular. It was certainly more upbeat than what one writer called him: "the stumpy Canadian."

The Tidbit was born Goodwin George Rosen in Toronto on August 28, 1912, the fifth of eight children. Two years earlier his Jewish parents had fled the pogroms of czarist Russia.

"I always had a lot of trouble convincing people I was a Jew because of my pug nose. I banged it up during a football game in high school. There was a strong rumor when I was with the Dodgers that I was only pretending to be a Jew so I'd be popular in Brooklyn."

Rosen wasn't designed for the bash and smash of football, but he brought a certain amount of the game's bellicosity over to baseball. Summer mornings were spent shagging balls at Maple Leaf Stadium, and Rosen was always ready for a scrap. But now and then he realized it was better to fight from a distance.

"When I shagged for the Maple Leafs they used to give me a couple of old balls as a reward. One day Joe, the chap who ran the field, saw me with some balls and decided he wanted them back. He came after me. The

fence in center field then was about a hundred feet high, and I climbed it. He was looking up at me and cursing me and telling me what he was going to do to me, and I thumbed my nose at him and said, 'I earned 'em.' And he said, 'Don't you ever come back here.' Of course I was back the next day."

When he turned eighteen he and a boyhood chum named Bobby Medline decided to hit the road in search of careers in baseball. They had spent the fall making standup Mutt 'n' Jeff ashtrays, sold them to Eaton's, and headed for Florida, where they had heard winter baseball was being played.

After hitchhiking to Washington, they spent most of their savings on a 1926 Ford touring car with a snap-down convertible top, which cost them $150 at a police sale. Its first tiny weakness proved to be a hole in the gas tank—"We'd fill it up with gas and half an hour later it would be empty" —which was soon joined by a hole in the convertible top. "By the time we got there the whole car was flapping." They sold it for $8.

Winter baseball, as it turned out, had been canceled because of the Depression. So after scraping together a little cash by pruning orange trees at twenty-five cents an hour, they tried hitchhiking to Arkansas, where one of Rosen's brothers lived. They were a strange sight in their Toronto winter coats and galoshes (later pawned for a square meal), and nobody gave them a lift.

So they hopped a freight car and joined the legions of hobos making their way across the continent. Just outside Little Rock the railway police mounted an assault, firing live ammunition.

The two of them managed to escape, but Medline fell and cut his leg. In searching for something to wash the wound with, Rosen ran into two of God's creatures he had never seen up close before—a black person, in a shack he approached for help, and a cow.

" 'Get yo' ass out of here, white trash,' I heard this deep voice say from the shack. So I got out of there and figured this cow out in a nearby field was my next best bet. I'd never been near a cow in my life, but I had this little tin can. And I said, 'Whoa, now, just whoa for a minute,' and I got a little out of him, enough to clean out the cut. And then we saw the police watching us. They'd followed us but when they saw me with the cow they doubled over laughing. Lucky for us, because if they caught you they'd put you in a chain gang."

Rosen's stories are full of laughter, but he isn't. He feels far more comfortable with a Jimmy Cagney glare, as he puffs on his trademark cigar,

Goody's first life memory is of fighting for a baseball, right here, in this alley. (Michael Rafelson)

than he does with a smile. The voice is warm, if gruff, the welcome is genuine, the courtesies are generous and there's humor in the air. But the face belongs to a flyweight and was long ago chiseled into a chin-first, make-my-day expression. He's been there.

Rosen and Medline got to try out in Little Rock. But Rosen made a small guy's mistake — he hustled too much. "I jumped back and forth during batting practice between left and right field, depending on whether a right-hander or a left-hander was hitting, trying to catch a lot of balls. And I made some good catches.

"But then they said, 'Let's see what you can do with the bat.' And I couldn't do anything—I was too goddamned pooped from all that running around."

He was cut in Little Rock and cut in Memphis, and finally slunk back to Toronto, where he played senior amateur ball with Saint Mary's parish until the Rochester Red Wings came into town to play the Leafs. He shagged balls for them, was given a chance to work out at practices and ended up in Rochester for a tryout, turning down the $150 the St. Mary's manager raised to try to keep him in Toronto.

In Rochester he met Warren Giles, then business manager of the Red Wings and later president of the National League. Giles was the first to give him the good-news-bad-news assessment that would dog all his days: "Son, you've got a lot of ability, but you'll never be a ball player. You're too small." Goodbye, Rochester.

A year and a half later his brother Johnny (who was not involved in the snatching-away of Goody's rubber ball) got Rosen a tryout with the Louisville Colonels of the American Association.

He made the team after a rude initiation. "My first time in the locker room the trainer came up to me and said, 'Son, we don't need a batboy.' I told him I wasn't a batboy. He stared at me with this disgusted look on his face. 'Then exactly where the hell do you think I'm going to get a uniform to fit you?' he asked me. And he was right — I had to wear one bunched up at the knees."

Having finally signed a professional contract, Rosen appeared hell-bent for happiness. In the next five years he hit more than .300 four times. In 1934 he married Molly, one of his sister's best friends, employing his characteristic brash approach: "He didn't even ask me — he just told me he was the guy for me, and that was it," Molly recalls, still shaking her head. There was joy. He and Molly had a son. More joy. A radio poll declared him the team's most popular player. What a guy! And what a ball player, gushed the *Toronto Star Weekly*: "[Rosen] made good with a thumping zest, hammering out a steady staccato of base hits and galloping over acres of outfield pasturage on twinkling toes."

When picking the Colonels' all-time all-star team several years later (a team that included Pee Wee Reese at shortstop and Earl Coombs in the outfield), the Louisville *Courier-Journal* not only selected Rosen, but designated him as "the greatest outfielder we ever had."

When Louisville pilot Burleigh Grimes was called up to manage the "Daffiness Dodgers," he took Rosen with him. Babe Ruth was the Dodger first base coach at the time and took a liking to Rosen, kidding him and giving him tips in batting practice.

"Babe's locker was right next to mine, and we got along real well. But one time he accused me of stealing his cigars, even though I smoked corollas and he smoked panatellas. I said 'I didn't steal your damned cigars, but I'll help you set a trap for whoever did. So I sent out for some firecrackers, and we stuffed them in half a dozen cigars on the top of his box.

"That night on the train all the guys were playing cards. Babe patrolled one car and I patrolled another, and we could see each other through the door.

"All of a sudden I saw this catcher we had, Babe Pratt, pull a cigar out of his pocket, and I knew what was going to happen. I caught Ruth's eye and signalled him to hurry. Which he did, but he was still about three steps away when Pratt took his fifth or sixth puff and the thing went off.

"Well I never seen anything so funny in all my days in baseball. You talk about shocked and scared—Pratt was sitting there with a black face and wild eyes, not knowing where he was, with Babe Ruth whomping him on the back yelling 'you thieving son of a bitch, you've been stealing my cigars.' "

Despite showing minimal power, Rosen played well with Grimes at the helm in 1937 and 1938, hitting .312, then .281, twice ruining no-hitters with the only hit of the day and leading the league in fielding percentage in 1938. But he still weighed less than 150 pounds, and when Durocher, the team's combatative shortstop, took over as manager in 1939, Rosen's future darkened.

"Leo and I never got along that great. I'm not saying he wasn't a good baseball man — he knew baseball, that's for sure. But he had some real faults. He was the type of man that if you were going real good he'd be there to pat you on the back and tell you how great you were. But if you were going bad you could see him looking at you in an entirely different way."

Leo begged Goody to play hurt, then discarded him. (Randall S. Echlin)

When Rosen got sent down after playing hurt it looked like he might disappear entirely. He played the balance of the year in Montreal, then got sold to St. Louis, but played for the Cardinals farm team at Columbus for only a few weeks before St. Louis backed out of the deal.

"The manager in Columbus, Burt Shotton, said to me as soon as I got there: 'I'm going to cure you—you're a rebel and I'm going to put you in your place.'

"So I said, 'Up yours—if you weren't so old you wouldn't be talking to me like that.' All through spring training he never let up on me. Opening day I charged a ball in the outfield and let it get by me, and he accused me of not hustling, which wasn't true. One thing led to another, and four days later I packed my bags and left for home.

"I was home for a day or so, and I got a call from MacPhail in Brooklyn. He said, 'I can sell you to about ten different clubs. Where do you want to play?' I said nowhere and hung up on him. To make a long story short, he called me a couple of days later and I ended up in Syracuse."

Rosen built a decent life for himself with the Syracuse Chiefs. Syracuse wasn't too far from his family in Toronto, he was getting extra money under the table and he was captain of the team. He led the club to two Little World Series during the next five years.

Rosen was also smart enough to have a clause written into his contract specifying that if he were ever sold to another team he would get a percentage of the deal. By 1944 he was still bitter about his aborted major-league chance, but had adjusted nicely to life in Syracuse. "The season was about a week old, and they said, 'We can send you to Cleveland or to Brooklyn.' I said, 'I ain't goin' anywhere. They said, 'Your price is $50,000 and two ball players, so you'd get $6,500. That was in addition to the $1,500 Rickey gave me to sign and the $6,500 the Dodgers paid me. So I did it, and I did all right."

In 1944 he hit .261 for the Dodgers as a reserve outfielder—no big deal. The Dodgers finished seventh. At the beginning of 1945—despite the fact that Durocher scrambled his lineup several different times—Rosen didn't start in any of the first ten games.

Then rookie Red Duvrett, who had been playing center field, ate some bad fish and got sick. It wasn't exactly Wally Pipp's headache. But it was enough to rescue Rosen from obscurity.

On April 28, 1945, Rosen subbed for Duvrett in center. He drove in three runs in a 4-3 triumph, including the winner with a bases-loaded single.

And so it went. After being inserted in the lineup he hit in twenty-seven of his next thirty games. On May 18, his bases-loaded homer put the Dodgers ahead for good in a 15-12 win over the Cubs. On May 31 his thirteenth-inning triple off the right-field wall scored two runners for a 6-4 win over the Pirates. On June 5 his two-run homer clinched a 6-3 win over the Giants in the fourteenth.

Rosen attributed his success to having put on some weight (he now tipped the scales at more than 170 pounds) and having come up with a cleaner swing. Although he had figured out the new swing himself while taking extra batting practice, he gave credit to coach Charlie Dressen, a potential successor to Durocher. Rosen knew how to carry a grudge.

The writers loved him. They called him "the little man with the big fat cigar." Columnist Dick Young said he was "the hottest thing in Brooklyn since they shut down the Star Burlesque." He revealed that Rosen had been discouraged in spring training, but that Dressen had talked him out of quitting. "Durocher couldn't lift him out of the lineup now without fighting every fan in Ebbets Field."

By June 11 Rosen was hitting .363, second to Tommy Holmes of the Boston Braves in the batting race (.385), and ahead of the great Mel Ott (.353.)

Brooklyn had a large Jewish population, and Rosen was naturally a favorite with them. One story he told the reporters went over particularly well, about how a gang of five football teammates in high school had descended upon him after a party at which he had refused to eat a ham sandwich, forcing a piece of ham down his throat. After which he sought them out one by one and kicked the hell out of every one of them.

"It was true," he remembers. "They not only forced the ham down me, but they pulled my pants down and pulled out my pecker—wanted to see if I was circumcised or something. But I told 'em, 'You're all gonna pay for this.'

"And I got every one of them. Every day at recess I took one out back. My brother Dave said if I didn't beat them, he'd beat me."

Three times in the spring of 1945 Rosen mounted ten-game hitting streaks. Holmes set a new modern-day mark by hitting in thirty-seven consecutive games, but two weeks after the streak ended Rosen was leading him in the batting race, .367 to .366.

The Associated Press put out a story stating flatly that Rosen was "crowding Dixie Walker [who had won the previous year's batting title] in the Flatbush popularity race," noting that on that day Rosen had made "three of the finest running catches seen this year."

Mullin, the famous New York *World-Telegram* cartoonist, drew a portrait of Rosen with the following caption: "Last year Dixie Walker's name was on every lip in Flatbush as he battled Stan Musial down to the wire for the batting crown and won with .357. Today the Good Pipple of the lovely borough of Brooklyn have another cherce . . . BABYDOLL ROSEN."

Al Vemeer, another famous artist-correspondent, depicted just how sweet it was:

> Goody is in the chips now, and could well afford to take a taxi to the ball park, but that is not the way a hero behaves in Brooklyn. A fat cigar stuck in his face and an open shirt revealing his manly chest, Goody walks the same route every day to give the natives an eyeful. Dogs bark joyfully and worshippers kneel to polish his shoes while Rosen stops to sign autographs. Little tots, already accepted into Brooklyn's strange baseball family, shout up the steps: "Hey ma, here he is."

Rosen did not win the batting crown in 1945. He hit .325, collecting 197 hits despite not being in the lineup for the first ten games, and finished second to Holmes, who hit .352. He collected eleven triples and a dozen homers with his new power, driving in seventy-five runs from the number-two spot in the batting order.

But he tired at the end. It was something like the day he'd tried out for Little Rock and overextended himself in the outfield. The Brooklyn outfield could be an exhausting place to hang out.

"I had Dixie Walker playing on one side of me and Augie Galan on the other, and they were good players, but a bit slow afoot. I had to take a lot of their balls. They wore me out—I just got tired."

He was nevertheless named to the National League All-Star Team. But there was a hitch. In the history of the All-Star Game, which dates back to 1933, there was only one year it wasn't played: 1945. The fuel saved on transporting players to the game was baseball's contribution to the war effort.

In 1946 Branch Rickey, with stars like Pete Reiser, Carl Furillo and Duke Snider waiting in the wings, traded Rosen to his archrivals, the New York Giants. In his first games in his new uniform Rosen banged out five hits as the Giants swept a doubleheader from the Dodgers. But later that summer he crashed into the outfield wall in Pittsburgh. He spent twelve weeks with his arm in a cast and was finished as a major league player.

Rosen had been given just enough time to prove his point, that the Dodgers never should have sent him down. The year after the injury he succumbed to pressure to play briefly for the Maple Leafs in Toronto, but the jig was up. During his career Rosen had worked during the winter with Biltrite Industries, the Toronto rubber company owned by Lou Sherkin. Sherkin gave him a position in the company after his baseball days were over.

"Goody could be a very ill-tempered person if you rubbed him the wrong way," recalls Sherkin. "He didn't like to be suckered. But kids always liked him, and the truth is he's a great guy and a real gentleman."

A gentleman you'd want on your side.

13

RON TAYLOR

Toronto, Ontario
January 10, 1988

"Ron's just like anybody else," says Jerry Koosman, Ron Taylor's room-mate when they both pitched for the New York Mets. "He's got a serious side and a humorous side and the ability to mix the two."

"Ron is like nobody else," says Paul Beeston, the Toronto Blue Jays' vice-president. "If I had one word to describe Ron it would be *weird*. There's nobody I'd rather send a person with problems to than Ron. But that certainly doesn't take away from the fact that he's weird."

Koosman is right about there being two sides to Taylor. He certainly has a serious side: they smile more at the morgue. Yet those who know his humor swear by his wit.

On the other hand Koosman may be suffering from memory twitch when he contends that Taylor is "just like anybody else." In fact there is no resemblance between Ron Taylor and anyone else in baseball. You'd have to search the planet. What Taylor is best known for — dramatic World Series moments — isn't especially what he wants to be remembered for. "What I would like to have people know me for is my confidence and diligence," he says.

It seems like such a dreary word: diligence. Why talk about diligence when you could be talking about ticker-tape parades? You were in one. Hey, you, sitting up on that convertible, with people stripping chrome off the doors and buttons off your sleeves and screaming your name and pelting you with confetti — is that what got you there? Diligence and con-fidence, confidence and diligence? And what are you going to do after the parade is over? Be a doctor? Be a *doctor*! You crazy?

In 1955 Taylor was seventeen. He and his buddies wanted to go to New York for the Labor Day weekend. See the big city, catch a couple of ball games, the works. The Giants had won it all in '54 and the Dodgers would

It's not that Ron didn't appreciate the two World Series wins and the
ticker tape parade. He did. But he wanted more. (Michael Rafelson)   103

finally beat the Yankees in '55, so there was first-class baseball wherever you went in New York.

Instead Taylor landed in Cleveland. The Indians were still good value; nobody knew the pennant they'd just won would be their last for at least a third of a century. But Taylor was there because Chester Dies, a Toronto-area scout, wanted him to show his stuff at an Indians' tryout.

Taylor had begun with the Leaside Baseball Association in Toronto when he was eight. He was shifted from first base to the mound as a peewee because of the zing in his arm, and by the time he was fifteen he was throwing against twenty-one-year-olds.

He not only had a good arm, he also had exceptional control for a young pitcher. His father, Wes, would practice with him, moving the catcher's mitt around, setting out targets and challenging him to hit them consistently.

The Indians yawned at first, telling Dies he should have taken the kid to the regional scout in charge of Canada instead of bringing him to Cleveland. But they agreed to let him work out, and what they saw snapped them awake. By the time the weekend was over Taylor was throwing to the glove of Al Lopez, the Hall of Fame catcher who was managing the Indians at the time. On the Sunday he threw batting practice to stars like Vic Wertz, Al Rosen and Larry Doby. Mike Garcia, one of the tribe's fabulous starting rotation, even went out of his way to chat him up and make him feel at home.

The Indians signed him for $4,000. His parents had to wire their consent. Taylor, an honors student at North Toronto Collegiate, had just finished grade twelve. After signing his contract he kept up his grade thirteen courses until late in the winter. He then did the kind of thing that makes educators sigh in despair: he headed for the Indians' minor-league spring training camp at Daytona Beach, where a locker with his name on it waited right opposite one belonging to another kid hoping to make an impact on the baseball world—Roger Maris.

That year Taylor pitched for the Daytona Beach team in the Florida State Instructional League and compiled a 17-11 record, good enough to identify himself as a legitimate prospect. At which point he felt he had accumulated enough credibility to ask for something foreign to the world of baseball in the fifties.

"I had decided that I should go back to school after winning the seventeen games. So I asked them if I could just not go to spring training for five years, to finish school every year instead and then just join whatever minor-league team I had been assigned to with the season in progress.

104

"They said, 'Fine — you're one of our best prospects, if that's what you want to do we'll support it.' So I went back, got my grade thirteen, and took four years of engineering at U of T."

In the summer he worked out of places named Fargo, Minot, Reading and Salt Lake City, winning more than he lost and fashioning respectable ERAS. Back in Toronto he did even better: he stood third in his graduating class in engineering.

It was obvious he was on the threshold of something special in baseball. It was much better hidden that in the classroom there were also bigger things to come.

At fifty-one, Taylor has a face that looks like it went another ten rounds after his body hit the canvas. It was put together with some special amalgum of granite and rubber, and it changes expressions about as often as an Easter Island head.

Even when he was eighteen, playing for the Daytona Beach Islanders in his first year of baseball, Taylor didn't exactly ooze frivolity. A Daytona Beach reporter did one of those frothy little surveys of this team of happy-go-lucky youngsters to see what they thought of pro ball:

"Ace hurler Ron Taylor, 18, of Toronto, who leads the mound staff with an 8-2 mark, tersely commented: 'Now it's your job and you have to make a living at it.' "

It's not that Taylor doesn't have a sense of humor. "He's extremely quick-witted," says Koosman.

"His humor hits you when you least expect it," says Rhona Taylor, his third wife, who met him when she was a nurse and he was an intern at Mount Sinai Hospital. "We'd be involved in some tense medical situation and he'd start talking about how there was a full moon and the moon rocks were pulling on our brains, or make some off-the-wall comment that would make everybody lighten up and function better. He was very well-liked."

But not what you'd call a full-time comedian. Mostly a serious man, an intense man, with missions he treats with grave respect. Not an easy man to live with or to work for because he is such a perfectionist. "I didn't say it was easy," says Rhona with a laugh. She sympathizes with Taylor's staff. "But it's fascinating. I wouldn't trade it for the world. He's always in deep thought, and some of the things he comes out with — his knowledge just astounds me."

Taylor's intellect didn't get in the way of his baseball, or of good times. Tony Kubek let it slip out at the batting cage one day that no matter how serious Taylor's demeanor is now, Taylor and Koosman had more than their share of adventures when they roomed together. Taylor is evasive. "I don't want to get into talking about carousing or chasing women. I'm not sure it would be appropriate now. Let's just say we were a couple of relaxed, fun-loving ball players."

The locker room is most often a not-so-delicate mix of sweat, vulgarity and low humor, but Taylor never seemed to think he was too good for the company he was in.

"Sure, I had education, but I never equated education with intelligence or intellectual capacity. Besides, I just thought playing baseball was a tremendous experience. It wasn't one that was going to be ruined if it didn't always offer intellectual companionship. I had friends, but I used to go my own way a lot. I could aways go off and read a book, go to a theater, go to a museum."

He broke into the majors with the Indians in 1962 after pitching twenty-one scoreless innings in spring training. His regular-season debut was what the Cleveland *Plain Dealer* called "one of the most remarkable rookie pitching performances in all baseball history." He fought a scoreless duel with Boston's Bill Monbouquette for eleven innings before Carl Yastrzemski opened the twelfth with a triple off him. Two intentional walks later Carroll Hardy hit a home run to win it for Boston, but Taylor had shown he belonged, even if he ended up going down for another year of seasoning at Jacksonville.

Over the winter he got lucky—the Indians traded him to St. Louis for first baseman Fred Whitfield. The Cardinals were studded with talent, both old—Stan Musial, Curt Simmons, Dick Groat, Ken Boyer—and new—Curt Flood, Bob Gibson, Ernie Broglio and, in 1964, Lou Brock. In 1963 the Cards finished second to the Dodgers. But in 1964 they finished first, beating out the Reds and the Phillies by a single game.

Taylor figured out early on he wasn't going to survive trying to blow people away with fastballs. He developed into a sinker-slider pitcher who challenged batters and moved the ball around well. "I like him," said Cardinals manager Johnny Keane, "because he's not afraid of the bat." In 1963 he was named Rookie Pitcher of the Year with a 9-7 record and 2.84 ERA, in a mix of starting and relief. In 1964 he had a better record, 8-4, although his ERA was 4.62. But he saved the best for the end.

The Cardinals won the National League pennant and Taylor made two appearances in the World Series. The first one was critical. The Yankees took a 2-1 lead in games, and appeared headed for a rout when they exploded for a 3-0 lead off Ray Sadecki at Yankee Stadium in the first inning of the fourth game. Ken Boyer hit a grand-slam home run in the top of the sixth to nudge the Cardinals into a 4-3 advantage. Taylor was called in to try to hold the lead.

Which he did, brilliantly. Over the next four innings he allowed no hits and exactly one base runner, walking Mickey Mantle on a 3-2 pitch after Mantle had barely managed to foul off what would have been strike three. The Cardinals hung on to win 4-3 and Taylor got the save. He had saved not only the game for the Cards, but the series: they won it in seven. Taylor faced only one other batter in the series, getting Yankee pitcher Jim Bouton to line into an inning-ending double play.

Glory. But the next year he was traded to Houston. He was hospitalized for six weeks with a herniated disk and pitched poorly. His combined ERA for the Cards and the Astros in 1965 was 5.60, and in 1966 it climbed to 5.71. It looked like those four innings in the 1964 World Series were going to be the pinnacle of a brief and not particularly remarkable career.

But expansion had opened up terrible teams for troubled pitchers. The Mets picked him up after he cleared wavers in 1967. They'd finished ninth the year before, up from tenth in 1965 and tenth in 1964 and tenth in 1963 and tenth in 1962.

They slipped back to tenth in 1967, but Taylor's personal rebound had begun. He posted an ERA of 2.34 and recorded eight of the bullpen's nineteen saves. The next year the Mets were ninth, but if you looked closely you could see something happening. There were new names on the mound, like Koosman and Ryan. The bullpen had thirty-two saves. Taylor had thirteen of them, with an ERA of 2.70.

Then came 1969, which was, of course, *amazin'*. The Mets won a hundred games, to capture the Eastern division, and went into the NL playoffs as underdogs against the powerful Atlanta Braves. The starting pitching, the Mets' main strength, faltered. The Braves hammered Tom Seaver for five runs in seven innings in the first game, but Taylor came out of the bullpen to pitch two scoreless innings and get the save, as the Mets won 9-5.

As columnist Rex Edmonston put it: "Old Ron Taylor came to Seaver's rescue and was as reliable as a mother's smile."

In the second game he pitched to five batters, gave up one harmless hit, struck out two and got the win. The Mets swept the championship series three games to zip and went into the World Series as 8-5 underdogs against the Baltimore Orioles.

The Orioles won the first game 4-1. Taylor, the only Met with World

When Ron threw the crucial pitch, Mrs. Payson, the Mets' owner, couldn't watch.
(Randall S. Echlin)

Series experience, pitched two innings of hitless, scoreless relief. Paul Blair was the only base runner, drawing a walk. Taylor picked him off first.

The second game was a nail biter. The Mets couldn't afford to go two games down to the mighty Orioles, anchored by Frank and Brooks Robinson and the breathtaking Boog Powell. The Mets took a 1-0 lead in the fourth on a home run by series hero Donn Clendenon. The Orioles tied it in the seventh as Blair singled to break up Jerry Koosman's no-hitter, stole second and scored on a single by Brooks Robinson.

The Mets went ahead in the top of the ninth on two-out singles by Ed Charles, Jerry Grote and Al Weis. When Koosman walked two batters with two out in the bottom of the ninth, Gil Hodges brought in Taylor.

To that point in his post-season playoff career Taylor had been in five games, had pitched ten innings, had given up three harmless hits, had walked two, struck out nine and given up no runs. None. History was asking for one more batter, who was Brooks Robinson. Robinson had hit twenty-three home runs that year and driven in eighty-four runs. The following year he would hit eighteen home runs and drive in ninety-four runs.

"It was a nice cool day," remembers Taylor. "I knew the importance of the game. I had good stuff. I felt strong."

Taylor threw two balls, then a curve for a strike, then another ball to bring the count to 3-1 and raise the prospect of the third walk in a row, and what then, a fourth? Back to the traditional Met days of goofy ways to lose?

The next pitch might have been outside, but it had enough movement on it that Robinson swung and missed: 3-2. Robinson fouled one off. "I was pretty damned worried," Taylor later told reporters. So was Mrs. Joan Payson, owner of the Mets, who had endured so much during the team's short but pathetic history. She covered her eyes with her scarf.

Taylor threw Robinson a sinking fastball on the inside part of the plate. Robinson hit a two-hopper to Ed Charles, the Mets' journeyman third baseman, who made an awkward, short-hop play on the ball, managing to pull it into his midriff. The runners were going on contact so Charles had no chance at a force at third. But for an agonizing moment he moved toward the bag with the apparent intention of trying to beat the runner.

Thinking better of it, he threw to first. In the dirt. Clendenon dug it out. Watching the play on the big screen in his recreation room, Ron Taylor winces. He wants Charles to make that play the way it should have been made, easily. But the tape also shows Taylor watching the play unfold from the edge of the mound. If Clendenon had had trouble with the throw, shouldn't Taylor have been scurrying to back up a throw to home in case the play came to the plate?

Ah, who cares. Taylor threw the right pitch and Mrs. Payson was able to uncover her eyes. The Mets won the game and the Series, just like the Cardinals had five years earlier. In ten and one-third pressure-packed post-season innings Taylor didn't give up a run or even a hit that meant anything. If they ever draft a twenty-five-man roster of all-time World Series performers, they'll have to put Taylor in the bullpen, right beside Larry Sherry of the 1959 Dodgers.

What he did on the playing field, and the glory he reaped from it, is hard to match in civilian life. "The ticker-tape parade is something that really stands out in my memory," he says quietly. The flamboyance of a parade doesn't mesh with the understated Taylor style — the videos show him, even in his moments of triumph, walking off the mound like nothing much had happened. But gliding between the skyscrapers in an open car was another story.

"It was just overwhelming. Here we were, going down Broadway, and all this tremendous roar, and all this ticker tape coming down on you, and people were tearing the molding off the car as you were going along, tearing buttons off your suit. What I was thinking about was that, you know, here I am going along the same route the astronauts went down, that Kennedy went down, that MacArthur and Lindberg went down. Here I am, a member of a team, being able to do this. It was a real gift."

So what next, sports hero? You want to be a manager? You want to be an engineer? You *still* want to be a doctor? You crazy old man.

There were two more years with the Mets, but Taylor was winding down, and at thirty-four it was over. He went home to Toronto. He had the engineering degree, which he'd always known he'd need when his athletic career was behind him, in his back pocket. He got some offers, many of them in sales. "They wanted to hire me not so much because of my sales ability, but because of my name. So there you're trading in something that means less to people every day, so you're dealing from diminishing value. I didn't want any part of that.

"I thought maybe I'd get my Ph.D. in engineering and work in computers. But I'd always thought it would be nice to be a doctor. I had two friends who were surgeons, and they gave me mixed messages. One said go for it. The other said, 'Don't. You're too old.'

"I had no idea how difficult it is to get into medical school. I went to see the assistant dean of medicine at U of T and I said 'I'd like to enroll at medical school next year.' He looked at me as if to say, 'What planet does this guy come from?' He said, 'How old are you?' I told him I was thirty-four. He said, 'That's pretty old. We don't accept anybody over thirty except in rare cases. And we have thousands of applications for two hundred and fifty spots.'"

They came to an agreement that Taylor would do a makeup year consisting of four difficult courses in honors science. If he pulled off the kind of first-class marks he had in engineering a dozen years earlier he would be considered. But even then, he'd only have a fifty-fifty chance at best.

Taylor responded with the kind of line that forced Beeston to declare him weird. "I said, 'Those are good odds. I'll take them.' That surprised him."

So he studied organic chemistry and physical chemistry and biology and molecular chemistry. He had married during his second year of engineering but that ended in divorce, so there were few distractions. He threw down a mattress in a room in his father's house and started to slap his brain around.

110

"I would go to school from nine to around five, come home, sleep from six to around eleven, get up and study from eleven to eight, and go to school again. I really think it's the toughest thing I've done in my life. I studied standing up because of the pain in my back."

He got his As and waited. He was out in Alberta managing the Lethbridge Lakers amateur baseball team when he got the news. "Not only did I get accepted, but we won the pennant out there.

"So I went to medical school, and medical school was even tougher. I did the same routine. I kept to myself. There was a joke going around campus: *Q. How do you get into medical school? A. Get straight As or be an ex-big-league pitcher.* But it didn't bother me. They didn't know my academic record. The first year in medical school they thought I was the janitor. I had a dirty old warm-up jacket, and I'd sit at the back of the class, and I think they thought I was going to take out the garbage or something."

A lot of medical school is memory work. Taylor had been taught not to memorize in engineering: memorizers failed. So he took his middle-aged brain and forced it to adapt to memorizing vast amounts of complicated information.

"And I passed. I had a few rough times, but I won the battle. I had that commitment. I wasn't going to quit." The intensity may have had some side effects. During his second year of medical school he married a woman he had dated in New York. It didn't work out.

He interned at Mount Sinai, where Rhona says he was greatly respected. "He was obviously a workaholic. He was intense and demanding. But he had that nice sense of humor when you least expected it, and he didn't strut. He was humble—he treated the cleaning staff with the same respect he showed other doctors.

"One day we were sitting in the cafeteria talking about what we'd like in a man, and he was coming through the line, and I said whoever I married will have to have the qualities that man has."

And now she is married to him, and they have two young boys, and baseball equipment hanging in the kitchen, and he works incredibly long days. He has a large general practice and a sports medicine clinic at Mount Sinai, which emphasizes early therapy. He is club physician to the Blue Jays, which allows him his own locker and uniform; he likes to pitch batting practice when he can.

"During the week I can't get down to the park until game time, and on Monday and Thursday I have clinics, so I have to get somebody else to go. Monday I start at the office at eight o'clock, and leave about ten-thirty at night. Tuesday I work in the office from eight in the morning until seven at night, and Wednesday I start at eight, and have a clinic at eight at night and get home at nine or ten. Then Thursday I start at eight and work until around ten-thirty, but Friday I knock off around four or five." On Sunday mornings he does paperwork when Rhona and the kids are at church.

He is, quite simply, very demanding of himself, his staff and the people he lives with. "He likes things perfect," says Rhona. "And he can be so quiet when something has gone wrong at the office. I've seen him shattered when he's had to tell somebody bad news. He really cares about his patients."

"The real extra," says Dr. Ron Taylor, "is having gone through the ups and downs of the life of a big-league ballplayer. And the trauma of marital problems. Having lived all that in a compressed period of time helps me deal with people. A big part of general practice comes down to emotional problems, and if you've worked through a few of these things yourself, it helps."

"He's terrific with people with problems," says Beeston.

"He cares so much," says Rhona.

"I'm my own drummer," says the guy who sat on the convertible, the ticker tape streaming down. Call him somber. Call him weird. Call him diligent and make him happy. On the mound, off the mound, always searching for the perfect pitch.

14

GLEN GORBOUS

Calgary, Alberta
January 15, 1988

Blessed are they who can bring a baseball to life with their throwing arms. For they are the chosen, known by the simple but sacred inscription scrawled majestically across their scouting reports: "Great arm."

One of the greatest of them all belonged to Glen Gorbous, born in Rosedale, near Drumheller, Alberta. Tommy LaSorda called him "the all-Canadian boy with the all-American arm." The arm took Gorbous to the majors. It also got him into the *Guinness Book of World Records*. Think about a football field and think about throwing a baseball one and a half times the length of it. Then whistle. Glen Gorbous did it.

"Great arm" is the most reverent of all assessments. It means, "Anything is possible, kid, even if you can't hit soup with the bat yet and you run like you've got your shoelaces tied together."

It's no guarantee. If it's attached to a pitcher, he's going to need the right mechanics; if it's attached to a position player, he's going to need some speed or power, too. But it's kind of like having a 160 IQ if you want to go to university. It's a nice place to start.

A ballplayer with a great arm may be a spiritual cesspool when he's in street clothes. No matter. He will still radiate a kind of religious aura when warm-ups begin. A mystery surrounds his gift. If his arm is skinny, so much the better. That only enhances the magic, bequeathed, no doubt, by some diminutive prehistoric ancestor who wowed his buddies with a spear when the behemoth hunt was on.

The biggest part of the mystery is that you can never tell who's got an arm just by looking at him. Outfielder Jimmy Wynn, who stood five feet nine and weighed 165 pounds, was called "the Toy Cannon" when he played for the Houston Astros in the sixties for the way he could blow away base runners.

On the other hand, Kirk Gibson is six foot three, weighs 215 pounds and can powder a ball into the upper deck and most likely outrun an antelope

and tear it to pieces with his teeth. But no amount of throwing instructions and no amount of practice are ever going to change the fact that he'll never bruise a baby throwing a baseball.

Then there was Glen Gorbous. Who would have thought God would have sent one of history's great arms to the little coal town of Rosedale, five miles out of Drumheller, on July 8, 1930? But Gorbous probably could have thrown Jimmy Wynn farther than Kirk Gibson can throw a baseball.

Not many players who hit just .238 in only 115 major-league games were selected for the book *Who's Who in Professional Baseball* when it was put together in 1973. In fact, there's nobody else in the book with numbers that modest. But the editors couldn't help themselves.

> Gorbous had six games with Cincinnati in 1955, 91 with Phillies. Hit .244 that year. Following season in 15 games batted .182. Went to bat just twice in 1957, one hit. His 66 hits in majors included 13 doubles, 1 triple, 4 homers, 29 RBIS. No stolen bases. Gorbous isn't remembered by many people . . . not much of a hitter, and not much speed afoot. But OH, how he could throw! *The Sporting New's* reports that he made the longest throw ever recorded in baseball — 445 feet, 10 inches. Was accomplished 8/1/57 at Omaha.

"I wish I was as good a ballplayer as I was a bullshitter," says Glen Gorbous, sitting in his modest office in downtown Calgary. He is Calgary sales rep for an Edmonton-based firm that services oil rigs, often in the far north. Office decorations are sparse — three calendars (one for last year, two for this year) and three maps (one of Alberta, two of the Mackenzie Valley area of the Northwest Territories).

Behind the only desk in the office sits a beak-nosed, big-boned man who isn't really a bullshitter, but who likes good yarns and has a nice memory for things other people try to forget.

Like the first ballpark he played in as a professional. He was in Oregon with the Medford Nuggets of the Far West League, at the lowest end of the Dodger organization: "It was a rodeo grounds with a skin diamond. I hit three-sixty-something and made the all-star team, but I had sixty-four errors at third base. Our shortstop was a terrific fielder, and he had eighty-eight. It was tough fielding there — you'd find yourself catching pop flies in the bucking chutes.

"There were lots of hoofprints and lots of horse turds. You'd go down for a baseball and come up with a turd. And there are more lights in this

On the evening of August 1, 1957, Glen stuffed the last of a hot dog into his mouth and wound up his arm. (Dan Turner)

office than there were in that ballpark, so sometimes it wasn't that easy to tell the difference." (With sixty-four errors, you *know* there were some horseshit throws to first).

In his second year in the minors Gorbous was playing with the Bisbee-Douglas Copper Kings of the Arizona League. Life was not a beach there —in fact life was a bus, winding endlessly through the southwest, dumping its human contents at one ball field after another. If the windows were closed, the bus became a broiler. If they were open they did an imitation of washroom hand dryers.

The bus would stop in Tombstone, Arizona, where the players were given a chance to empty their bladders. Which Gorbous and his chum, a catcher named Gus Buono, were doing at four in the morning in the Boot Hill Cemetery, on Wyatt Earp's grave.

"You know, Glen," said Buono, pondering the earth beneath him and life in the Arizona League, "that dead cowboy is better off than we are." The next day the two jumped the team and lit out for Calgary. They finished the summer playing semi-pro ball for the Purity 99 team Gorbous had been with before he signed as a pro.

Both were suspended by the Dodgers. Buono was never reinstated. But Gorbous was a prospect, even if his beginnings wouldn't have predicted it. He had learned his rudimentary baseball by a fluke in an open field near the Rosedale mines. The owner of the lumberyard happened to be an American who knew the game. Gorbous took to it, and when there was nobody around to play with he'd take an old taped ball and throw it straight up into the air, over and over and over again.

"I don't know whether you ever tried to throw the ball straight up in the air, but it's hard. I didn't have naturally strong shoulders, but that developed them. I used to try to throw it right out of sight. People were amazed at how high I could throw it.

"I used to catch them all when they came down, too. The catching part never seemed to help much later on, when I played pro ball. A guy would hit one out to right with the bases loaded, and I'd have trouble surrounding it. It must have been the pressure."

When the family moved to Vulcan, Alberta, Gorbous, then sixteen, played with a senior team. He later moved to the semi-pro league in Calgary, where super scout Howie Haak signed him for $500 when he was seventeen. "Son," said Haak, "you have a fair arm." Meaning *great arm.*

Although he never stole a base in the majors, Gorbous could run. But he'd never been trained to run the bases. "I had good speed for stealing hubcaps, but we were very crude ballplayers. It didn't seem that way at the time, but I found out we were when I went with the Dodgers and had to learn everything all over again."

A left-handed hitter, he had also developed an uppercut swing—natural enough for a kid wanting to hit the ball over a fence, but full of blind spots against top-caliber pitching.

Gorbous was invited back to spring training the year after his defection. He'd tried a little outfield in Calgary, and at Dodger training camp, always peopled by hundreds of prospects, Gorbous began sneaking batting practice with the outfielders as well as the infielders.

He became an outfielder by accident one day when a coach got confused and dispatched him to right field in a game. He never went back to third. "Nobody noticed," he recalls with a shake of his head.

He made his way through the Dodgers' minor-league system, thrilling people with his shotgun arm and hitting more than .300 several times. He finally hit his way to Montreal, the Dodgers' Triple A club, only to get demoted again when the Dodgers sent Sandy Amoros down. That winter two players would be drafted off the Montreal roster—Roberto Clemente, by the Pirates, and Gorbous, by the Cincinnati Redlegs.

The 1955 Cincinnati team he reported to was one of the strongest hitting clubs in baseball history, featuring Gus Bell, Wally Post, Ed Bailey and the massive-armed Ted Kluszewski.

"I'm 175 pounds and looking starved. The first time I walk into the Cincinnati dressing room big Klu takes one of my thirty-one-ounce bats, puts it beside his big thirty-eight-ouncer, picks mine up, and starts picking his teeth with it. It broke everybody up."

Gorbous was hitting a lofty .333 for the Redlegs (6-for-18) when he got traded to Philadelphia. But he hit only .237 for the Phillies in a platoon role over the balance of the season. It hadn't taken long for big-league pitchers to discover his flaw.

He was a pull hitter who couldn't go to the opposite field, an uppercutter who couldn't flatten out his swing. Pitchers started placing the ball on the outside corner and letting him hit deep to center field.

"What good were a lot of 410-foot outs? They knew I was going to try to pull everything, and they had me." The pressure at the top, he says, took a lot of the fun out of it for him.

Still, there were a few delicious moments. Carl Erskine tried to put a high fastball by him the first time he faced the Dodgers, and Gorbous hit a deep fly to Duke Snider in center. Erskine tried it again the next time around and Gorbous hit this one onto Bedford Avenue, outside Ebbets Field.

117

During one night game the Phillies were two runs behind with two runners on when the game was called because of a city curfew. The next day Gorbous came in as a pinch hitter to lead off the resumption of play and whacked a three-run homer to win it.

But while his throws from right field brought oohs and-ahs, his hitting simply wasn't consistent enough. The Phillies tried desperately to alter his swing, but in 1956 he hit only .182, and except for going 1-for-2 in 1957, that was it in the bigs. The all-Canadian boy with the all-too-Canadian skill gaps was gone.

But gone or not, as far as the world records are concerned, 1957 was Gorbous's best year. The Phillies traded him to the St. Louis Cardinals, and the Cards sent him to their Triple A team in Omaha.

There he ran into Whitey Reis, a veteran minor-league player who doubled as a stand-up comic at local bars whenever he could talk local bars into letting him perform. Reis had an eye for promotion and it came to his attention that Don Grate, another minor-league outfielder, had recently thrown a baseball 445 feet and 1 inch. Grate broke the previous world record, which had been held by one Sheldon LeJeune since 1910.

Reis knew that (a) Gorbous had an incredibly powerful arm, and (b) that it was in extraordinary shape for long-distance throwing. Gorbous had been doing a lot of it. Feeling loose and who-gives-a-damn after the intensity of the big leagues, he liked to amuse folks during warm-ups by popping bulbs in the faraway light standards.

Minor-league ball survives as much on promotions as it does on the game itself, and Reis convinced the team's owners that Gorbous should be given a shot at the record.

Gorbous demurred at first, on the grounds that there was nothing in it for him. "I said I don't think I want to do it. They said, 'We'll give you two hundred bucks.' I said, 'I no longer think I don't want to do it.'"

On the evening of August 1, 1957, just before dusk, the band was playing at the Omaha ballpark and leathery old men were testing the public-address system. It was hot and muggy with the hint of a breeze from left field to right, where stakes and flags had been set up marking Grate's record.

At first Gorbous was nowhere to be seen, but finally he emerged from behind the concession stands, a root beer in one hand, a hot dog in the other and his glove under his arm. A smattering of applause went up, the old man at the public-address system outlined the enormity of what was to take place, Gorbous crammed the last of the hot dog into his mouth, wiped a trace of mustard off his lips and ambled to the left-field corner.

118

"What are ya wearin' your glove for?" bawled someone in the stands, and Gorbous thought about it and shrugged. There was no answer to that, other than he'd never thrown a ball with his right hand without a glove on his left hand, and this didn't seem like a good time to start. "Balance!" he yelled back knowingly, wondering if that made any sense.

When he got to the launching area behind a demarcation string, Reis tried to give him some advice about how Grate had gone about setting the record. Gorbous sucked back the last of his root beer and waved Reis away. "I'd played against Grate and I was sure I could beat him. I was always like that with throwing—like Muhammad Ali. I never saw a guy I was afraid to throw against. I saw Roberto Clemente throw — he had a strong arm, but he threw three-quarters and you've got to learn to come overhand to get the right lift and a true throw. I'd never be afraid of him in a contest.

"And when I was with Brooklyn they tried to get Carl Furillo [known as the Reading Rifle] and I to throw against each other. It never came off. I think they were afraid . . . well, I know he had a good arm, but I knew I could beat him.

"Not much of a hitter . . . but OH, how he could throw." (Glen Gorbous)

"Anyway, I says to Whitey, 'I don't want to know how Grate did it. I'll just throw the ball as long as I can—what's the big deal about that?

"I had warmed up good, and I was sweating, and I looked at the flags and I remember thinking 'Whew, that's a long ways.'

"Anyway, I backed up to the fence, which gave me about ten or fifteen feet to run, and I ran toward the string and let it go. And I'm telling you, that was the best throw I ever made in my life. And I looked up and the ball had fallen about ten feet short. I said 'Whitey, I can't throw any harder than that.

"And he said, 'For a start you stopped six feet short of the string. And you've got to throw it higher, like Grate did—you're not trying to throw hard and low to get a guy at third, you're trying to throw high and far. And you've got to back up and get a better run at it.'

"I say, 'How am I going to get a better run at it? I'm right against the wall now.'

"But Whitey was smart—he had them open the groundskeeper's gate. And I go outside the fence and all of a sudden I am in the parking lot all alone. And I'm saying to myself, 'I should go across the street and have a beer while all these people are waiting for me to come through that gate.'

"But I took a run and came up to the string and threw higher, and the ball landed in about the same place.

"And by this time I figure I'm done for, because that is the second-hardest I've ever thrown a ball. But Whitey says, 'You're still not throwing it high enough and you've got to get an even bigger run, because that's the way Grate did it.'

"By this time I'd given up. A lot was gone out of my arm. But I went way back and the public-address announcer was saying, 'Gorbous is going to give it one last try,' and I ran like a madman to the string and Whitey is yelling, 'Higher! higher!' and I threw it up so high it felt like it was going straight up — only I got a poor release, and I just said, 'Screw it,' and stomped away.

"And people started screaming and shouting and Whitey said, 'You beat it.' And it didn't seem like any big deal at the time, really. The other players said, 'We know who's buying the beer tonight.' And sure enough, Whitey drank most of it."

15

REGGIE CLEVELAND

Calgary, Alberta
January 16, 1988

When Reggie Cleveland quit at the end of the 1981 season he was one of 396 pitchers in the history of major-league baseball to have won a hundred games.

About five thousand pitchers had tried, so Reggie finished in the top ten percent of his class. It was a career worth celebrating, and it has been celebrated. Cleveland was inducted into the Canadian Baseball Hall of Fame in 1986. He wears his red, diamond-studded membership ring proudly.

He was *The Sporting News* Rookie Pitcher of the Year in 1971, and two-time winner of the Rolaids award as best relief pitcher on his team — in 1978 with the Texas Rangers and in 1980 with the Milwaukee Brewers. Nice career.

So when Reggie Cleveland sits there sipping his drink in the living room of his modest bungalow in suburban Calgary, flashing his smile and looking content with life, it's only natural to ask him about the great times he had playing ball. And without the slightest hesitation he tells you about them. For awhile.

And then, after he has paid tribute to several wild and crazy teammates he ran with over the years, it's also only natural to ask him what *he* was like. He takes a sip. He sighs. Nothing is said for a few moments. "That's a good question," he says finally, his winning smile tucked away for the moment. "That's a really good question."

Like many Canadian kids who end up playing pro ball, Cleveland had a father who didn't mind kicking around sandlot ball fields. Bob Cleveland had served in the air force during the war, became a ticket clerk with the Canadian Pacific Railway and rejoined the RCAF as a corporal when his son was seven.

Bouncing around from air base to air base might not seem like an ideal

121

training ground for a ballplayer. But everywhere they went Reggie's father would get involved, making sure there was organized baseball, helping to raise money for uniforms and equipment with raffles, draws and bingo games.

First it was Saskatchewan — Little League and Pony League in Moose Jaw. Then Alberta—senior ball in Cold Lake, Bonnyville, Provost and Two Hills. Then Saskatchewan again—Swift Current, Moose Jaw, Regina, Melville and Qu'Appelle.

By the time he was thirteen, Cleveland was six feet tall and weighed 165 pounds. When he was fourteen he was playing with eighteen- to twenty-one-year-old juniors, and when he was fifteen he was pitching regularly on men's senior teams, finally playing for a team coached by Jackie McLeod, best remembered for his stint as coach of the Canadian national hockey team.

The scout who discovered Cleveland wasn't really a scout. His name was Sam Shapiro, and he was a four-foot-eleven-inch free spirit who moved a small carnival around the prairies in the summer and umpired intra-squad games in Florida during spring training. Through the umpiring, he'd become a friend of Cardinal manager Red Schoendienst. Shapiro's hobby was looking in on sandlot ball games, and after watching Cleveland pitch one night in Swift Current he wired Schoendienst and tipped him that the kid was a prospect. He later used to laugh that nobody ever repaid him the $4.85 for the telegram.

Cleveland was seventeen years old and no dummy when he signed for $500 with the Cardinals. He'd maintained an eighty-five-percent average all through high school and had plans for university. But he had cravings. Food—his nickname would be "Double Cheeseburger" with the Cardinals —baseball, and warm weather. "I was in grade twelve. The Cardinals sent me a contract in December saying that I could go to spring training. Spring training! I thought, 'Forget school'—I figured I'd make Triple A my first year and be in the majors when I was nineteen."

When he got to spring training in 1966 he discovered his pitching arm wasn't getting much help from his legs and upper body on the mound. But he learned quickly and by 1969 he'd made his debut with the Cardinals: four innings, four runs. Oh, well . . .

He'd married while playing A ball in Florida ("I got lonely") and his wife Kathleen had given birth to their first child the night he pitched a one-hitter for the Arkansas Travelers (a scratch single erased in a double play).

He tried to crack the Cardinals lineup once again in 1970, but went 0-4 with a 7.62 ERA in twenty-six innings. But there was at least one highlight.

As a pitcher, Reggie finished near the top of his class. But he has some regrets and advice. (Dan Turner)

As soon as he reported late in the season Schoendienst stuck him right into a game the Cards were losing.

"We were in Philadelphia, and I took the mound in the bottom of the seventh. I pitched the seventh and the eighth, and I was incredible—I just blew people away, struck out four or five of them.

"I was so hyped up that come the bottom of the ninth I was going out to the mound when I noticed nobody was with me. It hadn't clicked with me that we hadn't scored any runs and the game was over—we'd lost. I'm just sayin' 'where is everybody? Let me at 'em again.' "

The next year, 1971, proved to be Cleveland's year. He got off to a rocky 0-2 start, to make him 0-6 lifetime, before running into Hall-of-Famer Juan Marichal. Marichal had beaten Cleveland for his 205th lifetime victory a week earlier and had dodged a start against the mighty Bob Gibson the previous night to try to rack up his 206th against easier competition.

Cleveland still savors the irony. "The night before was one of those rare occasions where Gibson got his ass kicked, so Marichal could have had an easy win. Then I beat him 2-1. They had the bases loaded against me in the ninth, but [Moe] Drabowsky came in and saved it for me."

You ask Reggie Cleveland about the high times he and his pals had in the majors, and Drabowsky's name comes up time and again. There is the story about the night Drabowsky threw the TV set out the San Diego hotel room window into the swimming pool. There is the story about the lady who vomited into Drabowsky's lap, and the story about the night Drabowsky came into the game in relief and lost the game in Houston. And then . . .

"We got back to the hotel and Moe started drinking Manhattans, and he was feeling pretty good. He picked up this big tree they had potted and set it on the bar. The bartender told him to take it down, but Moe told him where to go and walked out. It took four guys to lift it down.

"Meanwhile the hotel—it was the Marriott—had these little globe lights a little over head high all the way down the lobby, and Moe proceeded to break all of those.

"Moe went to his room and started mixing his own Manhattans. And we had this pitcher with us whose name was Joe Grzenda,—Shakey Joe. [It was to be Shakey's last year in the bigs.] And Moe was sitting in his room, still drinking Manhattans, and he'd gotten a tray of highball glasses somehow. So he'd mix himself a Manhattan, take a few sips and go hunting Joe, and when he found him he'd throw the glass and ice at him. I remember Joe going down the hall with one of those fold-up tables, using it as a shield."

Cleveland chortles for a moment when he tells this story, savoring his second complete year in the majors. He was twenty-four. "The biggest thing with a young guy in the big leagues," he says, speaking quietly now, "is that you have a tendency to try to live up to everybody else. You say, 'Here I am — I'm with the Joe Torres and Bob Gibsons and Dal Maxvills and Moe Drabowskys — I'll try to keep up with them.' "

It was glamorous, a long way from harsh prairie winters. He bought a home in St. Petersburg, his wife's home town. "I'm settled in and there's no way I want to go back home," he told a reporter. "This is it."

Later, when Cleveland took out American citizenship papers, he actually got a death threat in the mail from an irate Canadian fan. He shrugged it off. America was where the action was. He wasn't in Hollywood. But he was close.

He was 12-12 in his first full year with the Cardinals, with a 4.01 ERA, which improved to 3.94 the second year, when he went 14-15. In his third year he was 14-10, with a 3.01 ERA. It seemed like he was beginning to bloom. Then two things happened to him in Venezuela, where he had gone to play winter ball.

First he hurt his knee — he thinks on a checked swing — and started to have trouble with his slider, which complemented his sinking fastball and had been essential to his success. And second, he got traded. In Spanish.

"My roommate, Mickey Scott, went down for breakfast one day during the first week of December. He came back up and said, 'I can't read Spanish too well, but I think you've been traded.' I tried to decipher it and decided he was probably right.

"But I didn't hear anything from either side. Finally I got back in late January and called Dick O'Connell in Boston, and said, 'I think I'm playing for you guys, but I'm not sure.' He said he was pretty sure I was."

Boston would more or less set the pattern for his career. His weight went down every spring and ballooned during the season; his ERA rose and fell in one- and two-year cycles. It was never terrific long enough for him to become a star, but never bad long enough for him to be dropped by the wayside.

He was useful because he could start and relieve. "Boston is where I got into the role of a swing man, starting sometimes, relieving sometimes. They'd say, 'Let's use Reggie as the swing man because he can do anything we want him to.' But my knee was so bad I couldn't run between appearances." Things didn't go well that first year. Lynn McGlothen, one of the pitchers who went to St. Louis in the deal, had the best year of his life, with a 16-12 record and a 2.70 ERA. Cleveland, who had been 14-10 with a 3.01 ERA the previous year, slumped to 12-14 with a 4.32 ERA.

"Boston's a strange baseball town. If you do well there they love you. If you're terrible — inept — they can forgive you. But if you're mediocre, watch out. They can't stand mediocrity. And the first year there, I was overwhelmingly mediocre."

He would have three more years in Boston: 13-9 with a 4.43 ERA in 1975, 10-9 with a 3.07 ERA in 1976, and 11-8 with a 4.26 ERA in 1977.

Although his ERA was highest in 1975, the year Boston made it to the World Series, he'd gone 10-3 after July 6 and won four straight games at the end to help stave off a late-season drive by the Baltimore Orioles.

During that 1975 Series, he pitched in the game immediately before and the game immediately after one of the most famous World Series games ever, the incredible Sixth Game, in which Boston beat Cincinnati 7-6 in twelve innings to tie the series at three games apiece. Unfortunately Boston lost the games on either side of that one, and Cleveland pitched in both of them.

The sixth game might have won it all for Boston if Cleveland had been sharp the day before, but Don Gullett beat him 6-2. After nursing a one-run lead into the fourth, Cleveland gave up a homer to Tony Perez, then a single to the pitcher, Gullett, and a run-scoring double to Pete Rose in the fifth, then a three-run homer to Perez in the sixth, capping a walk to Joe Morgan and a single by Bench.

Bench's single was actually a miscue by second baseman Denny Doyle, who misread a double-play grounder, moving toward second only to let it slip through where he had been standing. Which made it 5-1 instead of 3-1, and goodbye, Reggie.

He made an appearance in the final game, with Cincinnati leading 4-3 in the top of the ninth, walking Bench and inducing Perez to fly to right for the third out. He stood to win the game had Boston come back with two runs in the bottom of the ninth, but the Beantowners went down one, two, three. Cleveland's consolation prize was small: he was the first Canadian ever to start a World Series game. And his memories of that game are hazy. One newspaper report referred to him "berating the umpire, gesticulating wildly," before he was lifted.

In 1976 he not only came back to win ten games and fashioned a fine 3.08 ERA, but he gave up only three home runs all season — an incredibly small number, considering the confines of Fenway Park. Two of the three wouldn't have gone out of any other park. It was a lovely year for the

Reggie had a talent that would bubble up, and ebb away, and bubble up again. (Boston Globe)

talent that would bubble up and ebb away, bubble up and ebb away, during his thirteen years in the major leagues.

In 1977 he went 11-8 with a 4.26 ERA. In 1978 he was traded to Texas, where he again came back, with twelve saves and a fine 3.08 ERA, which qualified him to play the lead role in a *Sports Illustrated* article on the collection of affable cast-offs and oddballs that peopled the Rangers' bullpen.

He was liked in Texas — people always liked easy-smiling Reggie — but the Rangers ran into financial problems and he was sold to Milwaukee, where he pitched for three years in the culmination of a career that should have peaked with the Brewers' appearance in the 1982 World Series. In 1980 he pitched well, going 11-9 with a 3.74 ERA, after coming to manager George Bamberger in the spring and saying, "I'm going to make you proud of me." Bamberger was doubtful. Cleveland was getting older, he was coming off a mediocre year, and it seemed late in the game for him to be getting his act together. But he came through, and for one more season everyone was proud of him. But he waned again in 1981, picking up only two wins and a save, and by 1982 there wasn't much left of Reggie Cleveland to attach an arm to.

"Right from the start it was too much of too much. Too much of everything. And it's easy to let it happen, because it's such a glamorous lifestyle. It got to the point where I had a problem — a serious problem. There's no doubt in my mind that the biggest problem with athletes in the big leagues is booze.

"The booze is a lot worse than the drugs ever thought of being or ever will be. Not that the drugs are so great. You remember the big scar-faced pitcher who won the Cy Young Award? I won't mention his name. But his idea of pitching was to take so many amphetamines that you couldn't stay still, then after the game drink twenty-four beer to come down off it.

"Anyway, I had a problem. Beer? Sure. But anything. If it was alcohol, I drank it. I married too young. And baseball makes it worse. I was away from my wife and kids most of the time—from March to September I was by myself.

"After I went to Milwaukee my days were consistent because the family was still living back in Texas. So at home or on the road, at noon or one o'clock I'd wake up and go down for breakfast, then go to the ball park at two or three in the afternoon. You'd play cards for awhile with the coaches and go to the bullpen for the game and maybe get in and maybe not, although in my last year I didn't get in a whole lot in the last two or three months.

"Then afterward you'd have four or five beers in the clubhouse, maybe six beers in the clubhouse, and then go right from there to the bar, and close down the bar, maybe have another dozen beer, or booze, or whatever, and go home or go back to the hotel and crash, and get up at one o'clock the next day and do exactly the same thing, day after day after day.

"And it was like that in Boston, except I was younger and could keep going better, except I rolled my car in a tunnel one night after a ball game. How do you roll your car in a tunnel? I still don't know. There was a little blurb in the *Globe and Mail* the next day—'Reggie Cleveland was in a car accident, blah, blah, blah . . . '

"I had a good year in Texas, but they were hard up for money so they sold me to Milwaukee. I was really pissed off, because I had bought a twenty-acre farm in Texas. So I went to Milwaukee, and really had a shitty year. Then the next year I told myself I'd better have a good year or I'd be gone, so I did. But then I started having some family problems again, and the booze and everything was really catching up to me.

"But nobody was telling management about my problem because I was such a good drunk. I'd built up my tolerance so I could drink twelve or fourteen beers without showing it, and where I was drinking wasn't that far from the hotel, so I just walked back, without falling down. But I realized I was falling to pieces.

"So I'm hitting the booze hard, really hard, and of course not having a good year and all, and then we had the players' strike. I'd spent everything on the farm and my cash flow was poor. Then we go back after sixty days and I've got to get back in shape in a hurry, and so I hurt my arm a little.

"So now I'm not pitching worth a shit either, and when I do pitch I get my ass kicked, and that makes me drink some more. And then finally we had to play off for our division title, and I went to Buck Rogers, the manager, and I said, 'You've got a team in the playoffs, and you don't have any confidence in me, and I don't have any confidence in me. Get somebody you're going to be able to use,' I said, 'because I've got to get out of here or I'm going to end up in the tank.'

"Harry Daulton, the general manager, came down and told me he didn't realize things were going so badly for me. I said, 'I got to get out of this life-style for a while. My family's falling apart, I'm falling apart and I'm drinking myself into a stupor every night.'

"When I look back, doing well in the major leagues depends mostly on whether you can adapt to the travel and the endless bullshit. You start out as a young kid, very impressionable. And a lot of times you develop bad habits. In baseball you finish up in a strange town at eleven, eleven-thirty at night. You can go back to your hotel room and look at the walls or watch television or read a book, but everybody else is going down to the bar. So you go down there for the camaraderie, and then you see that good-looking girl in the corner, and let me go talk to her for a minute . . . That's another thing in professional sport—there's peer pressure to screw around. It gets to be, 'Did you score last night?'

"I wanted to be one of the guys—it's that simple."

Cleveland finished with 105 wins and 106 losses, just about breaking even. He returned to Canada, he says with a rueful smile, to escape continuing pressure from his first wife and the United States Internal Revenue Service. He had signed for a $500 bonus at the beginning of his career and gone away to stay. When he played, toward the end, he earned close to a quarter of a million dollars a year. When he came home he was broke.

Calgary is a refuge. He shares his bungalow with his second wife, Charlene, and her two sons. He sells cars for Shaganappi Chev-Olds. He still has that roguish smile, but the drink he keeps sipping on is coffee. "Once in a while, but not often," he says, to the inevitable question about whether he still takes a drink.

"I've seen it both ways, 105-106 and 106-105," he says with regard to his record. "But it's really 106-106. I'm sure of that."

Not according to the *Baseball Encyclopedia*, or the Hall of Fame Library in Cooperstown: it was 105-106. There were, of course, all kinds of chances to pick up another couple of wins over the years. Most of them, the candid man with the charming smile will tell you, were pissed away in urinals from St. Louis to Boston, Texas to Milwaukee and points in between.

16

JOHN HILLER

Iron Mountain, Michigan
February 5, 1988

The snow squeaks as John Hiller makes his way to the barn to feed the cows. The evening is shadowed, blue and quiet all the way to the horizon, where a pink and orange sunset takes over and gives off a faint reminder of warmth. Soon the deer herd will come where they've scattered the grain, breathing clouds of vapor into the brittle air.

Michigan's upper peninsula is about as remote as a ballplayer can get from spring training. But not for long. Tonight is for goodbyes. At six in the morning Linette will rev up the pickup and drive John Hiller down through Wisconsin and over to the Green Bay airport. A few hours later he'll be in Lakeland, arriving early because of the fantasy camp. He and Al Kaline and some of the others will take to the practice fields and bars with a couple of dozen well-to-do Detroit businessmen, squirreling away a little extra money before the pitchers and catchers show up.

Sixteen years ago Hiller had a little fantasy of his own. He thought he could rekindle life as a professional athlete after suffering a heart attack at twenty-seven. It was a stupid idea. Baseball people thought some mix of youth and fear and sense of loss had come together to addle his mind. But with a courtesy unusual to the business of baseball, they at least tried to drag their feet a bit before telling him his time was up.

He used the time well. He spent some of it in a cockroach colony, which was appropriate enough. Because a fringe relief pitcher — even a left-handed fringe relief pitcher — whose heart muscle is damaged and who can't throw away his jockstrap and face reality is about as useful as a cockroach in the clubhouse.

But in the end, after a year and half of pressing his nose against the window, Hiller came back to baseball and did what he'd never been able to do before. He pitched brilliantly. As comeback stories go, this one ranks with the rolling away of the stone in 33 A.D.

He is bald and handsome, with warm brown eyes. He acts and moves like a kid, except for the circulation problem in one leg, which forces him in out of the cold, into the cozy, beamed kitchen he and Linette, his not-yet wife, have restored around a wood stove. They're both refugees from former marriages, and the farmhouse, brimming with plants and antiques and knickknacks, seems like an ongoing celebration of their getting together.

Hiller talks and dresses like a country boy, but he grew up in Scarborough, on the east edge of Toronto, which he tried to move back to a few years ago. It didn't work. As he said in the local newspaper when he got back to Iron Mountain:

"Toronto is a beautiful city, but it has grown to almost four million people and was so changed and unfamiliar to me that it did not seem like home any longer."

Growing up there, though, John Hiller was a city slicker. He was familiar enough with trees—Scarborough has its share of trees—but not cows and the like. Which would mean a clumsy entrance to farm life when he finally decided he was a man of the soil.

Not only didn't he train himself to farm in Scarborough, he didn't train himself to do very much. At school he was preoccupied with having fun and eating lunch, right up until his final year in grade eleven, when he got some decent marks. "I left it a little late. But I don't think an education would have done me any good anyway. I never would have been happy in a suit and tie."

He yearned to be a hockey goalie, but wasn't much between the pipes. He was athletic, but once he turned sixteen and could tool around in a car he didn't go out of his way to keep in shape. He played baseball and pitched when he wasn't playing outfield, but didn't think of himself as a prospect.

"Until I was sixteen I was nothing. I mean I always had a good arm, but I was just another kid who pitched one day and played the outfield the next. When I pitched I always reared back and threw — I didn't worry about my arm. I threw with a strange kind of hotdog motion, and I got people out on fastballs.

"But you couldn't say I was anything special. One day when I was about seventeen somebody took me down to let Charlie Dressen, the manager of the old Toronto Maple Leafs, have a look at me. I went with another kid who could throw a lot harder than I could. After we both threw, Dressen came over to me and asked me if I liked hockey. I said I did. So then he said, 'Well, you'd better trade that glove in for a new pair of skates because you're never going to play baseball for a living.' I said that didn't bother me because I didn't want to play baseball for a living anyway—I played for fun. And I wasn't kidding—I just never took it that seriously."

But Hiller got bigger and stronger and when he was eighteen his coach, Bob Prentice, now chief of Canadian scouting for the Blue Jays but then connected to the Tigers, brought a Tigers scout from Buffalo named Cy Williams in to sign him.

What Prentice remembers liking most about Hiller, besides his control, was that he was strong and durable. "He'd still be throwing as hard in the ninth inning as he did in the first. Some other scouts—I remember there was one guy from the White Sox — looked at him and didn't seem that interested. Which was fine with me. I'd just finished up as a pro infielder and I knew I had something here."

After Williams saw Hiller pitch he talked to his parents before talking to their son, thereby saving himself some money.

"My dad's a brilliant man — not educated, but brilliant," says Hiller fondly. "He had talked to Williams on the phone and Williams had said the Tigers were going to give me $2,000 to sign. And my dad said, 'Don't you dare. If you give him $2,000 he's going to think he's the greatest thing in the world and the greatest thing ever to hit Scarborough. If he's going to make it he's better off without the money — he'll make it on his own.' And my dad was right. If they'd given me $2,000 I would have gone right out and spent it on a car and stopped thinking about anything else.

"But I didn't know they'd talked. When Williams came over to the house and I asked how much they were going to pay me if I signed, and he said $400 a month, I just said, 'Holy.' I'd been making $12 or $13 working on weekends, and $400—wow!

"And I said, 'How about all these bonuses I keep hearing about?' And he said, 'We don't give Canadian kids bonuses because we can't be sure from the caliber of kids they've been playing against whether they're any good.'

He chuckles. "That made sense to me. And he said there were a couple of pairs of spikes in the car, and if one of them fit I could have a pair and he'd give me a glove later. I never got the glove, but one of the pairs of spikes more or less fit."

Hiller headed for Florida at nineteen, never having been out of Metropolitan Toronto for anything other than a nearby ball tournament. Three weeks later he called home and told his father he was having a great time, but added he'd probably be home soon. His father asked him why. "Look, Dad," he said, "this is fun, but I can't compete with these guys."

But he could, and they kept him. He made progress and put down U.S.

roots. He played for Duluth, Minnesota, in the Northern League, married a local girl and settled there. He made the Tigers in 1967 and proceeded to have four pretty good years, in which he won more games than he lost, 23 to 19, gave up fewer hits than innings pitched, had a strikeout-to-walk ratio in the neighbourhood of 2 to 1 and an ERA of 2.39 in 1968, 3.99 in 1969 and 3.03 in 1970.

He appeared in two games in the 1968 World Series and was cuffed for six hits and three walks in only two innings, but didn't do any damage and the Tigers won. So . . . not bad. Not nearly as mediocre as he remembers: "I remember myself being very average. In my mind I was a fringe pitcher who got to stick around because I was a left-hander."

He and his wife, Janice, had two children, and on the basis of his $20,000-a-year salary he bought a new house in Duluth. He drank his share, smoked three packs of cigarettes a day and hefted 210 pounds on his six-foot-one-inch frame. But then he was only twenty-seven, in his prime. Or so he thought.

On January 11, 1971, at nine-thirty in the morning, Hiller had just returned from a weekend of snowmobiling. He recalls setting his coffee mug on the kitchen table of his new home in Duluth, lighting up a Marlboro and taking a deep drag. At which point he felt a slam of pressure in his chest. Something to do with his lungs, he thought, and stubbed out the cigarette.

Half an hour later he tried a new cigarette. Same thing—wham. He was gasping. The heaviness in his chest got worse; sudden sharp pains stabbed down both his arms. He called his family doctor, who seemed calm enough but told him to come down to the hospital. Hiller was sweating profusely.

For some reason he thought he might have pneumonia again—he'd had it in 1966, the only time he'd ever been sick. When he went out to get in the car he realized the trailer was hitched to the back of it, with a snow-mobile up top. He unscrewed the hitch and tugged the heavy trailer up into the yard. Now he was clammy with sweat.

He made it to the hospital. They went through a few quick checks, put him in a wheelchair and took him to the coronary unit. "I don't want you to worry," said one doctor. "But you've had a heart attack."

He wasn't allowed out of bed. He thought his situation through. With a lack of medical knowledge gleaned from years of skipping health classes, he decided he would get a couple of weeks of bed rest and report for spring training. But when a doctor asked him if he had training in anything other

John had this little fantasy. He thought he could still play after
suffering a heart attack at 27. (Dan Turner)

than baseball, the message started to seep through. Two weeks before spring training began he realized he wasn't going to Florida.

He called Jim Campbell, the Tigers' general manager, with the news. Campbell was flabbergasted, then annoyed that Hiller had waited so long to tell him. "But it wasn't like the end of the world for him," says Hiller with a smile, "it wasn't like the destiny of the Detroit Tigers was riding on my arm. I was a fringe left-hander."

Tests showed one of the main arteries leading into his heart was sixty percent blocked; another was thirty percent blocked. Bypass operations were new; one was recommended. But he was offered a second option. Removing seven feet of his large intestine would arguably reduce the amount of cholesterol produced in his system and give him a better shot at getting back into baseball than would a heart operation.

He decided it was worth a shot. He had the operation at the University of Minnesota. When he came out of the hospital he was down to 142 pounds and so weak he could hardly walk. Weak but fierce.

"The doctor who treated me first said I'd never play baseball again. I couldn't believe him, saying it that bluntly to me. And that made me mad. I guess he knew I was uneducated and what my family situation was, and he wanted me to get on with my life in a different area.

"Well, I'm basically lazy. If someone had said that with hard work, and so forth and so on, you might make it back — then I might not have. But when they told me I never would, I'm dumb enough and stubborn enough that I was determined I would.

"I went over to the YMCA in Duluth. They had such a small track you had to go around it thirty-five times to run a mile. I did four laps and fell flat on my face and thought, 'Oh, no, this isn't going to work.'

"Two friends of mine had a furniture store, and I needed work, so I went to see them. And I remember climbing the steps to the store and having to stop at the top. But they were good — they let me work out when I wanted to, and I worked hard. When I ran at the Y I would focus on some guy's heels, and squint my eyes and pretend I was on the mound again. And I worked with small weights, and played paddleball, and threw a baseball against a chalk-marked square I had drawn on the basement wall at the Y.

"One of the brothers who owned the furniture store watched me throw once and said he could hit that kind of pitching. There was a sofa in the store worth $700, and I said I'd pay him $1,000 for it, even though I didn't have a nickel, if he could touch his bat to one pitch and put it down in fair territory, but he had to give it to me if he couldn't. I won the sofa.

136

"The doctor who did the operation, I think he was pretty sure he could stabilize my cholesterol situation with his operation, but I don't think he was too sure he could reverse it. Anyway, as far as I've heard I was the only one it worked with up to that point, and the only one since.

"The doctor was ecstatic, and so was I. The tests showed that the artery that had been thirty percent blocked was clear, and the other one was only five percent blocked. I called the club and told them I was coming back. But the reaction was kind of . . . *sure* you are. They didn't sound at all convinced. I was deflated, but they said they wanted me to come to Detroit to get tested, so I decided I was pretty happy after all, since I knew I'd pass.

"But what I'd forgotten was that Chuck Hughes of the Detroit Lions had died of a heart attack right on the field the previous fall. The doctors in Detroit kept talking about the pressure I'd be under on the mound, and I could tell they'd made up their minds. Finally Campbell called me and told me they couldn't bring me to spring training as a pitcher in 1972, but I could come as a kind of a coach and scout. I didn't have much choice. I had to stay close to them."

Hiller reported to the Tigers' minor-league camp in the spring but was a lousy pitching coach, he admits. "I was too concerned about showing them what I could still do. Every time another coach would come by I'd grab somebody and warm up, on the excuse I was going to throw batting practice to the kids. The kids may not have got much out of it, but I did give of my time freely in the storytelling department. It was good for my ego to see all those young kids, green as grass, hanging on to my every word listening to a big leaguer tell it like it is."

The big-league camp was only about five hundred feet away, but Hiller stayed away from it. "I didn't want people feeling sorry for me and mouthing all kinds of sympathy. I found out later that my old roommate, Mickey Lolich, was pulling for me, and talking to Billy Martin, who was the manager then, about me. Martin even told me at the time that he wanted me on the ball club and that he would do anything in his power to get me there."

And then they were all gone, headed north for the season. Hiller's scouting and coaching contract paid him $7,500 a year. He had been getting $280 every two weeks and sending $260 of it home; that just about covered the mortgage payments and installments on the loan he'd made to cover household expenses and medical bills. His wife and two children, Wendy and Joe, had moved in with Janice's family back in Duluth.

He weighed about 160 pounds and was in good shape because of all the exercise and a regimented, low-cholesterol diet. Which was hard to maintain at Tigertown, where he was living on a tighter budget than the minor leaguers he was working with.

"When the team went they left behind some ham and part of a salami, which I ate until they started to go green. Every morning I went to a place and got myself a bowl of oatmeal—it was filling. There was a counter, and when the gal would go back to get the oatmeal, I would reach in and grab handfuls of soda crackers and shove them in my pocket. That was my lunch.

"I had quit drinking, but I still liked the taste of beer. So there's a nice place in Lakeland called the Foxfire. A mug of beer at that time was seventy-five cents. And on Friday night I would walk over there—it's about two and a half miles—and sit at the oyster bar. They had soda crackers and those little fish things. And I would sit there for hours, nursing a beer and watching the floor show, off to the side.

"I told the club I didn't have any money to get an apartment, so they let me stay in the manager's office in the clubhouse at the training complex. I was sleeping on a mattress on the floor, and the first night I turned out the light, and in about fifteen minutes I heard this scurrying all over the place. I turned on the lights and there were thousands of cockroaches—there weren't just hundreds, there were thousands. I'm not squeamish, but I'm thinking that when I'm sleeping these things are crawling all over me. I couldn't help thinking, 'If I were Al Kaline, would this be happening to me?'

"I had eight dollars, and the next day I went over to the hardware store and spent it all on fumigation stuff—every penny I had. But it didn't help a bit. Finally the Lakeland parks and recreation department opened up the team dormatories and let me stay there."

Campbell came to Lakeland, sat in the stands watching an instruction session and called Hiller over when it was finished.

"I could see it in his eyes. I knew he was there to release me as a player. But I didn't give him the chance. I said, 'If you've come to release me, you can forget it. I haven't come this far to let that happen.' Later Campbell admitted that's what he'd been there for. "But with John feeling that strongly, I just couldn't do it."

The Tigers' team physician was the one person in the club's upper hierarchy who thought Hiller might be able to make it back. He made arrangements with Dr. J. Willis Hurst, then president of the American Heart

His name was etched right up there with Ty Cobb, Hank Greenberg, Mickey Cochrane...(The Detroit News)

Foundation and former president Lyndon Johnson's personal physician, to see Hiller, making it clear that Hurst was the last hope.

"But every time I'd have an appointment set with Dr. Hurst, Johnson would have a heart attack. [Johnson died of a heart attack in January, 1973.] It was unbelievable. It happened three times.

"Finally I got to see Hurst, and they put me through incredibly extensive tests. And at the end he winked at me and said, 'Be patient.' I went back to Lakeland but it was hard to be patient. I was lonely and just about starving. Finally I told the Tigers I'd had it — I was going back to Duluth.

"I was only home for three days when I got a call from Campbell. I couldn't believe it — I had the okay. Later I read that the doctor had said if they wanted me to avoid a heart attack, they'd better let me play. I went to Detroit as a batting-practice pitcher and threw about five times. The only negative thing is that Jim Campbell — he and I are good friends, and this is the only negative thing that ever happened between us — he put a contract in front of me that said $17,000. I said, 'This is $3,000 less than I made last year.' And he said, 'Well, we don't know if you can pitch.' Later on I told him that had been a lousy thing to do. Three thousand dollars meant nothing to the Tigers. But I was broke and it meant a lot to me."

There was a distinct lack of class to the way Hiller rejoined the lineup, as well. A twenty-three-year-old lefthander named Les Cain, who'd had a few decent years for the Tigers, had been having arm trouble. Martin sent Cain and Hiller to the twin mounds in the bullpen and told them to throw against each other — the better man would get the job. It meant the end for Cain.

"I couldn't believe they were doing it that way, but nobody was going to throw harder than me that day. They could have put Nolan Ryan beside me, and if he'd thrown 103 I'd have thrown 104. Les's arm was hurting, and he didn't throw well. Mine wasn't, and I did."

Chicago fans gave Hiller a standing ovation when he entered his first 1972 game against the White Sox. He was dizzy with triumph, crossing up Bill Freehan, his catcher, on signs, and giving up a home run to the mighty Dick Allen, the third batter to face him. But he was back. The tests, the long hours in the YMCA basement, the cockroaches and the soda crackers were behind him.

In 1972 Hiller had a fine half year, finishing with an ERA of 2.05. But in 1973 he entered another world. He pitched 125 innings, ranking near the top of the league for relievers, and gave up just 89 hits. He walked only 39 batters, several of them intentionally. And he struck out 124, a startling total for a pitcher who depended on deftness as much as power. His fastball was good, but probably didn't clock above the high eighties. He had a magical change-up, however, and mixed these two with a "slurve" — a combined slider and curve — with great success. His ERA for the year was a minuscule 1.44. He saved thirty-eight games — then a record — for an ordinary, third-place team.

ERAs can be deceptive for relief pitchers, because they can come into a game in a tight situation, give up a hit and the runs that score are charged to their predecessor. But there was nothing cheap about Hiller's ERA. "I didn't let one of anybody else's runs score that year. Not one crossed the plate. Not on a sacrifice fly, a bunt — nothing. And I didn't give up one hit on my change-up. Once I threw it in Yankee Stadium with a one-run lead in the bottom of the ninth, the bases loaded and a 3-2 count on the batter. The guy just dropped his bat.

"It's hard to talk about, because it didn't happen to me. I still don't understand it. I'd go to bed shaking my head. I knew I was pitching better — I was in the best shape of my life. But this was a dream." It would take ten years for Dan Quisenberry to come along with forty-five saves to break the record.

In 1974 Hiller came back with a 2.64 ERA for a sixth-place team, rebuilding with kids. He won seventeen games and pitched a staggering 150 innings in relief. In 1975 his ERA was 2.17, in 1976 2.38, in 1977 a less exciting 3.56 and in 1978 it was 2.34. Only in his last two years, in 1979 and the spring of 1980, did he start to wear down. When it happened — and the forgetful in the stands started to boo — he got out. Although he pitched only eleven games in 1980 before quitting, Tiger owner John Fetzer honored his contract for the remainder of the year.

On May 31, 1980, he bowed out at Tiger Stadium between the third and fourth innings. Sparky Anderson had to push him back out of the dugout for a curtain call to finally bring the standing ovation to an end.

There have been sad times since — he and Janice ended up divorced. And happy times — he met Linette not long afterward, and they've made it through hanging wallpaper together with no signs of dying romance.

And funny times. When he moved to Upper Michigan from Minnesota he spent a lot of time learning how to milk a cow with amused neighbors watching. But the community seems fond of him — his trophies decorate the local bar.

And proud times. When Detroit fans named an all-time, all-star Tiger team, his name was etched right up there with Ty Cobb, Hank Greenberg, Mickey Cochrane, Al Kaline . . . "I felt really good about that."

But not as good as walking out to the mound again in Comiskey Park in 1972 and giving up a home run to Dick Allen. "I didn't care where he hit it. All I knew is that I was pitching it. I can't tell you how good that felt."

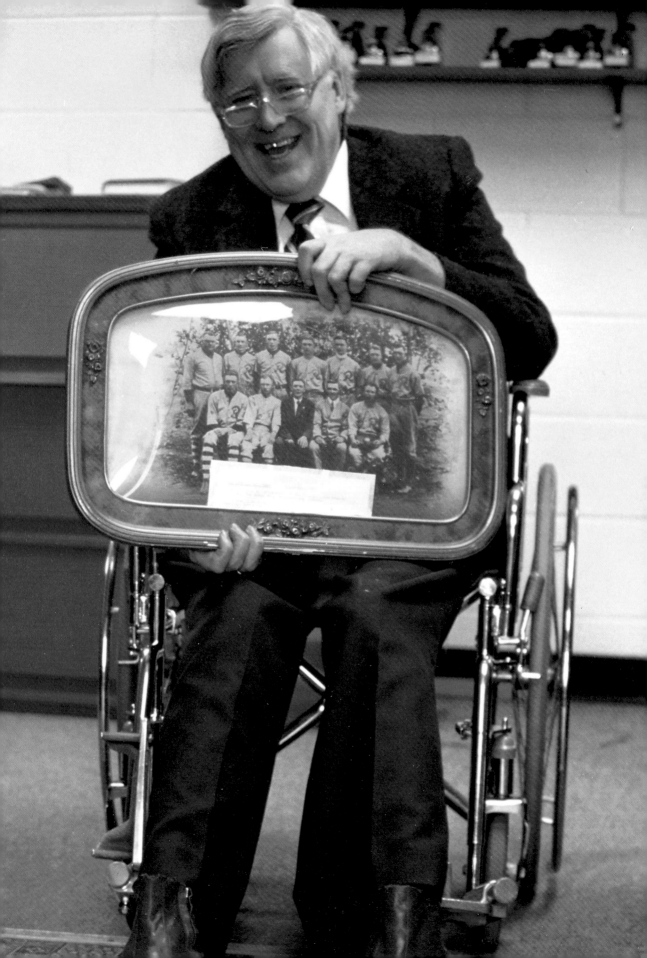

17

DAVE SHURY

North Battleford, Saskatchewan
February 16, 1988

"Baseball! God, if you came from the Prairies, you had to remember the baseball. There was nothing else to do. You'd work your land and put in the seed and watch the Russian thistle knock out the new wheat or barley and then the blistering heat would come and you could see everything shrivelling. Then you'd get, maybe, the grasshoppers, and that was it for the year. No crop insurance, nothing, but there was always the baseball.

"If you had a car you could get to a tournament every weekend. All through Manitoba, Saskatchewan, Alberta, and teams used to come out from the Okanagan Valley too. I remember one team that came from Penticton, I think, and they rode the freights to get to a tournament at Vulcan.

"Each town would have a sports day, beginning early in June and running right through to Labor Day, sports all over the country. There would be men's fastball, just ordinary baseball, and then there was softball, and a men's and women's senior team and usually a girls' and boys' or junior teams. Most towns, if they were big enough, and they had the surrounding farms and villages to draw on, they had four teams, and there were some damn good teams. I've seen some senior teams from towns in Saskatchewan which could go up against anybody in the country today. It was just that they were stuck out there in the wilds and nobody ever heard of them, but some of that pitching was strictly big league. Mostly fastball, you understand. There wasn't much slider or curve. The boys got up there and for seven or so innings they just threw that ball as hard as they could and nobody can tell me there weren't a couple of potential

Dave's multiple sclerosis slows his words down, but has never
been able to blunt them. (Dan Turner)

Dizzy Deans or Lefty Groves out there in the Thirties. Hell, those fellows had nothing to do except practice, and they just loved to play baseball. I've seen men of 40 playing just as hard as a guy of 20, and some of their women, whew! Those gals could play. Softball, of course, but you get a big, hefty Ukrainian girl throwing a big softball and it just comes screaming in.

"Each town would have a tournament and they'd get the prize money, hook or by crook, from entries, admission charges if they could, although not always, because a lot of it was cow pasture ballparks, and gifts from the merchants and the banker, and perhaps a rummage sale or two. Some of those pots got up to $500 and even for a place like Swift Current or Weyburn or Brandon or Wetaskawin or Lethbridge even higher. As much as $1,000, and that was enough to bring real good teams from all over hell's half acre and including up from the United States if the entry was allowed. I've seen 10 teams playing, in the men's senior, on three diamonds, from 10 in the morning and when the last fly was caught just as the sun was going down several thousand people would have watched.

"They were big events. Real big. An awful lot of fun. Some teams used to bring in ringers, a Yankee, or a guy from the East, if the pot was big enough. There was nothing wrong with it, I guess, but the ringer never got the royal type of welcome he probably thought he deserved. Not even from his teammates because if he was that good, then he'd make a deal to take a third of the pot, and a third could mean a lot of dollars from the other guys' pockets.

"There was one guy that Stavely brought in and he was a pitcher, a fastballer, but he had a nice curve and a curve wasn't seen much at those tourneys, and he pitched a no-hitter the first game, a one-hitter and a two-hitter, and Stavely won the tournament. Naturally, and if you don't believe it you can look it up in Robert Ripley's *Believe It or Not*. Three great games in one day. The big gink had played pro ball for Seattle or San Francisco and hadn't got the attention he probably thought he deserved, but he sure did on the Canadian prairies.

"Sports days were fun days. Everybody came, and there was a dance and a lot of drinking, out in the cars and trucks parked around, and sometimes a fight or two. The cops usually stayed

144

away, let the folks have their fun. Not like a Polish wedding
where they stayed parked at the corner of the hall just waiting
for the bomb to explode. They were good times, not prosperous
times, but everybody did what they could to help the next
fellow, and a lot of planning by the ladies and the committee
went into them tournaments. Some of the rivalries between
towns got pretty fierce, at the ball park level for the big prize,
but otherwise it was just people of Saskatchewan or Manitoba
or Alberta trying to make the best of a tough situation.

"Sitting in the little bleachers most towns had at the
fairgrounds, you wouldn't know that if you dumped everybody's
pockets, everybody in the stands and along the sidelines, you'd
be lucky to come up with $50 spending money. Nobody really
cared that much. One thing I've always thought I'd like to have
seen. Like to have seen some of those town kids and those big
farm boys get a chance to try out for some big league team.
Likely they wouldn't have made it, but then again, you might be
real surprised. Some of those boys were real good."
—from Barry Broadfoot's *Ten Lost Years*.

It is well known that if you hit a ball hard enough in Saskatchewan it will
roll forever. When Terry Puhl was growing up in Melville, for instance,
nothing he hit ever stopped until it came up against the foothills of Alberta.

We're talking freedom thoughts here. All you need to conjure them up
them are a round, seamed brain, a big sky and prairies all around. None
of these are missing on the road between Saskatoon and North Battleford,
where David Shury practices law.

If you're going to meet Dave Shury you're thinking big sky and prairies
anyway. His people have lived within a few miles of North Battleford since
his grandfather left the railway in Buffalo in 1905, having emigrated from
England some years earlier.

And you're certainly thinking baseball. Shury was there at the founding
meeting of the Saskatchewan Baseball Association in 1954, and served as
president for a year before becoming the organization's official—and now
not-so-official—historian. And he's president of the Saskatchewan Baseball Hall of Fame.

But it's harder to think freedom. Especially when Shury's wife, Jane,
uses a ton of affection and some hidden reservoir of weightlifter's strength
to pick his six-foot frame from his wheelchair and dump it in his living-
room chair. WHUMP! This is the sound of the hangman practising with a

two-hundred-pound sack of sand, and it takes Shury a few minutes to right himself from a flopped-over-sideways position to a straight-on hunched position, dead legs stretched out front of him.

Shury is fifty-eight. He's had multiple sclerosis since he was twenty-four, fresh out of law school at the University of Saskatchewan. When he talks you don't think of baseballs rolling free. The words wheeze forward as though each is a sixteen-pound shot his larynx has to tumble out of his mouth.

He laughs, in his gasping way, when telling you how he finally realized there was something seriously wrong. There had been occasional earlier signs — a bloody nose from not moving his glove quickly enough on a grounder when he was seventeen, difficulty with sweeping during a curling match in university, trouble making his legs work when he was chasing a bus once.

But it was the spring of 1955, when he was filling in as coach of a North Battleford juvenile hockey team, that he was sure. The team was visiting nearby Wilkie. "The stick boy and I had put the equipment on the wrong bench, and they told us the visitors' bench was on the other side of the ice. So we grabbed the sticks and walked over, the stick boy and I, and all of a sudden, for no reason at all, I slipped and fell flat on my ass." He guffaws, his lively eyes dancing merrily as the thought of falling on his ass.

He was diagnosed, and his nerve fibers began to deteriorate in a predictable way. "The hard schlerotic patches produced by the disease," says the *Encyclopædia Britannica*, "eventually result in permanent paralysis." But Shury's arms still move.

His daughter, Debi, was born in 1956, and his son, Brent, in 1963. Shury's symptoms worsened until he was confined to a wheelchair fifteen years ago. Since then they've stabilized. After he was diagnosed in 1955, he took on the presidency of the Saskatchewan Baseball Association.

Baseball, he says simply, has always been his grand passion, and his ally in his fight against paralysis. "It gives me something to live for. I don't know what the hell I'd have done if it wasn't for baseball."

Well, for a start he would have lived a much more tranquil life. For if there is one place no quarter is asked or given it is in a minor athletic association annual meeting. Over the more than thirty-year existence of the Saskatchewan Baseball Association, Shury was never the fastest talker, and lost his share of the disputes. But he always had the last word — he wrote the newsletters and reports and, in 1985, *Play Ball Son!*, the history of the association.

146

Shury is often referred to in the third person in *Play Ball Son!* and depicted as a man forever doing battle with the devil. Lament with the author, for instance, the failure of a 1962 committee of five to properly designate the responsibilities of the association's first full-time man in the field: "Shury, who had worked for six years to make this a reality and who had been primarily instrumental in raising the monies to make a fieldman's salary possible, was left off the committee. It may have been due to this omission that the project failed the following summer."

Saskatchewan Premier Walter Scott pitched in the Qu'Appelle Valley in 1886. Baseball has been a grand, sustaining passion. (Saskatchewan Archives Board)

Or sympathize with the plight of the same chap who, as a member of the association's finance committee, came to realize that too much money was being designated for baseball clinics: "Shury could see the money he had collected for advertising being eaten up by these ball schools and to force some sanity into the Organization he handed in his resignation."

That was in 1963. But this guy Shury's resignation was not accepted. Instead the association backed down on sponsoring the clinics. Then in

1986 Shury was bumped rudely from his post of league historian by a new guard, who cleared out a lot of Shury's pals, as well. In his 1986 review, the ousted historian — still recording, you'll notice — calls it the Year of the Great Purge: "Shury was told his services as Historian were no longer required — no explanation was ever given to him."

Is it possible that Shury got bumped because he had been on the wrong side of too many regulatory debates? As he points out, most minor baseball meetings are dominated by two perennial squabbles. How many innings a week should a pitcher be allowed to throw? (The instigator's impassioned logic may vary from year to year, depending upon whether his squad has several capable chuckers or just one he'd like to see build up his arm.) And how strict should the league be about enforcing boundaries designating the territory each team can draw from? ("Curly wanted to throw it wide open, so I says, 'Hey, Curly, how many kids you got stashed over the border?' ")

Perhaps the association's new executive, as appreciative as it might have been about all the chronicling during all the years, wearied of Shury's bluntness — and who knows, perhaps even a lack of historical evenhandedness? — when sides were taken over heated issues.

Was it fair of him to say of one Little League coach that the association "had had trouble with [Slim] Streek from the outset. [Slim] was secretary of the Regina Little League Association and felt himself above rules and regulations. In fact he made up his own rules as he went along. When he was challenged he pleaded ignorance."

Can we trust the association's highly respected historian when he observes that "some of the executive were spending money like drunken sailors"? Perhaps. Probably. But one can see how a new executive would find itself wary of its historian.

Shury says he doesn't care that he has been ousted. In fact, just this day the proofs have come back for his latest *Saskatchewan Historical Baseball Review*, and the association's year will be part of the reportage. "I just told them, 'I don't care whether you make me the historian or not. I'm still going to collect the history.' "

Besides, collecting the SBA's history has never been more than part of what he perceives as his duty to baseball in Saskatchewan. He spends half his days on law, half on baseball, and has a secretary, Troylene Patterson, who only deals with baseball. As president of the Saskatchewan Baseball Hall of Fame and Museum he has a basement full of archival material; the hall hasn't been built yet.

He writes a weekly baseball column, "Prairie Diamonds," for the Battleford *Telegraph* and is active in provincial and national amateur base-ball. He personally financed the first Canadian national team, a ragtag collection that played at the Can-Am games in Winnipeg in 1967 and upset the swaggering Cubans. And his annual *Baseball Review* is filled with nuggets.

Some of them are his own, depicting, among other things, how his roguish Uncle Billy raided the Hot Stove League's coffee tin filled with money for the town team's uniforms, leaving in its place a cheque for $132.60 drawn on the long-defunct Home Bank of Prongua.

But his contributions come from all over the province and beyond, and the quality is often remarkable. Denis Gruending, of CBC Radio in Regina, wrote a book called *100% Cracked Wheat*. Shury read it and excerpted the poem "Chucker Chatter", exposing his readers to some of the best baseball poetry written anywhere:

> *hudda buddy*
> *hudda buddy*
> *now you go now you go*
> *fireball fireball*
> *righthander*
> *shoot to me buddy*
> *shoot to me buddy buddy*
> *fireball now fireball*
> *righthander*
>
> *ohhh*
> *now you smoke*
> *now you smoke buddy now you smoke buddy*
> *buddy*
> *now you hot*
> *now you hot shot ohhh*
> *now you hot*
> *buddy buddy*
>
> *c'mon babe c'com babe*
> *c'com shooter*
> *c'com shooter buddy buddy*
> *you 'n me honey*
> *all they is*
> *honey*

> *all they is honey honey*
> > *buddy buddy*
> *way to mix*
> > *way to mix now righthander*
> > *now you work*
> *now you work buddy*
> > *now you hot buddy*
> *now you hot buddy*
> > *you push to me buddy*
> *push to me buddy*
> > *push ball*

> *push ball*
> *you 'n me honey*
> > *all they is honey honey*
> *all they is honey*
> > *buddy buddy*
> > *buddy buddy*

Shury himself doesn't write poetry, unless . . . Well, sometimes the most prosaic presentation of words — even something as rigid and pragmatic as a list—can turn itself into a poem. In a 1984 column Shury simply noted that the Saskatoon Exhibition had held a continuous baseball tournament, except for 1924, for forty-seven years, begun by a man named John C. Cairns "to fill the gap left the year before when the professional Western Canada League folded."

The winners and runners-up were as follows:

    1922 Conquest 14—Rosetown 13
    1923 Kinley 10—Wadena 5
    1924 No Tournament
    1925 Kinley 5—Milden 2
    1926 Floral 4—Fiske 3
    1927 Rosetown 6—Ruthilda 0
    1928 Lucky Lake 9—Lanigan 4
    1929 Bruno 5—Lucky Lake 4
    1930 Lanigan 5—Cory 4
    1931 Neiburg 5—Bruno 3
    1932 Wakaw 8—Radisson 6

1933 Bruno 13—Battleford 5
1934 Neiburg 8—Lanigan 3
1935 Neiburg 7—Lanigan 6
1936 Neiburg 9—Blaine Lake 2
1937 Neiburg 14—Lanigan 6
1938 Rosthern 4—Lanigan 0
1939 Neiburg 18—Kenaston 5
1940 Lanigan 6—Viscount 0
1941 Wiseton 5—Neiburg 2
1942 Delisle 10—Hughton 1
1943 No. 4 SFTS 12—No. 7 ITS 7
1944 Dundurn Recces 7—Aberdeen 5
1945 Aberdeen 9—Rosetown 2
1946 Wiseton 4—Viscount 0
1947 Aberdeen 9—Melfort 6
1948 Richlea 4—Aberdeen 3
1949 Sceptre 4—Delisle 1
1950 N. Battleford 3—Saskatoon 3 (tie)
1951 Sceptre 13—N. Battleford 6
1952 N. Battleford 3—Saskatoon 0
1953 Kamsack 8—Sceptre 3
1954 Saskatoon (4 team round robin)
1955 Delisle 8—Langham 2
1956 Delisle 1—Langham 0
1957 Rosetown 16—Delisle 12
1958 Delisle 6—Kindersley 3
1959 Delisle 7—Kindersley 4
1960 Kindersley 7 N. Battleford 2
1961 Unity 3—Neiburg 2
1962 Unity 7—Kindersley 3
1963 Kindersley 2—Unity 0
1964 Neiburg 4—Unity 2
1965 Asquith 14—Delisle 10
1966 Neiburg 11—Rosetown 2
1967 Unity 11—Kindersley 7
1968 Unity 4—Colonsay 0
1969 Unity 7—Eston 1

There is a sound of railway whistles to these names, and the feel of an abandoned station when you get to 1969. The tournament was cancelled in 1970. "It seemed it became too much trouble to run the tournament, so it was scrapped," huffs Shury in the *Review*. And then his personal boycott: "I have vowed never to return to the Saskatoon Exhibition — rock bands and tractor-pulling do not seem to excite me."

What does excite him is having to rule that a third baseman named Harvey was ineligible for a tournament in New Brunswick some years ago, then having Harvey and his mother visit him on their way to Banff to tell him they had appreciated his decision. That not only excites him, it makes him weep. "You meet the best people in baseball," he says snuffling. "And the worst," he adds, his face spreading into a grin. "They're the ones who want to win too much."

What also excites him is finding some long-ago pitcher's first name, or the missing score from a tournament during the Depression, and sharing it with his readers, with Troylene at the typewriter.

"There is a ball park in Ruthilda, where that 1926 team I showed you played." He is tired now, and his words struggle with fatigue. "And there's nothing special about that park, other than a little rise in the outfield, out in right. But I can go to that ballpark and just imagine all the great prairie ball players who have played there, and it just lifts me up."

18

NATIONAL BASEBALL INSTITUTE

Vancouver, British Columbia and Seattle, Washington
February 27, 1988

John Douris, the tall, skinny pitcher with the hot brown eyes, has a fair idea of what he'd like to do when he's done with baseball: "Sports medicine, physical education — probably one of the two." He smiles. Randy Curran, the gargantuan first baseman, knows what he wouldn't like to do, ever again. "I hated making lawn mowers. The boss is all over your ass all the time." He shudders.

Which is why both these twenty-one-year-olds have their schoolbooks with them as the National Baseball Institute's team bus departs Vancouver, headed for the University of Washington and a doubleheader that will kick off a thirteen-game road trip down the coast of California. Hey! These kids are Canadians, it's still February, and they're off to soak up some sun and play some serious ball. Hallelujah!

If the team name — the National Baseball Institute Blues — sounds strange, it makes a twisted kind of sense. Calling Canada's national college baseball team an "institute," *Vancouver Sun* columnist Archie McDonald has observed, "makes it sound like reform school, and in a way that's the case. It is trying to reform the image and the quality of baseball in Canada." As for "Blues," well, Labatt's has some money in this project. One of the team coaches, in fact, is pondering the name as the bus rolls toward Seattle. "You know," he says, "this is a Canadian national team. The obvious name for it would be the NBI *Canadians*." Chuckles all around. Molson's should live so long.

The National Baseball Institute is largely the brainchild of Wayne Norton, a forty-five-year-old Vancouverite who used to play center field between Reggie Jackson and Joe Rudi in Double A at Birmingham. The heavy-hitting Jackson and Rudi were on the way up, the light-hitting Nor-

ton on the way down. Never mind. The good-looking, smooth-talking Nor-ton had his share of skills on the field, and more than his share off it.

Now program administrator of the NBI and development coordinator for Baseball B.C., Norton is both an organizer and a hustler. He hustled Pat Gillick of the Toronto Blues Jays and top executives at Petro-Canada and Labatt's into coming together with Baseball B.C. to set up the NBI.

Gillick and Bob Prentice, head of Canadian scouting with the Jays, had already had discussions with P.N.T. Widdrington, chairman of the board at Labatt's, about establishing some kind of Canadian baseball academy to develop top Canadian players. When Norton came along with the NBI concept, Gillick was ready for him. And when federal bureaucrats were slow in bringing Baseball Canada into the picture in 1986, Norton and his private-sector pals went ahead without them.

It only took only a few months for the feds to realize they had been left in the locker room, and Baseball Canada has since joined as a full partner in the five-sponsor venture. Cooper, adidas and Wilson supply equipment, Agency Press helps with printing and Canadian Airlines transports bodies when the bus won't do.

Heading south to Washington and California, the bus will do fine. Its passengers are both students and ballplayers. Whereas quitting school and heading to the minors at a young age used to be virtually the only avenue to the major leagues, college ball has become an increasingly sig-nificant springboard for professional ballplayers in the United States. More than one hundred and fifty Canadians currently play for American college teams. Many of them are in the States because there was no place else to go; Canada has never had a significant college baseball program.

But this bus is filled with high-school graduates from British Columbia, Alberta, Ontario, Quebec and New Brunswick, and they're going to school at UBC, Simon Fraser University or one of Vancouver's community colleges or technical schools. They get between $1,500 and $4,000 a year for aca-demic expenses, and they are required to keep up their studies. There probably isn't one of the twenty-six players aboard who doesn't want to play major-league baseball. But failing that there is minor league ball, coaching, and the possibility of making the Canadian Olympic team going to Seoul. There are trips like this to California, and there is the gravy of getting something better than a high-school education.

To Kitchener's Randy Curran, the first baseman with the wicked bat and suspect glove, the education isn't the important part. "I'm taking business at Vancouver Community College. I just go and try to pass — I don't do too well in school."

Catcher Dean Croy, of Lethbridge, Alberta, has great arm, uncertain bat. (Dan Turner)

To Toronto's John Douris, the slim righthander who's been developing as the team's number one starter since Denis Boucher left, the school is more important this year than last, when John Harr, the NBI's head coach, had to do some growling. Douris also goes to VCC. "I was a good student at Neil McNeil High School in Toronto, but I guess I didn't think college would be very tough. I concentrated mainly on my performance on the field, and then my school marks came down, and then my game came down, and I was a mess at both." Since then he's put both his game and his studies back together. "I know I'll need the schooling."

To Lachine's Denis Boucher . . . Hey, where the hell is Boucher? He isn't on the bus. Didn't he do a great job working on his English in his first year here? Didn't he get the win in Canada's first game at the Pan-Am games? Didn't he say how much he was looking forward to the Olympics? Where the hell is Boucher?

It's February 27 in Seattle, which isn't exactly the heart of the sunbelt. Spring training for major-league teams is barely underway in Florida and Arizona. Kids' baseball, even junior ball, won't be getting underway in most Canadian cities for another two months. But the University of Washington is ready for the new season.

The campus diamond is green and groomed. A chap at the entrance grabbed the NBI roster as soon as the bus arrived, rushed off and made photocopies and is now handing out scorecards as the crowd arrives. Crowd? There are probably a hundred people filing in. And just for a pair of exhibition games unconnected to the university's NCAA schedule. There is a sound system and a game announcer, who gives the crowd a jab of rock music between innings. There is a concessions booth, with drinks, popcorn, potato chips, hot dogs, hamburgers and condiments that just won't stop. There are *two* recorded anthems, three properly uniformed umpires and portable toilets. And even a nice offering of spring sunshine.

This is a dream, an escape from hibernation and, most of all, an opportunity. Because, for all the fantasies that young kids have about playing major-league ball, the odds against making it for anyone living in Canada have always been prohibitive. The occasional pitcher slips through, because there are fewer skills to develop. But it's different for position players. Perfecting a major-league batting stroke and inculcating the myriad skills needed to go with it require thousands of hours on the diamond.

Terry Puhl is the only living Canadian who's had a long run as a full-time position player. There is big money to be made playing baseball.

Americans, Puerto Ricans, Dominicans and South Americans pursue the dream relentlessly. One American, Greg Jefferies, who was the New York Mets' number one pick in the 1985 draft, works eight hours a day at his game, year-round. Californians play ball all year. California is by far the largest supplier of major league ball players. Canadians kids are lucky if they make it into thirty ball games a year. And even luckier if there's anyone around who can teach them anything. And luckier still if the competition they get is good enough to show them what they're lacking.

Enter the NBI. These boys on the bus do weight training and other types of conditioning during the winter, take part in indoor workouts complete with batting cages during January and play a ninety-game season against good U.S. college teams during the spring and fall. Many of them are graduates of the Canada Youth Team for sixteen to eighteen-year-olds, which Norton got started in British Columbia in the early eighties before headquarters were moved to Ontario.

The Youth Team — NBI combination is an enticing package, although Norton says some players still prefer the U.S. college route "on the grounds that if this is Canadian, it must be inferior." But the NBI has held its own against tough American competition in its first two years, when its players were primarily freshmen and juniors. Things promise to get even better.

Bernie Beckman, the team's pitching coach, is also a civil servant working for Sports Canada. He's responsible for making sure that Ottawa is getting its bang for its buck in baseball the same way it does in track and field, skiing, synchronized swimming and the like. "So far it's worked out very well," he says. "We have players who either left college programs in the U.S. or passed up opportunities to join them. Coaching here is ahead of U.S. college coaching. They don't have the experience of John, Ossie and myself."

John Harr, the head coach, is a physical-education graduate from UBC who played in the San Francisco Giants and New York Yankees organizations. Infield coach Ossie Chavarria was a utility player with Kansas City and Oakland before settling in Vancouver after a stint with the Mounties in the early sixties.

As for the Blues, they are getting battered in the second game of the doubleheader after having been crushed in the first. The boys are rusty. But they've beaten the Huskies more often than they've lost to them over the first two years, and there are all those games to go down in southern California.

Jays' V.P. Pat Gillick talking to NBI pitching coach Bernie Beckman in the stands. (Dan Turner)

Maybe they're nervous because Blue Jays vice-president Pat Gillick is in the stands. There he is, right over there, talking to Bernie Beckman. Hey, Pat! What the heck happened to Denis Boucher, anyway?

Gillick, relaxing in his favorite beige windbreaker, *loves* the National Baseball Institute. Not that he effuses when he talks about the NBI. Gillick is too much the suave, civilized man—friendly but reserved, funny but serious, relaxed but watchful, to gush about anything. But here he is, the biggest boss in one of the most successful baseball operations in North America, inhaling half a day from his busy schedule to sit here and watch the NBI get its season started.

"We got involved because we want to improve the performance of baseball in Canada," Gillick says with such a sense of goodwill that only the devil himself could question his motives. "We thought there should be an alternative for all those kids going to the States. It's going to be so difficult for Canada to win a medal at the Olympics if they don't have a high-profile program and the kids don't get better coaching."

He acknowledges that it will be easier for the Blue Jays to sell their product if Canada becomes more of a baseball country, which it will if the caliber of the game improves at the local ballpark. "That will be good for us, and good for the Expos."

He is impatient with the Expos' whining that they have never asked to be involved in the NBI, a complaint that various officials connected to the NBI have tried to explain in different ways. John Hamilton, executive director of Baseball Canada, has stated publicly that it has been because "I think that they see Quebec more as their market, whereas the Jays have taken a more positive approach about viewing the entire country as their market." Expos president Claude Brochu has vehemently denied this. In fact the Expos have been desperately scrambling to recover some of the non-Quebec market the Jays stole while the Expos were sleep-walking.

Relations between the two teams weren't helped by the Expos acting like haughty royalty when the Jays were trying to establish themselves in the late seventies and early eighties. The Expos treated the Jays like a minor league team. They made virtually no effort to promote the annual Pearson Cup fund-raising game between the two teams, as though it were really all too boring to bother with losers. The worm has since turned, and Expos owner Charles Bronfman has emerged hurt and angry, complaining to federal politicians that the Jays' attempts to corner the TV market in Ontario represent "reprehensible" threats to the Canadian fabric, isolating Quebec.

This may be true, but the Expos' lack of generosity back in the early Jay days invited retaliation. The Jays now deal with the Expos in a cold, businesslike way, and Norton is more forthright than Hamilton about why the Expos havn't been invited to the NBI ball:

"I admit I went to the Blue Jays first. They were involved in development programs with Baseball Canada, plus Labatt's had been involved in Baseball B.C. ever since I've been around, so I knew they were likely to have an interest. And after we got it going the Expos asked questions as to why they weren't involved, and whatnot, but I use the analogy that if you're going to get the private sector involved, you don't go to both McDonald's and Burger King."

What Norton seems to be saying here is that if the Expos had been paying attention in the old days they might have deserved a share of the NBI pie. Will failing to have a share cost them the chance to sign Canadian prospects?

Gillick concedes that "it's certainly another goal that maybe a professional player or two will come out of the program." But he's quick to add that the Blue Jays aren't trying to corner the market on Canadian ball-players through their involvement in the NBI. "You don't get that many professional players out of a program like this, anyway. And when they do come out of this program, they can do what they want. If they want to go to the Expos—if they want to go anywhere—that's up to them."

Which is . . . true. One of the advantages of taking the NBI route is that Canadian-based players aren't subject to the major-league draft. Players in American colleges have to either play for the teams that draft them or sit out a year. NBI players, if they prove their skills in college games or high-profile international events like the Olympics, can pick and choose. At least for the moment: there have been rumblings in the States that if the NBI is going to play against American colleges, its players should be subject to the same draft rules as American-based players.

So Gillick is right—the guys can go where they want. But while Norton and other NBI officials make funny gurgling noises when it's suggested that the Blues come off as a bit of a government-subsidized Blue Jays farm club, it would be silly to say that the Jays' NBI involvement doesn't give them at least an edge in signing NBI players.

Take the case of Denis Boucher. The Montreal Expos and the New York Yankees both wove generous amounts of clumsiness with miles of stupidity to come up empty on Boucher, so it's hard to feel sorry for them. It is fair to say that the Blue Jays were the only team of the three involved that was encouraging Boucher to stay with the books and participate in the 1988 Olympics instead of signing professionally. Until push came to shove. When it did, ask yourself whether the Jays didn't have an advantage.

Boucher, a left-handed pitcher who turned twenty on March 7, 1988, participated in each stage of a process that Norton had convinced the people at Sports Canada would produce not only Olympic athletes, but educated Olympic athletes. Boucher played for Canada's Youth Team at the 1986 World Youth Tournament, he joined the NBI program that fall and he got started on a college education in Vancouver. He pitched for Canada at the Pan-Am games in the summer of 1987, winning the opening game and then losing to the U.S. He has good mechanics, a nice fastball for his age (around eighty-five miles an hour), and came a long way, under Beck-man's tutelage, in developing off-speed pitches.

There was no question in anyone's mind that he was the ace of Canada's Pan-Am staff, the best pro prospect in Canadian amateur baseball, and the kind of starting pitcher Canada would need to compete with the Cubans and Americans in Seoul.

160

He also should have been God's gift to the Montreal Expos, who have yearned for, prayed for a quality French-Canadian prospect since the franchise was established in 1969. For two decades French-Canadian sportscasters have participated in the demeaning process of asking Expos ballplayers questions in English, having them answer in English and then recreating the interview so their questions at least, are in French, although the answers are still in English. They have always dreamed of the day they could rattle off a question in French and have the answer come rattling back in French.

Boucher was born to be an Expo. He would draw crowds. Even if he didn't make the grade, the Expos, owned by the English-speaking Charles Bronfman and his mainly English-speaking associates, would be seen to have tried.

The Expos brought Boucher to Olympic Stadium early in the 1987 season to work out in front of Murray Cook, the team general manager, who resigned shortly thereafter. Following the workout the Expos offered Boucher $5,000 to sign. *Arachides.* Either the Expos should have kept their hands off Boucher for patriotic reasons — he was preparing himself for the Olympic team — or they should have made him an offer that would have bought him more than a used Chevy Nova.

When the Pan-Am games rolled around in August, Boucher was the starting pitcher in the opening game, giving up only one run and five hits in six innings against Venezuela before tiring in the seventh, when the Venezuelans scored two more runs. Canada won 8-4.

This is when the Yankees got pushy. Dick Groch, former coach of Canada's national team, was not on particularly good terms with the new Norton-Beckman-Harr triumverate. He had on one occasion threatened to have the NBI blacklisted with the NCAA, which would have prevented it from playing against U.S. schools, on the grounds that it was recruiting Canadian players already on U.S. college rosters. (Beckman admits that when recruiting Canadians from U.S. colleges to play for the Canadian national team he doesn't mention he is also connected to the NBI. Last summer some national team candidates complained that they came under pressure to switch from their U.S. schools to the NBI so that Harr and Beckman could run a more centralized national team program.)

At any rate, Groch was in Indianapolis for the Pan-Am games and used his connections with some of the national team players to get Boucher out to dinner a few days before Canada's big game against the United States. Boucher says Groch made him an offer of $18,000; insisting the offer expired at midnight the same day.

This put a lot of pressure on Boucher when he should have been con-centrating on his pitching. Here, in the words of John Harr, is what hap-pened next: "Fortunately Serge Fournier from Quebec was one of the coaches with the team, and Boucher confided in him that he had a problem and didn't know what to do. That's when we—well, we didn't panic, but we knew we had to inform the Blue Jays that there was something up here and we had a problem and we're out in left field on this because [Boucher] didn't know what to do.

"I guess Bob [Prentice, the Jays' director of Canadian scouting] and Pat [Gillick] acted quickly and came down. We didn't want to lose him to somebody else. We didn't want to lose him at all, but if we were going to lose him we didn't want to lose him to somebody acting in an underhanded way. So Gillick came down and signed him, signed him there on the QT. It was just an upsetting thing for everybody, Denis and the coaching staff."

Signed him on the QT? Yes, for $20,000, according to Boucher. There were no rules broken, because Boucher didn't get the money until the Pan-Am games were over. And the Jays can't be blamed for stealing him from the Olympic team: Boucher himself says they gave him the choice of sign-ing, taking the bonus, and starting pro ball, or signing, taking a rain cheque on the bonus, and going to the Olympics. "I decided to play pro," he says simply, and it would probably be pushing it to blame the Jays for not trying to talk him into staying with the Olympic program. But wouldn't it be silly to say the Jays didn't have an edge in signing Denis Boucher?

"I don't know that we have an edge, really," says Pat Gillick, still stretched out comfortably in his favorite beige windbreaker. "After all, a kid's going to sign with the team that offers him the most money."

Which is . . . true. But the Jays are obviously kept well informed.

Beckman thinks that players not being subject to the draft and being able to market themselves to the highest bidder may be a detriment to the Canadian Olympic program. There are restrictions on when professional clubs can go after American college players, so good Americans stay avail-able longer for Olympic competition. Players like Boucher, however, hav-ing been groomed with federal and provincial money, can sign at any time. "Once this program gets stronger, the NCAA might start telling us how to run our program. And if we're going to remain competitive by playing with their teams, we may have to honor their rules. Our boys may be susceptible to a draft down the line.

"The commissioner's office has asked questions about it. I think our attitude right now is to play dumb, but I don't know how long we can get away with it. And this is also a concern of Sport Canada's. This is a high-performance program for training elite athletes, and they're saying: 'Hey, we're putting a lot of money into this — can these kids just sign at will? We're paying Bernie to develop this kid and then he turns pro — there's our amateur program shot to hell.' So in a way I'd welcome the draft a little bit, because it might help me keep amateurs on board a little longer."

POSTSCRIPT: During the first week of March 1988, the Toronto Blue Jays played a split-squad exhibition game against the Detroit Tigers in Lakeland, Florida. Denis Boucher had negotiated a clause in his first contract that required that the team take him to the major-league spring-training camp before shuttling him over to the nearby minor-league camp to begin his seasoning.

In the eighth inning of the game against the Tigers, Boucher was given his token opportunity to throw the ball. The Jays were losing 6-3. Throwing mainly fastballs, he retired the side without allowing a base runner in his first inning of work. Mixing in some curves and change-ups, he retired the side without allowing a base runner in his second inning of work. The Jays tied the game.

In the tenth inning he got two quick outs before giving up a single through the hole at shortstop. He then walked two batters to load the bases. The second walk came on a change-up on the outside corner that every scout in the park thought was strike three. In taking the ball back from the catcher Boucher moved to the front of the mound to glare at the umpire, but never lost his poise.

The Tigers sent Tom Brookens to the plate to pinch hit. Brookens was having a good spring—so good that when the American League season got started he was one of the early batting leaders, hitting .522 during the first week. Boucher struck him out swinging on a high, hard fast ball. After he did that, Boucher jumped in the air a couple of times to celebrate.

Bob Gebhardt, formerly with the Expos and now director of player personnel with the Minnesota Twins, was scouting the game and expressed his admiration. "The kid's never even played in the instructional league and he just did that — it's hard to believe. And the way he jumped off the mound at the end you'd have thought he'd just won the seventh game of the World Series."

Or an Olympic medal or something.

19

TED BOWSFIELD

Penticton, British Columbia
February 28, 1988

Ted Bowsfield, the San Jose Red Sox southpaw, is being hailed as
a possible second Robert (Lefty) Grove . . . the tall Canadian
moundsman really fires that tomato across the saucer.

Penticton *Herald*, 1955

The flight from Vancouver says goodbye to the Rockies and almost immediately settles over Penticton. The city's bungalows and modest two-story
houses present themselves in small-town garb, with porches here, specks
of color there, fences and clotheslines in between.

Nothing unusual, except there seems to be a net around everything. The
town is caught up in a web of bare-limbed fruit trees. There are crisscross-
ing lines of fruit trees everywhere in Penticton, in backyards, along bou-
levards, on hills, everywhere. The trees stand starkers for the moment,
straining to bud, waiting to show off.

Ted Bowsfield pitched here as a kid, but there hardly seems room for a
ball diamond. Maybe the outfielders perched in fruit trees, and Bowsfield
chucked apples to kids holding branches. The weather has started to warm
below, says the pilot as he prepares to land. The warmth will nudge the
trees along. Rebirth is at hand.

But Ted Bowsfield and his boys, Ted Jr. and Brad, have not come home
to celebrate rebirth. Frank Bowsfield, insurance broker, father, grand-
father and the man who stuffed his 1948 Hudson full of boys and drove
them off to play pickup ball against neighboring towns, has suffered a
stroke. He lies voiceless and paralyzed in the the local hospital. He is
eighty-eight.

From the ground the town appears as still and lazy in the spring sun as
it did from the air, as though any movement might disturb the sleep of the
orchards. It is Sunday in a town full of memories.

In the basement recreation room of Frank and Queen Bowsfield's Penticton home their son absently watches Orser and Boitano skate for Olympic gold, waiting for the evening to visit his father. His mother is resting in the other room, also very ill. She is eighty-six and it hurts, but her voice is clear and strong.

Ted Bowsfield, left-handed veteran of seven major-league seasons, is fifty-two now. He is still handsome, with an easy smile and a relaxed, unhurried manner. He compiled an ordinary 37-39 record over those seven seasons, but there is a presence to him that suggests he might have owned the teams he played for.

"That old Hudson," he recalls with a wistful grin. "We could put more kids in that car. We'd put the whole team in there and do it in one trip, with everybody sitting on everybody else's lap. When that car unloaded, it was a sight to behold."

He remembers homemade uniforms. And while he is remembering them a disembodied voice, eighty-six years old, remembers them with him from the other side of the half-closed bedroom door. "We used to take up the old senior team's uniforms," the voice says. "Sometimes they didn't fit just right," the voice adds. *Oh well*, the voice seems to shrug. *We did our best. And didn't we all have fun.*

Other kids who piled out of that old Hudson might have had a chance in pro ball, Bowsfield thinks. Particularly his friend Sam Drossos, the catcher, who would fling himself anywhere within several feet of the plate to stop the widely scattered rockets coming from the mound. But Drossos' father told him that if he went away to play ball the family motel would be gone when he got back. Sam Drossos stayed.

Bowsfield shakes his head. "Sam didn't get to follow his dream. When I come up from Seattle I always drop in to see him. We're still good friends."

It was Frank and Queen Bowsfield's son who had the awe-inspiring talent. He followed the dream and caught it. When he was fourteen Bowsfield was already pitching for a semi-pro team, established in Penticton just in time to nurture his gift. When he was sixteen he pitched a three-hitter against a visiting Cuban all-star team. They were adults, he wasn't shaving yet, but he only lost 2-1. He had no breaking ball, no change-up. What he threw left whiffs of smoke. "I threw harder than grown men. The arm really was a gift. Not only did the ball come in hard, but it came in moving. I didn't know what God had given me. I'd pick up a football and throw it the length of the field without trying. I'd skip stones on the river and they'd go and go and go . . . "

But his smoke looked like it might evaporate when he fell from a cherry tree that same year, a typical Penticton injury. "I didn't know what I had done. I tried to pitch in Summerland and my elbow got all puffed up. It turned out I had a hairline fracture on my funny bone. It was my dad who came through. He found me the best doctor available, in Vancouver, and if it had been another doctor the chances are things wouldn't have worked out very well. But this doctor set [the arm] for me and it healed perfectly."

The scouts, who had been hovering, backed off after the injury. But Bowsfield was soon throwing hard again, aiming the ball in the direction of Yankee Stadium. "I had this thing about the Yankees. They were the best. I either wanted to play for them or beat them." Bowsfield would never play for them. But there's a form in his file at the British Columbia Sports Hall of Fame: "What were the highlights of your career?" it asks. "Beating the Yankees," is the ever-so-sweet reply.

Bowsfield was drafted by the Boston Red Sox. His favorite scout and fishing pal, Tony Rubello, was with the St. Louis Browns, but the Browns were becoming the Orioles and Rubello was concerned that the organization was in such flux that Bowsfield might not get handled well. He recommended that his prodigy sign with Earl Johnson of the Red Sox, which Bowsfield did. The Sox sent him to San Jose, which was Class C ball, and Johnson went along to nurse him through the homesick days.

In 1955 Bowsfield had a 9-7 record with San Jose, striking out 124 batters in 117 innings. His fastball was still virtually his only weapon, but it was a zinger. A Canadian Pacific telegram home early in the year smoldered with excitement: WON 3-1 PITCHED 7 INNINGS GOT TIRED STRUCK OUT 11 WAS VERY FAST TELL LILA. Lila was a contestant for the Penticton Peach Queen title and was to become his first wife and mother of his two sons. "Was very fast" was an expression the sportswriters would get used to using when describing Bowsfield during his four years in the minors. Control wasn't his forte; speed was. An article written later when he pitched with Oklahoma City, the year he won the ERA crown in the Texas League, included him on a short list as "the fastest of the fast." Never mind that he threw off a stiff front leg and seemed to put a lot of strain on his throwing arm. The kid threw hard; you don't tinker with that.

Bowsfield never did develop much of a curveball, particularly in the minors. "It was a little wrinkle, something between a half-assed slider and a nickel curve, and sometimes it didn't do anything, it just sort of spun." But, hey, breaking balls were for guys who couldn't throw heat, old men

Throughout his childhood Ted dreamed about the Yankees. Then he grew up and killed them. (Dan Turner)

167

with washed-up arms. Not the Penticton Peach, as Boston writers would later dub him. Not a guy in there with the fastest of the fast.

But by 1958 Bowsfield was at least making an effort at complementing his fastball with some other pitches. Now throwing for the Minneapolis Millers of the American Association, he tinkered with a limited off-speed repertoire — a half-decent curve, a change-up and the beginnings of a screwball — to lessen the certainty that everything was coming in at the same speed. That was enough progress to get him to the league all-star game (he pitched two hitless innings) and to win him a promotion to the Red Sox toward the end of the year. He was twenty-two.

His memories of his first game at Fenway Park are a blur: Jim Bunning pitched a no-hitter for the Tigers. "Williams, Piersall, Jensen — he was mowing those guys down like they weren't there. Ike Delock went eight for us and then they brought me in. I didn't know where I was at. I tripped over the chalk line going to the mound, I was so nervous. All I know is that I got three guys out. The rest is a complete blank."

But Yankee Stadium was indelible. "Those impressions are very vivid — they'll never leave me. I came up out of the dugout and there was Mantle swinging the bat. He was ripping shots all over the place, and all the flags were flying, and there were the three statues in center field: Ruth, Gehrig and Miller Huggins. I was really in awe — it was a dream come true. That was my favorite team, from listening to Gillette and Mel Allen. They were really a great ball club — Mantle, Berra, Skowron, Howard, McDougald, Richardson, Kubek, Carey, Boyer, Enos Slaughter. I was in awe.

"The first thing my teammates showed me was the spot where Mantle had almost put the ball out of the stadium. It was hard to believe a ball could be hit that far. I thought, oh, what a thing to show me just before I'm going to pitch my first game here."

And what a game it was. The league championship was all but clinched for the Bronx Bombers, who would go on to win it by ten games over the runner-up Chicago White Sox, with the Red Sox three games farther back. The Yanks would then fight back from a 3-1 deficit and win the World Series against the Milwaukee Braves and the great pitching duo of Warren Spahn and Lew Burdette. Mickey Mantle would hit .304 with forty-two home runs for the season and add another pair of homers in the Series.

But not against the Peach. On August 10, 1958, Bowsfield warmed up in front of fifty-six thousand Yankees fans. "They were giving me jabs, yelling, 'Hey, rookie, hey, Canada, hey, rookie — this is the big leagues.' " He turned the crowd around, which isn't easy at Yankee Stadium. Throwing mainly fastballs, he held the Yankee Bombers hitless until the seventh, when he threw "a wrinkly little curve" to Norm Siebern, who stroked it for a double. He had come within eight outs of pitching a no-hitter and ended up with a four-hit, 9-3 victory.

"This youth is slick," said Casey Stengel, the venerable Yankee manager. "He has good stuff. He can do so darned many things and do them well." "He has a live fastball," said Elston Howard. "He was putting the ball where he wanted it," added Mickey Mantle.

The losing pitcher was Bob Turley, who went 21-7 that year.

Six days later Bowsfield pitched a complete game, a seven-hitter, to beat the Yankees again, 6-2. The losing pitcher was the master craftsman, Bobby Shantz. "I wish I had your arm," Shantz told him after the game.

Two weeks later Bowsfield went up against the Yankees one more time, beating Turley again. Stengel was generous in defeat. "I don't know how many, or how few, games he's won. But I do know that he beat the Yankees three times in a row, and no left-hander the Red Sox have had since [Mel] Parnell [in the forties] was able to do that. Not that many people beat the Yankees just like that."

Reporters called Frank Bowsfield at home. "He always wanted to play in the American League," he said of his son. "Just so he could beat the Yankees." No quote could have pleased Boston fans more. Next to winning the pennant, nothing elated them like beating the Yankees. Bowsfield was named the team's Rookie of the Year. He had gone 4-2 during the month and a half he had been up, and looked like a man for many seasons. There was nothing freaky about his triumphs. He was twenty-two years old and had one of the best arms in the American League. Or so it seemed.

During the next six years there were some fine moments. It's just that there were a lot fewer of them than everyone had expected. Between the ages of sixteen and twenty-two Bowsfield had an arm like a twelve-gauge shotgun. By the time he was twenty-eight, and supposedly in his prime, it felt like this:

"The problem was at the back of the shoulder. The muscles had been torn so bad that every time I threw the ball, adhesions would tear away and it would start bleeding inside. In Vancouver I got up one morning to get out of bed and I had to lift my arm out with me. It had no movement —it had no life to it at all."

Bowsfield can't be absolutely sure what killed it, but it was probably a combination of things. Bad mechanics for a start: too long throwing too wrong—not unusual for pitchers coming out of Canada.

"I put a lot of strain on my arm. I think a lot of us could have prolonged our careers if we'd been taught the fundamentals, and a lot of us weren't. If you threw real hard nobody really tinkered around with you very much."

He landed hard on his front foot. And he threw across his body. "When I got up there and saw Ryan and Seaver and Gaylord Perry throw, I thought how great it would have been to have learned from them. Those guys don't put tremendous strain on their arms."

After his triumphant debut, Bowsfield went home to Penticton and constructed an unheated polyethylene tunnel to throw in. "It was overenthusiasm in trying to improve. And what I think I did was bundle up in too much clothing, restricting my arm, tearing some muscles in the shoulder."

He reported to spring training with his arm hurting, but followed the advice of teammates who said, "Pitch even if you feel like you've got a tiger on it, because if they find out it's sore you'll go down and never get back up again."

In 1959 he pitched through pain for nine regular-season innings, allowing twenty-five base runners before he was sent down. In 1960 he was traded to Cleveland, where Frank Lane quickly gave up on him. But in 1961 came expansion, and Bowsfield became an original California Angel. A catcher the Angels selected retired and Bowsfield was thrown in in his place. He had two good years with the Angels, going 11-8 in 1961 and 9-8 in 1962.

He was popular in Los Angeles, where the Angels played in their early days. "In a city which yawns at celebrities," exclaimed *Weekend Magazine* sportswriter Andy O'Brien, "he's an idol." Not quite, maybe. But pitching for an eighth-place team in its first year of existence, Bowsfield was the only Angels' starter with a winning record. He continued to take it out on the Yankees, especially their stars. In 1961 when Roger Maris hit sixty-one home runs and Mickey Mantle fifty-four, Bowsfield pitched six games against them, allowing them one hit, a double by Mantle.

"That's what kept me in baseball, being a left-hander and being able to beat the Yankees," He said. He found out how to get by as a rag-armed shadow of his boyhood days. "I actually turned into a pretty good pitcher." He laughs. "I just couldn't throw any more." But he came up with a deceptive screwball and won games for the Angels, including a three-hitter and a couple of shutouts. *The Sporting News* called him "the classy curver." Not as exciting as "the fastest of the fast," perhaps. But some consolation.

Bo Belinsky shunted Bowsfield out of Los Angeles and over to Kansas City. Belinsky, notorious for his love of nightlife and addictive substances (including Mamie Van Doren), was supposed to go to the Athletics as the player to be named later in a deal for right-hander Dan Osinski. Osinski-for-Belinsky had a nice ring to it, but Bo discovered that K.C. had been bragging to journalists that he'd soon be joining the team. The commissioner's office voided the deal because outside parties had been tipped off before the player involved was informed. "Bowsie," as the popular Bowsfield had become known, was the replacement, and the west coast newspapers screamed he was the fall guy. But he took the news with good grace and understanding. "Bo didn't want to leave California and Mamie. Kansas City was the end of the world for Bo."

And the last stop for Bowsfield. "The pain was getting pretty bad. It was taking a longer period for the cortisone to take effect. I started on it in earnest in 1960. The doctor would take a pen and he'd probe my shoulder with his fingers. He'd say, 'Does that hurt?' 'Yeah.' And he'd mark it with a pen. 'Does that hurt?' 'Yeah,' and he'd mark another spot, and then go from spot to spot with the needle.

"It got so you'd learn you could pitch with pain as long as it was dead pain. If it was a long inning on the bench you'd go out and the pain would

Ted was second from left, back row, his father second from right: "That old Hudson. We could put more kids in that car . . ." (Queen Bowsfield)

be alive again, so you'd have to pitch through it all over until it deadened again.

"Then in 1963 and 1964 and 1965 especially, the cortisone didn't work — nothing worked. I was taking snake oil from Mexico. You'd rub it on your arm and when it went through your skin you got a garlic taste in your mouth. It didn't do any good, but by that time I was willing to try anything."

Somehow during his last two years in Kansas City he managed to come heartbeats away from pitching two no-hitters, one of which was almost a perfect game. Against Minnesota in 1963 he got into the ninth, then gave up a hit back through the box to Vic Power to lose it. He ended up winning the game 5-1 on a two-hitter.

And in a game against Boston, Felix Mantilla led off with a double off the Green Monster, after which Boswfield set down twenty-seven men in order. Would the double have been an out in any other ballpark? Bowsfield chuckles and cringes. "No, it would have been a home run. He hit a rocket. He put a dent in the wall."

People who are born gifted and have the gift taken away from them can quickly turn bitter, but Bowsfield took what baseball gave him with a smile. When Power spoiled his no-hitter against Minnesota, he told reporters he hadn't deserved it anyway. "Mediocre pitchers aren't meant to pitch no-hitters," he said with a wave of his hand. "I've never felt I was good enough to pitch a no-hitter." In a world of massive egos, Bowsfield was known as a good sport.

He goes for a walk, down to the ball field he played on, over to the river where he skipped stones. The soft hazy sun is still massaging the fruit trees, and the ball diamond, remodeled since the fifties, looks almost ready to play on. "My mother used to come to the games," he says, kicking the spot where the old mound used to be. "She had a voice you could hear for ten blocks.

"And my father, my father was always worried about me playing the game right. When I was young I'd cry if I lost. I was a bad loser at any sport. He told me that was wrong, that you had to pick yourself up and come at them again.

"He'd watch me. He always wanted to know how I was doing. Sometimes I could look behind home plate, right directly behind home plate, and I could see that little face pressed up against the screen. And he'd be listening to a fastball—zap crackle and pop, and I'd see him for a second—and then I'd lose him, and he'd be gone."

On the first page of Bowsfield's clippings album there is a birthday card from his father. It says: "Have been proud of you as a boy, Ted, and expect to be proud of you as a man. Play the game hard, but play it clean. Dad."

When Bowsfield left baseball things went badly for a while. "Those were hard times," he says. He tried to pitch for the Vancouver Mounties and managed to go six scoreless innings before the pain sat him down again. He opened a small liquor store in southern California, but it didn't work out. He and Lila broke up. He went looking for work to the Caifornia Angels head office seven times, without success.

But the Angels were building Anaheim Stadium, and Cedric Tallis, vice-president for operations for the Angels, decided that Bowsfield, despite his lack of experience, had the stuff to run it. Tallis started him cleaning toilets and dumping out wastepaper baskets, and made him work as an usher and ticket seller and ticket taker until finally he was manager of the stadium. He was there for eight years, then became director of the Kingdome in Seattle for twelve years until he got sick of the politics involved and got out.

He runs his own stadium-management consulting firm out of Seattle now, and has more people wanting him to do work for them than he can satisfy. He is remarried. He is happy: "I'm one of those lucky people who hasn't had an unhappy day in his life."

He hasn't seen his father yet. He'll go over when it gets dark. At the ballpark, he flings a couple of imaginary balls at an imaginary plate. At the river he skips stones and can still do eight-hoppers: "Look at that one! Hey, can you believe that?" In a town full of memories, it's a sight to behold.

20

BUZZ BIALGOWSKI

Dunedin, Florida
March 12, 1988

"We were rejects, pure and simple."
—Buzz Bialgowski
Toronto Blue Jays

Anyone who'd try to convince you that that Buzz Bialgowski was the Blue Jays' first pick in the 1976 expansion draft—well, what's the guy going to try to say next? That Babe Ruth was born in Moose Jaw?

But in truth, if Buzz Bialgowski's great-grandfather, John Bialgowski, hadn't been so desperate for a job on the railroad in Pennsylvania and so worried that a Polish name would freeze him out, you'd have never heard of this other guy, Bob Bailor. You'd have had a big-shouldered ethnic name like Bialgowski to reflect Toronto when it was just in the process of shedding its tight-assed, Anglo-Saxon image. Ah, what's the use?

As surely as Toronto baseball fans are stuck with the name SkyDome, Buzz Bialgowski is stuck with the name Bob Bailor. And what if it is an unassuming little name? Bailor is an unassuming, droll, personable little guy, with a crooked little smile and youthful good looks that haven't changed much since the 1976 Grey Cup parade.

Which was a head-shaker for Bailor, whose nickname has been Buzz since he buzzed all over the place as a child. It made him shake his head because Bailor had never counted for a whole lot, even when he'd been healthy. He was ignored in the major-league draft when he graduated from high school, he was nearly released right after he finally did get signed and, although he developed into a pretty fair minor-league ballplayer, he was never able to crack the Baltimore Orioles' major-league roster. To cap it off he'd recently developed a sore shoulder that was threatening to end his career.

The Blue Jays' first player should have had a more exciting name than Bob Bailor. Other than that, Buzz was just right. (Dan Turner)

And yet there he was, in November 1976, sitting on a float with quarterback Chuck Ealey, riding down Yonge Street amidst throngs of freezing Torontonians.

He had at least three thoughts about sitting on that float, trapped in the national celebration of a country he'd never been near before. The first was, "When will this all be over? I have to be deer hunting tomorrow, and Dad and the guys are waiting for me." The second was, "Why is everybody speaking English?" Folks in Pennsyvlania had told him he'd have to learn French. He never would hear any French in Toronto except when the nice lady went bilingual on the Canadian national anthem and they booed her.

And finally he thought, "Is this really happening? I mean, they're making a big deal out of a theory. Here I am representing a team and we don't even have one yet."

Later, he says, he grew more comfortable with the fact that the Blue Jays machinery was in motion. "And I was the start of it all."

Being "the start of it all" wouldn't have bothered most professional athletes. Their egos are groomed from childhood to be at the center of things; and each cut they survive on the way to the top reinforces their belief that the center of things is exactly where they belong. But there were factors that made Bailor a different kind of cat.

The first was the Bialgowski family credo: Don't get thinking too highly of yourself, ever. If you take a nice, modest approach to your accomplishments you may actually turn out to be something; but if you get swaggering, wham! You'll be down, and you won't be able to figure out where up went.

Not too long ago Bob Bailor's father, Bob Sr., listened to a glowing description of how well his son had managed at A ball in Dunedin in 1987, how quickly the Jays had moved him up to Triple A ball in Syracuse and how natural a prospect his son was to manage in the majors some day. Bob Sr. is a retired railway engineer who refuses to consider moving out of the weather-beaten family home in Connellsville, Pennsylvania, overlooking the Yough Valley, the Youghiogheny River, and the Allegheny Mountains. After pondering Bob Jr.'s accomplishments and prospects for three or four seconds, Bob Sr. said, "Well, we don't want to get too far ahead of ourselves, do we? Bob never got too high on himself when he was playing—I don't see why he should now."

Once you get by the credo, you have to understand that the Bialgowski idea of heaven is to get as far away from the center of things as you can.

Bailor didn't learn he'd been drafted by the Jays right away—he'd been off in the woods with his buddies. "Me, my best buddy Mike and my brother Woo were just coming home with some wild turkeys we shot for Thanksgiving and we saw my dad standing on the front porch, a-hollerin' and a-yellin' and jumpin' up and down. 'Hurry up,' he's shoutin', 'you been drafted number one by them Toronto Blue Jays.' Dad, he was so damn happy. It was the best Thanksgiving we ever had."

But when the Jays asked him to appear in the Grey Cup parade, he gulped, said he guessed he could handle that but, um, no, he couldn't stay for the big dinner and the game the next day. The Pennsylvania deer-hunting season was starting on the Monday, and he had never missed an opening with his dad and brothers and buddies, holed up in a cabin away from the bustle of Connellsville (pop. 8,210), and he never would.

Bob. Sr. says you shouldn't get the idea that the Bialgowskis are a bloodthirsty lot because they like hunting so much. "It's mainly the outdoors, the companionship and getting away from it all, that's what we like." When Bob Bailor was born his father went out and bought a bunch of baseball equipment and was polishing up his hunting rifle when his son came home from the hospital. "Ah," he is reported to have said. "I got me a partner." You get the idea.

And finally, Bob Bailor never considered himself big stuff because he wasn't. He was small. Rico Carty, one of the original Jays, was known as "Beeg Mon." He called Bailor "Leetle Mon." Bailor was allegedly five feet eleven and 170 pounds when he signed with the Jays, but that was standing on his tiptoes after eating three pizzas. He had always been considered too small to be a prospect and had spent his youth fighting his own doubts that he was big enough.

Connellsville was football country: Johnny Lujack, the Notre Dame legend who became the glory of the Chicago Bears, grew up just across Edna Street from the Bailors. Bo Scott, who played for the Ottawa Rough Riders and Cleveland Browns, was from Connellsville. And the late Jimmy Braxton, O.J. Simpson's blocking back with the Buffalo Bills, was, too—a fact that nearly put an early end to Bailor's baseball aspirations.

"I had wanted to be a big league ball player since I was six. At first I played pretty well with kids my own age. I was thirteen and pushing 130 pounds if I was lucky. And I was real shy. But my father and some other people convinced me I could step up to Legion ball, where the kids were a lot older. Well, Jimmy Braxton, who later became a great friend of mine, was the first baseman on that Legion team. He was about six feet three inches tall and 220 pounds—no baby fat, all muscle. I'll never forget it.

They talked me into trying out for this team. I got out of my father's car, it was a white Dodge, automatic. And Bubby [Braxton] was the first guy I saw. Shit. I jumped back into the car and made them take me home. I told them if they were all like that I didn't want any part of Legion ball.

"My dad said it was up to me. And the next day I went back. But it was always like that. When I got to the majors I remember thinking, 'Well, here I am again, over my head.' "

This is the guy up on the float, symbol for thousands of Toronto baseball fans of the major-league team they'd dreamed of for decades. The good news, as Bailor was soon to discover, was that being in over your head didn't mean being out of place. The whole team was in over its head.

Bailor, wearing blue jeans, as is his wont, is sitting in the lobby of the Ramada Inn Countryside Hotel in Dunedin. Consistent with baseball tradition, it is as far away from the beach as you can find a hotel down here. He is on lobby patrol, enforcing curfews for the Jays' minor-league players, trying to keep them out of the bars and off the beaches.

It is baseball gospel that baseball and beaches do not mix. It is baseball people's deepest belief that summer is the Garden of Eden, with a ball diamond in there somewhere, as you would expect, and the beach is the apple tree, pure and simple.

Bailor remembers a night the previous season when somebody unaccountably booked his Dunedin Blue Jays into a hotel on the beach, halfway through their Florida State League schedule. "They were all out there, most of the night. That's one of the few times I had to call a team meeting and remind them what they were in this for. We dragged our asses the next day, and lost badly, but I kind of liked it. It proved a point."

Bailor never, ever dragged his ass.

In strictly statistical terms, he did well enough. Every expansion franchise needs a beacon of hope in its first year. Bailor didn't look like a good bet. He was a sore-armed minor leaguer who'd gone 3-for-13 in two brief trials with the Orioles: he'd hit .231, with 0 runs and 0 RBIs — almost a virgin. But at least his arm healed when he finally decided to quit nursing it, throw through the pain and see if it would get better. It did. How good would Peter Bavasi and Pat Gillick have looked if, as was just as likely, his arm hadn't come around? Bill Singer also had a sore arm when Bavasi and Gillick selected him fourteenth in that draft. And still did after racking up a 2-8 record with a 6.75 ERA. Bye-bye, Billy.

It would have been a shame to lose Bailor the same way. He was the kind of symbol a fledgling team needs. He was versatile, had grit and loved baseball. "When my friends were going out with girls, I was the one who'd leave the party to go out and throw a ball against the wall. When I was in the minors and everybody was complaining about the long bus trips, I was lovin' it, playin' cards and drinkin' beer and havin' a good time."

And playin' ball, imagining he was Wee Willie Keeler? Nah. Albie Pearson? Nah. Willie Mays? Yeah. "I wasn't drafted out of high school, which is a pretty bad sign. I kept going to Pirate tryout camps, and they kept telling me I was too small. Finally my American Legion coach, Herman Welsh, I figure must have sold his soul to an old friend of his, who was a scout for the Orioles, to get him to sign me to a pro contract. Of course now that I'm on the management side of things I realize what I was. I was a fill-in signee." Which is the rough equivalent of an extra on a movie set. You are there so the genuine prospects have someone to play with. It means you should have stayed in school.

But Bailor, although he'd signed on as an infielder, thought he was Mays. "I wasn't doing too well and my first manager called me in and said they wanted to release me, but he'd stuck his neck out for me. And he asked me if I had ever played outfield, and I said 'Sure,' even though I hadn't. But when I was a kid playing Whiffle Ball in the streets I used to jump into one particular pine tree to make catches and pretend it was a light tower at Forbes Field. My father whipped my rear end for jumping in it too much, but I kept doing it. I figured if you weren't in the infield, center field was the place to be. Of course it didn't help too much that I didn't have any power."

Bailor turned out to be a clever first choice. The main thing about an expansion team is that holes are constantly appearing, everywhere. Bavasi and Gillick knew Bailor could play everywhere, and he did.

He was supposed to be the shortstop, but . . . "We had this problem. We had a whole lot of outfielders, but none of them could play baseball very well. So I ended up in center field for quite awhile. And I loved it out there."

The guy *was* Willie Mays. He hit .310. Willie's lifetime average was only .302. A franchise is born.

Bailor remembers the very beginning: "It was mass confusion, it really was. The coaches didn't know the guys, the manager didn't know the guys, we didn't even know each other. We didn't have names on our backs, so we'd call each other by our numbers. Guys would disappear, and you'd

Spring training, in the beginning, was mass confusion. Coaches and managers didn't know the players, and the players called each other by their numbers. (Toronto Star)

say, 'Hey, where did number thirty-three go?' There were some guys you knew who had played on good teams, so you figured maybe they were pretty good. Like Jim Mason had played on the Yankees. But then you figured, if he's so good, why is he here?

"You take Jim Clancy. He's my best friend now. But I looked at Jim Clancy, and maybe I'm no baseball genius, but I wouldn't have paid ten dollars for Jim Clancy's chances of pitching in the major leagues. He was just a big, gangly kid who couldn't get the ball over the plate. But Pat and them must have seen something.

"And Ernie Whitt. I played against Ernie Whitt in Triple A ball. He never made an all-star team and he never stuck out. He was average this, average that. You weren't afraid to steal against him. We were all like that. We were all average or we never would have got drafted. We all would have been protected. We were rejects, pure and simple."

Roy Hartsfield, the Jays' first manager, wouldn't appoint a team captain, but the quiet Bailor came off as the unofficial version. His .310 batting average in his first season was a record for expansion teams. He played scrappy ball. He bruised his back trying to break up a double play and banged up his knee trying to steal third. It was a dumb play—there were two out when he did it — but he believes in taking what you can get. "It's fun to play all out. It's fun for the people to watch."

He hit only .264 in 1978, but upped his RBIs from thirty-two to fifty-two. His decline in batting average was attributed to the sophomore jinx. And besides, he was hitting second in the lineup, a difficult spot to hit for average. For the second straight year the writers voted him team MVP. Even more important than Bailor's versatility was the fact that he wasn't a whiner. Playing for a team that went 54-107 never dampened his enthuiasm or diminished his effort.

Meanwhile Toronto was turning out to be heaven for a backwoods boy. He liked it for itself — "It was kind of a small big city" — but mostly for its proximity to fishing holes. "Right north of Willowdale you've got some of the best fishing in the world." Which, if you check your atlas closely, is in and around places like Collingwood and Gravenhurst.

"Balor Moore and I would usually go after a Sunday afternoon game, fish for an hour or two after dark because that's good bass fishing, and then get up early and fish and still have time to get back for Monday's game. One time we got back from a long trip to the west coast and we didn't get in until six in the morning. We had no game on Monday, and I tried to get Balor to go straight up to Collingwood. But he was married and said his wife would kill him. I had to go alone. I got to know the people of Collingwood real well." One of his proudest moments was catching a fair-sized salmon in the *Toronto Star*'s Great Salmon Hunt. He cleaned it in the clubhouse sink.

"I loved it in Toronto. I never wanted to play anywhere else. When they drafted me in 1976 Peter Bavasi called me and told me how excited he was, and said I'd end my career in Toronto. And that's what I wanted to do."

In 1981 Bailor was traded to the New York Mets for Roy Lee Jackson, an inconsistent righthanded relief pitcher. The captain without a C had hit .229 in 1979 and .236 in 1980. His home run total remaining consistent: he hit one in 1978, one in 1979 and one in 1980. But the Jays' brass must have sensed he was not going to catch Willie Mays, and they were right. He was to hit only one more during the next five years.

He was disappointed that the organization wasn't quite as sensitive about dumping him as they were about drafting him. "Let's put it this way — they didn't do another parade."

New York turned out to be okay in one sense. He got a lucrative new contract, and since he never spends money on anything other than hunting equipment and fishing poles, he started to invest wisely. But moving to the Big Apple traumatized him. "I had culture shock. I didn't have a car and I was afraid I was going to get mugged. The only thing that saved me was the 1981 players' strike. I was the only one in baseball who wanted that strike.

"I got out of town, went to Pennsylvania, went to the nearest stream, put my pole in the water and just shook like a dog that's been scared."

Bailor played three years for the Mets and another two for the Dodgers. But the knee he'd smashed stealing third continued to deteriorate and diminished his value as a utility man. After so many years playing for bad teams, however, he did get into the League Championship Series with the Dodgers, going 0-for-1. The Dodgers lost that series on Jack Clark's famous home run. Up in Toronto, the Jays were losing one of their own to Kansas City.

Bailor was released in the spring of 1986 in what he calls "a dream firing." He didn't want to go, but there was a year left on his contract, the money was guaranteed, he had married, and Bob Bialgowski III was just a few months old. And the fishing holes were waiting.

The previous year, Jays' vice-president Paul Beeston had called him over before a game, blown cigar smoke in his face and told him when he got through playing to call the Jays before he called anyone else. "He was a guy who exemplified what this organization is," says Beeston. "He was a hard-working guy who would do anything necessary to win, never complained, and was both a student of the game and had a great affection for it. He liked to work hard and have fun. We wanted him badly."

After two years as a manager and one large promotion, Bailor still isn't sure whether he'll stay in the game. "I never grew up wanting to manage in the major leagues, he says." But he has enjoyed counseling the kids.

"I say, don't cheat yourself. If you never make it out of A ball, don't let it be because you didn't try. If your numbers are wrong, that's no disgrace. But if you don't give it everything you were supposed to give it, that's a disgrace."

Just part of the Bialgowski credo.

21

TERRY PUHL

Kissimmee, Florida
March 14, 1988

"Before Terry Puhl came down here we thought Canadians were mostly a little bland but decent, you know. But maybe the word for Canadians should be decadent instead of decent. You take this kid Puhl. He makes it to the bigs. Granted he's pretty young back then, but as soon as he starts popping the home runs he starts thinking big shot. He's up drinking all night, there's the cocaine, the fights, and finally the damn paternity suits. If that's your Canadian farm boy, I'd hate to see your city dudes."
—Billy Hatcher,
player representative,
Houston Astros Morals Committee

Hey, just kidding. Call off the libel lawyers. Not Terry Puhl. Not on your life. But you wonder. Babe Ruth boozed and womanized. If Puhl wasn't going to hit like the Babe, wouldn't Canadians at least have preferred that he act like him? Or take the wild-tongued George Bell. George plays in Canada. Would we have preferred a wild man like Bell to the gentleman Puhl as the best everyday Canadian player of the 20th century?

Are we satisfied with a guy whose nickname is TP? Couldn't he at least have called himself "the Saskatchewan Wheat Puhl"? Is flamboyance always going to be the Canadian f-word?

It's not that Puhl hasn't been a pretty special performer. But if baseball players were fireworks, Terry Puhl would be the burning schoolhouse: pretty enough during combustion, but you keep waiting for it to send up a rocket.

Unfair, unfair. We're not only talking about the Canadian player with the best numbers of this century, we're talking about someone highly respected by his coaches, manager and teammates.

He is also the one Houston player in the insipid twenty-six-year history of the Astros who fired when it really mattered. Nolan Ryan didn't — your typical Roman candle. Ryan had a three-run lead in the seventh inning of the deciding game of the 1980 National League Championship Series and couldn't hold it.

Puhl hit .526 in that series — ten hits in nineteen at-bats, including four in the final game—and came extra-inning close to single-handedly pushing the Astros into the World Series. In 1986, coming off an injury, Puhl got into another NL Championship Series as a pinch hitter, going 2-for-3. Totals in the big clutch: 12-for-22.

Yet a profile in *MVP*, "Canada's Sports Magazine," spent three pages yawning about Puhl. The most the article could muster in terms of enthusiasm was a comparison with a glass of milk: "both the outfielder and the drink are white, safe, and predictable." Well, now. We don't seem to be talking hero-worship here.

What's going on? Canadians have given every appearance of being hooked on big-league baseball since the Expos set up shop in 1969. Furthermore, when we're talking Puhl we're talking about the finest position player Canada has offered up since Tip O'Neill was with the St. Louis Browns in the 1880s.

In 1986, in anticipation of his thirtieth birthday, the *Houston Chronicle* printed a tribute to Puhl. If he had never quite lived up to his sparkling early promise, the article said, Puhl had still been a quality player. He might well have been even better, it added, if the Astros hadn't tried to meddle with his hitting so much. But "the native of Melville, Sask. is like so many Canadians — quiet, hard-working, and without excuses . . . Terry Puhl would never whimper a complaint."

Solid, determined, decent — Terry Puhl has obviously left the kind of imprint on Houston that Canada has left on the world. Damn. We hate that, eh?

The Melville Assassin — no, he wasn't called that, but let's think pizzazz here — was called up on July 8, 1977. It was his twenty-first birthday and Puhl was way ahead of himself. Few but the brightest stars climb out of the minors that early.

He hit .301 in half a season's play. He was six foot two, 190 pounds, elegant in the outfield and fast on the bases. He didn't show a lot of early power, but the Astros thought they could make a few adjustments. And if they didn't, well, he was built for the spacious plastic pastures of the

Astrodome anyway. He hit five triples that first year and would likely have been among the league leaders if he'd been up all year.

Nobody was sure how he had emerged out of Saskatchewan to become an everyday major-league player while still a child, but the gift was gratefully accepted by both the Astros and Canadian ball fans.

Wayne Morgan, who scouts for the Jays now, found him for the Astros at the first Canadian national midget tournament in Barrville, Alberta, when he was sixteen. Puhl had attended an Expos tryout camp the year before in Regina without triggering any alert systems. But he'd tried out as a pitcher and had been too young to sign, anyway.

Morgan didn't like him much as a pitcher. "He had fairly decent arm strength but he didn't have a good delivery and he didn't have a breaking pitch. But I liked him at bat. He was big and strong, he was an athlete and he was fast. He played the outfield when he wasn't pitching, but I couldn't tell how he'd throw from the outfield because his arm was sore from pitching."

So Puhl went back to Melville, and Morgan made his way to other parts of Saskatchewan, where he had friends, and hung out. Every few days he'd call and find out how Puhl's arm was, and after a few weeks, when it had finally healed, he showed up, set himself up at third base and had Puhl throw to him from the outfield.

If he didn't get his glove knocked off, he was satisfied, and Puhl signed one of those little Canadian contracts with those itty-bitty bonuses. Scouts don't offer much because they aren't as sure of Canadian prospects, who often haven't seen much top-flight competition. And the kids are usually eager to sign because they know the train isn't going to come by that often in the Great White North.

Puhl feels he made a sensible decision: "You start picking and choosing and you end up signing with nobody." And if he was worth more, he would have no trouble getting that back with compound interest later on.

He started out at Covington, Virginia, hitting .284, which was followed by .332 at Dubuque, .286 at Columbus, .266 at Memphis, .305 at Charleston, and — hey! — the major leagues. During his three and a half years in the minors he hit exactly six home runs, so the Astros must have known what was coming. Especially when half his future stretched before him in the Astrodome, home of the warning-track fly.

Despite the power shortage, the early years were wonderful. First came the .310 performance in 1977, followed by .289 in 1978, when he was named to the National League All-Star Team before his twenty-second birthday. That September he began a streak of 182 consecutive games without mak-

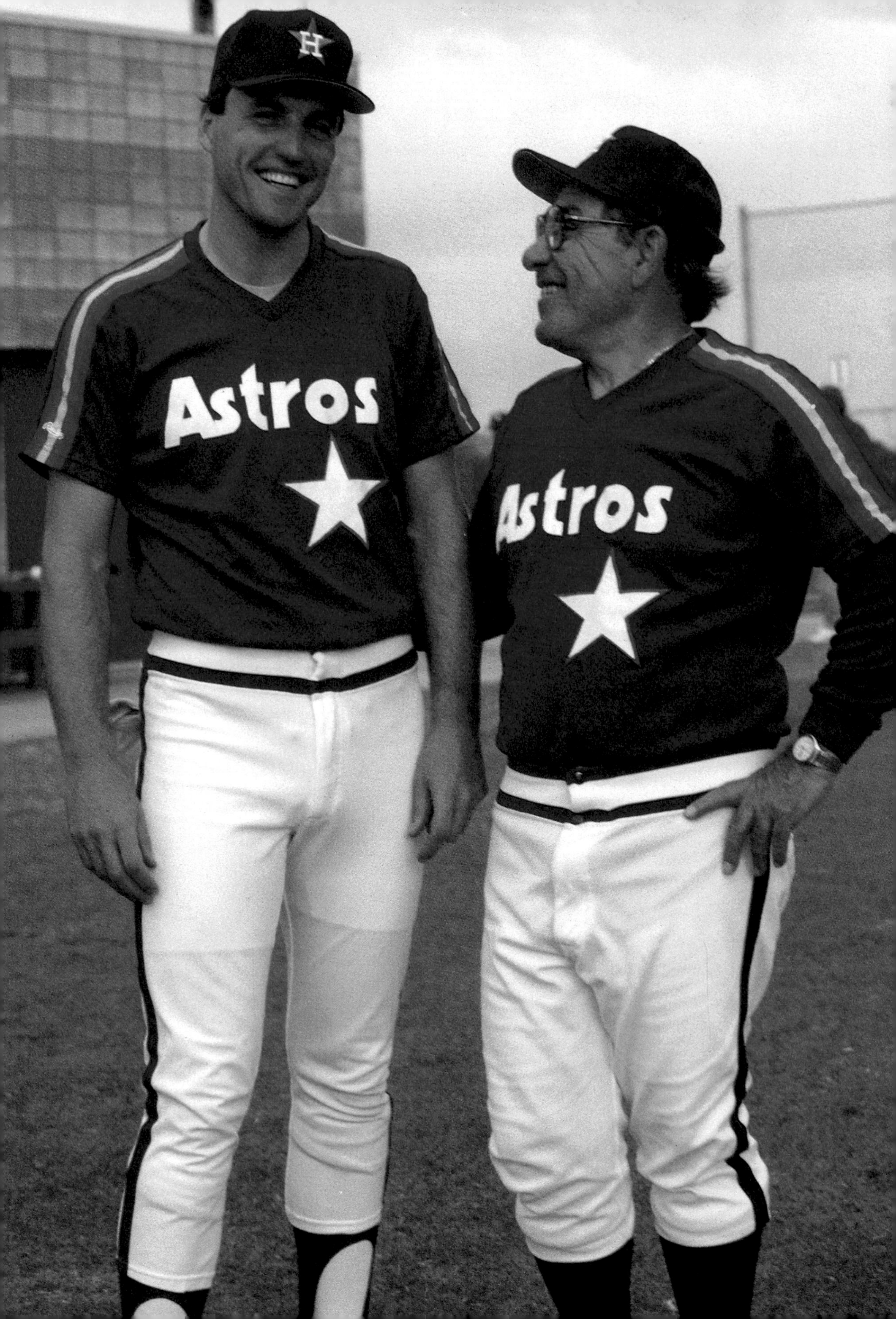
H
Astros
Astros

ing an error; the 157 errorless games he played in 1979 made him the first player in the history of the game to play 150 or more games in one season without making an error. That year he hit .287, giving him a solid .290 record for his first three years.

One remembers a delicious sun-drenched day in March 1980, at the Montreal Expos spring-training camp in Daytona Beach, Florida. The Astros were in town and Puhl was beaming. He'd gotten over being the green kid among all the veterans, although not without embarrassment.

"One day two years ago," he recalled that day, "when it was early and I was leading the league in batting, Pete Rose came over near the cage when I was hitting. And I heard someone say, 'How ya doin'?' But I couldn't believe Pete Rose was really talking to me, so I just went on swinging.

"Then I heard, 'How ya doin', kid? Whatsa matter, don'tcha talk to me just because you're leadin' the league?'" Puhl's clear white skin turned red under the Florida sky just thinking about it. "You talk about embarrassed—boy, was I embarrassed." So how did he finally respond, you are anxious to know, hoping for a dazzling example of baseball repartee. "What could I say? I said 'How ya doin', Pete?'" There you are. The young man had a sense for the baseball dialogue right from the beginning.

That spring Puhl was still enough of a kid to be excited about baseball cards. Not only had Topps Baseball Cards produced his third card, but they had put his picture on the outside wrapper of the box the card packages were delivered in. The folks at Topps said they'd chosen a shot of him because of his good-looking swing and for color considerations. (The Houston uniform tended to make a person look like his intestines were on fire.)

That kind of thing tickled Puhl in the spring of 1980 — "Right on the front of the box. I've got to get one of those." That and being young and an Astro. "Whatever happens I've got youth on my side," he said with a laugh, and he meant it. His manager at the time, Bill Virdon, agreed, but emphasized that Puhl had other qualities as well. "He's incredibly mistake-free," said Virdon, who had been a fine outfielder himself. "He's been the most coachable player I've ever dealt with. He's very attentive, very alert. You just know he's going to be a great one."

Eight years later, at another spring training, Terry Puhl would remember those years as his smug period.

It is the spring of 1988. The Astro veterans lie out on the training field and stretch. Puhl is uncomfortable with the idea of being photographed in these various contortions. The shots would simply be a reminder that he

The Melville Assassin has been solid, decent, quiet, hard-working and uncomplaining. Do we care? (Dan Turner)

has been the victim of a series of injuries that has come close to crippling his career in recent years. That's a tired old story, he says. He feels good. Real good.

And he looks good, moments later, when the left-handed batters take to the batting cage. When he swings a ferocity comes into his pale blue eyes that is nowhere to be seen when he doesn't have a bat in his hands. He still has that smooth, clean stroke that stings baseballs on wicked, hissing journeys down the right-field line. Yogi Berra grunts approval, still looking out of place in an Astros uniform, so far away from the Bronx.

"When I came over here two years ago he looked great in the spring," remembers Berra. "Then he got injured again."

There have been a few tough years. The spring of 1980 went well enough. Puhl lost his errorless streak seven games into the season, but he hit .282 with thirteen home runs — an encouraging show of power that was the equivalent of maybe twenty home runs anywhere other than the Astrodome. Then he hit his .526 for the Championship Series — still the record after all these years. The following year the Astros got greedy.

Al Rosen, the the Astros general manager, was desperate to give the punchless Astros some heft. He looked at Puhl, still six feet two but grown to two hundred pounds, and decided he could hit for power. The Astros worked tirelessly, revamping Puhl's line-drive swing, trying to give him more lift. *Au contraire.* The results: in 1981, the strike-shortened season, he hit .251 with three homers. In 1982 he hit .262 with eight homers.

In 1983 Dennis Menke came aboard as the Astros' hitting coach and Puhl was allowed to go back to his natural swing. He responded with a .292 average and eight home runs, following that in 1984 with a .301 year and nine homers. It became evident that by meddling with one of the prettiest swings in the game the Astros had temporarily lost a remarkably consistent and capable lead-off hitter, who almost surely would have hit between .280 and .305 for them for eight straight years, stealing 175 bases over the period and playing the most consistent outfield in the league.

The two years of fiddling screwed that up, but Puhl didn't whine. He was being well paid—he signed a four-year, $1.65 million contract in 1982 and would sign another four-year deal in 1986 for more than double that.

And his game was back together. In 1985 he was hitting well at the beginning of the season and was shooting for his third errorless season. He got it, but in only fifty-seven games.

First he pulled his hamstring. "I was running down to first in a game against San Diego in the eighth inning when I felt a stab and heard a pop like a balloon breaking. I rested it for two and a half weeks, which was the biggest mistake I ever made. It's a five or six week injury. You always want to get back as quickly as possible; there's nothing worse than sitting on the bench."

Ironically, trying to come back early marked the beginning of Puhl's career as a bench player. He was on the disabled list four times that year, three with the recurring hamstring and once with a hyperextended elbow. He still hit .284.

He stretched all winter and did wind sprints. New manager Hal Lanier penciled him into the number-two spot in the batting order. The *Chronicle* liked his chances for a comeback—after all he was still only twenty-nine. He was ready, said the newspaper, "to renew his quest for that one super season that has eluded him."

Early in 1986 spring training Puhl tore his ankle trying to jam his way back into first base. He was on the disabled list for three weeks in April and three weeks in July. He hit .244 in eighty-one games.

In 1987 the ankle still bothered him. He hovered around .200 all year. A late-season surge brought him up to .230 in only 122 at-bats. During his miseries, the inevitable had happened: the Astros had developed some good new players. Puhl describes them with relish.

There is Billy Hatcher in left. Using a corked bat only some of the time, he hit .296 in 1987 with fifty-three stolen bases. "Billy is very quick," says the Astros' former base-stealing leader. "He's probably the fastest guy on our team."

There is Gerald Young in center, who hit .321 with twenty-six stolen bases in only seventy-one games. "There's no telling what he can do. He's very mature for a young player, and he's got the potential to hit home runs, too."

There is Kevin Bass in right, who hit .284 with twenty homers and twenty-one stolen bases, the kind of numbers Al Rosen tried to squeeze out of Puhl. "He's a nice package: he can hit for average, he can hit for power, he's got good speed and a good throwing arm. He's probably the best all-around player on our team."

And there's Terry Puhl himself. On the one hand, "This is the year I've got to fulfill my potential. I've never felt I've put together the kind of season I'm capable of." On the other hand, "Right now I'm the fourth outfielder. It's hard to set any goals, because I might be coming in for an at-bat here or an at-bat there. It's not as bad as it sounds. It's been fun for me to be able to adjust to these different situations. I think they're going to use me a lot more this year than they did in the past few years. Remember, Jose Cruz [the former Astro left fielder] isn't with the team this year. He took up a lot of at-bats last year."

It is true, Cruz is gone. When Cruz was cut at the end of the 1987 season, Puhl, former rookie phenom, became the player with the longest service with the Astros. *Good grief.*

When Puhl first arrived to the Houston Astros' minor-league spring training camp at the tender age of seventeen, he found himself squeezed between two emotions: sadness and fear. There was the homesickness: "It was my first time ever away from home and my first time on an airplane. I had tears in my eyes." But most of all there was the fear.

"It didn't take me long to see what the real business of baseball is really like. It scared me, seeing guys get released, seeing guys get sent home with their dreams crushed. I thought, 'Well, that could happen to me.'

"I was in a room with four bunks. The three other guys got released. I went to a room with three other guys, and those three got released. And

Terry has always wanted to be more daring, and he's always craved that one great season. In 1988 he came pretty close. (Houston Chronicle)

no one else would take me in their room, because they were scared they'd get released if they did. So I had to spend the rest of the spring alone.

"I became very businesslike. I worked and worked and worked. I don't have the natural talent that some guys have, so my game has to be mechanically perfect. I worked at that. I've never been afraid of work, and I love the game. The hitting and running and throwing—I could do that twenty-four hours a day.

"I learned how to play the game right. The only thing in life that makes me really angry are people who are incompetent because they won't try hard enough. I see it all the time, from kids and veterans alike, and I hate it. So I made myself play good ball, and I progressed through the system, without my dreams being smashed.

"The only time I kind of got lost is when I had the early success with the Astros. I had already met my wife-to-be, Jackie. She's from Vancouver, but I met her in my hometown, Melville—she was working for an accounting firm there. I was was on the 1978 All-Star team at twenty-two, and there's no question that I stumbled through those times, personality-wise. I had that swelled ego. Jackie and I were dating, and she made it clear she didn't really like me at that time. Maybe I wasn't swaggering openly, but I was inside. And she was so close to me, she could see through me. I remember her going back home after the All-Star Game, and I remember her writing me a letter saying she didn't like what she saw in me there. I had to rethink things and put some stop signs out. She was right. This game can gobble you up if you're not careful."

Terry Puhl's smug period was over. He had diligently learned the game. He was known for playing it carefully and well. Now he would put his ego away and learn to live life carefully enough not to fall prey to baseball, not to crush his own dreams. "I've seen players go through women and fancy cars. I've never seen it really make them happy, though." He bought a big Cadillac Coup de Ville in 1978, the year of the All-Star Game. He still drives it.

He became religious. "It's a personal relationship with Jesus Christ, whether you want to call it born again or whatever." He got into the investment business as a broker with teammate Craig Reynolds. He specializes in picking out safe investments for people who can't afford to gamble with their money.

Safe, Puhl acknowledges, is his style. It may stem from being seventeen years old, three thousand miles from home, and watching his roommates disappear around him. Or twenty-two years old, and watching his personality disappear around him. Or who knows? Maybe just being from a conservative little farm town on the Prairies. There wasn't anything flamboyant about him, even then. "He wasn't a holler guy," according to Doug Senyk, a friend and former teammate in Melville. "But he worked hard and set an example for others to follow."

Puhl has a daughter, Naomi, who is six, and a son, Stephen, who is four. Earlier this day he and Jackie have taken them fishing. "It's just getting them to try things, to see how they react to new challenges, see how they react to ice skating, roller skating, throwing a ball, whatever. I'd feel bad if they were scared to try things. They're good about that, not being afraid to fail.

"It's like baseball. You don't see the brilliance if you play cautiously. If there's one thing I could really change over the years it would be that I wish I had risked more at the game, just let things fly a bit more, instead of left foot, right foot . . .

"I'm always being branded that kind of player, of always getting the job done, hitting the cutoff man, this and that. Sometimes I wish I had booted a couple more balls in the outfield but made a brilliant play somewhere along the line."

He has two years left on his contract. Will he play like that? He laughs and sighs. "Now that's a good question. Maybe you should ask me two years from now. You know my role has changed now. Now I'm really at the point where I have to be more regimented, because you can't afford to make a mistake when they put you in in a key situation.

"But then again, you're right. I've still got plenty of time to turn that part of my game around. And I think I'd have more fun at the game by fearing less and risking more."

Maybe this year, eh?

22

JIM McKEAN

Dunedin, Florida
March 15, 1988

"I only felt bad when my fooling around hurt the quality of my work . . . if I had kept quiet and concentrated on my job I would have been a better umpire. But I wouldn't have enjoyed myself as much . . . I was simply having a good time and I wasn't afraid to show it . . . talking and joking around were my only skills on the field."

—Ron Luciano,
The Umpire Strikes Back

But then Ron was born a buffoon. Luciano would probably have been more at home in pro wrestling than he was in baseball. But if you were in a carnival mood at the ballpark — and who isn't sometimes? — Luciano was good for a laugh. Once, when he was behind the plate, he broke Tommy John up so much by calling a baseball John had inadvertently dropped out of his hand a strike that John gave up two walks and two hits and had to leave the game. Ho, ho, ho.

Another time he was reading something on a paper airplane that had been thrown from the stands when he was supposed to be making a call at second. He guessed, and he still isn't sure if he got it right. Hee, hee, hee. What a guy, that Ronnie.

"If only I had funny stories to tell, to reassure people that their innocent faith in baseball is justified."

—Jim McKean,
American League umpire

Jim McKean, is big, like Luciano, and used to play football, like Luciano, and . . . well, that's about it. McKean can turn his hangdog look into a big, easy smile very quickly, but he isn't into slapstick. Luciano is probably

the guy for you if you're there for the hot dogs and beer. But McKean's your man if you're deeply into a ball game, and hoping the ump is, too.

In fairness to Luciano, he was bluntly honest about the farce he sometimes made of the game. McKean is bluntly honest, too, about a subject that makes baseball promoters nervous: baseball = business, yes; baseball = romance, no. His thesis is simple: professional baseball has become so deadly serious to most of the people involved in it that it's almost irrelevant to connect the word "game" to it.

McKean likes professionalism — he'll take a real umpire over Luciano every time. Slapstick isn't what he misses: "I couldn't do what Luciano did, and I wouldn't want to." But he yearns for something in between, something that fits between asinine slapstick and somber pinstripes, a mixture of excellence and fun. "The game has lost its soul. And I can't see that it's going to come back."

Most good umpires are athletes, and McKean has always been a jock. Growing up in Montreal, he made the Quebec baseball all-star team. But football was his game. He played backup quarterback with the Montreal Alouettes and for a long time held the record as the youngest player to compete in the CFL. He was only seventeen when a second-quarter injury brought him in as pivot in a game against Edmonton. He threw two touchdown passes and Montreal won 16-14.

"I was pretty good," he says, weighing his words, pursing his lips, trying to be objective, like any good ump. "I should have gone down and played college football in the States, but the Alouettes wanted to keep me around so they sent me to university in Montreal."

McKean backed up Bernie Faloney with the Alouettes between 1963 and 1965 and did the same for Ron Lancaster with the Saskatchewan Roughriders in 1966 and 1967, making it into the Grey Cup with the 'Riders before a ruptured kidney ended his career.

In the off season he refereed hockey, including a Memorial Cup final, and would occasionally umpire a kids' baseball game around Montreal. After football he marked time for a couple of years, trying to adjust to civilian life but still feeling the call of the field. One day a Shell "sports short" on television caught his eye. It focused on an umpires' school operating in Florida under the direction of veteran National League umpire Billy Williams.

"I said, 'Hell, why not?' I decided to go to every Expos game they played until Williams came out." When he finally showed, McKean was com-

"Imagine going to work every day and having the worst obscenities spit in your face in front of the people you work with . . ."
(Michael Rafelson)

195

pletely unprepared, sitting in the stands in cutoff shorts and thongs with a buddy who'd already gone through a few beers. Williams came by the screen at cozy Jarry Park. McKean froze. His buddy, topped up with anti-freeze, did not: "Hey, Billy, this guy wants to talk to you about umpiring!" For reasons best known to himself, Williams came over, looked the pair over, and told McKean to visit him in the umpires' dressing room after the doubleheader.

McKean went home, showered, shaved, changed and came back to the ball park. He was used to CFL clubhouses, so the site for his conversation with Williams should have been familiar.

"But it was a different world in there, seeing the lockers and the names and the food and the uniforms. That was a big-league situation I just wasn't used to. I was in awe."

McKean composed himself quickly enough to assure Williams he didn't have a police record. Moral authority is at the heart of umpiring, and there are very few opportunities for ex-cons. The following spring McKean found himself at Williams' training school, where they weed out the never-wills from the prospects as quickly as the ball clubs do at instructional leagues.

"I had to buy the equipment I needed in the States. We didn't have wire masks and that stuff in Canada. A lot of our umpires wore postmen's jackets."

McKean quickly found out how important physical presence was. "I saw little guys with thick glasses, and it didn't take long to figure out they didn't have a chance." At six foot two, carrying 230 pounds with grace and authority, McKean did.

"If I were rating myself after we finished our training I would have said I maybe stood about twentieth out of fifty. I just didn't know the rules as well as most of them, had never worn an outside protector and didn't know the stances. Then I found out that's the kind of guy they like. They want someone who's totally green with an athletic background and good coordination. If he can move around, they can take him and develop him. They don't like to see a guy come in with ten years of college experience, because he has too many bad habits you can't change.

"Anyway, I didn't think I'd done so well. I'd never really failed at anything I'd tried at, and this time I seemed to be cutting it pretty close. Then I went to the banquet at the end, and I was sitting out there at the back. And they have this award that goes to the umpire with the most potential to make it into the major leagues, and I heard them call my name. Honest to God, I pulled one of those Miss America jobs and said, 'You've got to be kidding.' But they weren't.

"I lucked out my first year. I got to work the Florida Class A League, which has the best minor-league stadiums because they're used for major-league spring training. I really struggled in my first year. I didn't have the experience. But I'd hustle, I'd run, and I was never out of position. I'd get there and make the wrong call, but I was never out of position.

"It was a tough year. Rookie umpires get called some pretty terrible things by people, from the dugouts and the stands. They're taking out their frustrations from their own crummy lives. And I struggled, even though people said I was doing a hell of a job. I figured if I was doing a hell of a job the other guys must be brutal. I nearly quit, but I'm glad I didn't. Because what I didn't realize was that the players were doing as bad a job playing as I was umpiring. Bad play makes umpiring more difficult. There are always balls skittering in the dirt, and there are more close plays because the infielders have more trouble getting the ball where they want it. And the pitching is more erratic.

"From there I went to the Eastern League — from Lakeland to Three Rivers, just like that. One day a gruff old guy came into the dressing room in Waterbury, Connecticut, and started to compliment the home-plate umpire on the job he'd done that night. Then he turned to me and began to rip me apart — 'You gotta do this, you gotta do that, you shouldn't talk to this guy, don't straddle the white line.' Then he introduced himself as supervisor of American League umpires. So I figured, jeez, he's not too happy with me. I'd better be thinking about the other league if I'm going to go anywhere. But then when he said that about not straddling the line [it is the National League style *to* straddle] I thought, hmmm, at least he's interested."

That Christmas McKean got a letter telling him the American League was taking an option on his contract. After splitting most of the following year in the minors, he was called up to the majors in September. It was 1973, four short years after McKean had staked out Jarry Park looking for Billy Williams.

He got off to a hairy start as a regular in 1974. The Yankees were playing in Milwaukee in the Brewers' opening series at home. McKean was handling first base. The Brewers were losing 9-7 in the bottom of the ninth, with the bases loaded and two men out. Dave Pagan, of Nipawin, Saskatchewan, was on the mound for the Yankees. As he was about to go into his windup, New York first baseman Chris Chambliss called time out for

Yankees' manager Billy Martin. McKean threw his hands in the air to signal time out, but Pagan threw the ball. The Brewer's batter hit it out of the park. The crowd went wild with joy. McKean called "no pitch." The crowd went wild with bile. In Latin America it might have meant a lynching. McKean's schedule was altered. The league kept him out of Milwaukee for a while.

"That'll give you a few sleepless nights, if you do that in your second year. Because up until five years in the game you're always thinking, 'Oh, boy, there goes my job.' " Eleven years later McKean was umpiring third when veteran NL umpire Don Denkinger blew the call at first that probably cost the St. Louis Cardinals the 1985 World Series.

"Of course, I felt for him. You always have the feeling that it could be you. You have nightmares that it will happen to you, and sooner or later it will. It's very hard to tell you what the pressure is like until you put the uniform on and go out on that field and get behind that plate with twelve cameras on you, and all they're looking for is for you to make a mistake. A mistake like Denkinger made can ruin your career. The only thing that got him over the hump is that he was an eighteen-year veteran."

For McKean, still only forty-one, it has been fifteen years now. Fifteen years of watching, deciding in haste and immediately informing the participants and the assembled masses of your decision. Fifteen years of hunching, peering, gesturing, checking bats, dodging, scurrying, arguing, soothing and rubbing up baseballs with Chesapeake Bay mud. Fifteen years of playing at least one game of racquetball and running three miles a day to stay in shape. And most of all, fifteen years of traveling, always traveling, until your wife and the baby, now four, seem like a far-off dream.

And what is it like on the field? It seems, from the stands, that there might be a lot of pro-wrestling-type hype to it: the manager barrels out of the dugout, goes jaw to jaw with the ump, spits tobacco juice to the left and the right of him, shows off the veins in his neck, kicks dirt and is finally given the old heave ho. Gotta be theater, right? Grown men wouldn't . . .

Yes, yes, they would, says McKean.

"I've never had a manager shouting at me who wasn't serious. That's the part of the job I hate the most. Imagine going to work every day and getting the worst obscenities spit in your face in front of the people you work with, not to mention a park full of people and everybody at home in

Jim nearly got lynched in Milwaukee when he first came up. Now he's an umpiring chief's delight. (Toronto Star)

their living rooms watching on TV. It might look like a charade on 'This Week in Baseball,' but it's real. And it's disgusting."

There are things McKean likes about baseball. "For six or seven dollars on up you can take your family out and spend three hours in the sun and not feel any pressure. That's cheap compared to other sports. And the nicest thing about it is the lack of violence you get in other sports."

And there are things he doesn't like about baseball as it has evolved in recent years. The increasing length of games, for one thing. Few people realize how arduous it is to stand on a ball field for three hours or more, night after day after night, without the half-inning breaks the players get nine times a game.

"They're trying different things to speed it up, like calling higher strikes and so on. We'll see. The reason we haven't been calling the higher pitches strikes is that they're pitchers' mistakes, and you don't like to call a mistake a strike.

"What I'd like to see is automatic intentional walks and making the batter stay in the batter's box unless he's swung at the last pitch. And making the guys bring more than one bat out with them. The batboy can take care of an extra bat—he's not doing anything anyway. Jeez, I've lost guys. A guy breaks a bat and he's gone. He goes into the clubhouse, he can't find a bat, he comes out, he brings the wrong bat, he goes back and gets another one, he puts pine tar on it—I've stood there for ten minutes waiting for one bat."

Without losing his temper. McKean looks like such a big, good-natured bear that you'd guess he has pretty good control. "I'm low key until situations arise, then all of a sudden I'll blow my stack. But I think I've mellowed. Everybody does it differently—some guys are high-pressure all the time. A lot of new people, whether they're managers or players or umpires, the first year they're gung-ho to fight everybody. But you get so darned tired from fighting you say, jeez, there's got to be a better way. The guys who set me off are the guys who are blaming me for their own shortcomings." However high he'd like to blow, McKean doesn't think he's ever lost control of a situation. "I'm a pretty good policeman."

A 1984 *Sports Illustrated* article focused on increasing complaints that umpires had become too arrogant, thin-skinned and quick on the trigger, particularly after the umpires' strike of 1979. It pointed out that baseball officials consider the best umpires to be the ones who do their jobs unnoticed. Dick Butler, in charge of umpires for the American League, used McKean, who he promoted to crew chief, as an example. "He has the best attitude of any umpire I've ever had."

McKean is proud of his style, but when *Sports Illustrated* contacted him to tell him what Butler had said, he was quick to defend his more volatile colleagues. "If it seems that we're willing to take less, maybe it's because we're getting more," he said. "We may have changed, but I think the players have changed too. They don't have as much respect as they used to."

As a crew chief, McKean often finds himself protecting a new colleague. "I just make sure the benches stay off him. I say, 'Stay off him and let him umpire. You know what it's like at the start. If somebody hadn't give you a chance you wouldn't be here, and if you don't give him a chance he's not going to be here tomorrow. And if you don't give him a chance you're not going to be here today, because he can't work if you're going to scream at him. Hell, I can't work if you're going to scream at me. So either let me work or you're not going to sit there.' "

Butler said McKean wasn't arrogant, thin-skinned or quick on the trigger. He didn't say he wasn't tough, blunt and firm.

It's not just the loss of respect McKean laments. It's the loss of joy. "There used to be a lot of fun on the field. I don't mean the Luciano stuff. But there was a lot of kidding around, a lot of joking. Now, once you get by spring training, it's simply a business from the first pitch of the season to the last day."

McKean figures his timing hasn't been too good. When he first came up there was still some fun to be had. "But in the early days I had to work so hard to survive that I didn't have time for much fun. Then, when I got over that hump, the players started making so much money that the whole atmosphere changed. You see a ballplayer at the airport and he's got an attaché case. He looks like a businessman. There's no more sitting around and talking about the game. As soon as the last ball is in the air, they're gone.

"And it's hard to kid around. Guys take offense at everything that happens. Look at the Kirk Gibson thing. [At the beginning of 1988 spring training, new Dodger Jesse Orosco spread shoe polish on the band of Gibson's hat. When Gibson discovered the stuff on his forehead, he stormed off the field and refused to play.] That kind of thing used to be part of the team concept. Now there are fights all the time, and this guy doesn't get along with that guy, and this guy's not getting along with his manager. The players are running the game, and guys who have big cars and lots of real estate don't like to be made fun of. They think they're too important. You show up a guy like that and he says to himself, 'Don't they know about all the property I own? Don't they know how important I am?' "

Ask Jim McKean what he's gotten out of the game, besides a career, and he will tell you he was proud to have been in two World Series and two All-Star games and several playoff series. "I've got a Grey Cup ring, I worked a Memorial Cup in hockey. I've had a well-rounded career. I really can't complain. Except . . . "The game has changed totally. The fun is gone."

Say it ain't so, Jim. And he'd love to. But he won't: he's made his call. At the moment retired umpires can't start collecting their pensions until they're fifty. McKean hopes the age will soon be lowered. Because in about five years he'd like to make his last out call. And then get out himself.

The Blue Jays raved about Rob's perfect attitude. Then they changed their minds. (Dan Turner)

23

ROB DUCEY

Dunedin, Florida
March 17, 1988

Boomer Wells, the big, spike-haired relief pitcher, is dumbfounded. "This is your own car?" he asks from the passenger's seat, speaking with disbelief. Rob Ducey smiles and nods, doing a little hand jive to "The Pleasure Principle" as it explodes out of the stereo speakers and spills out the windows of the brand-new burgundy fully loaded mean-as-anything Chev Iroc-Z. "Your very own car?"

Ducey giggles and accelerates, leaving a little rubber. He surely has the most spectacular smile and the greatest set of teeth in modern baseball history. His agent has made a deal for him with Schlueter's Chev-Olds in Kitchener. He gets a car every year. This year it's an Iroc. Next year, he thinks maybe he'll take a Corvette. That's what it sounds like he's saying, anyway. But it's hard to tell for sure. The speakers are doing their job.

"My girl is on fi-ire,
You're my dee-sire . . . "

"Got it for being the most improved player at Syracuse last year." Ducey laughs, driving with his left hand, dancing with his right. In fact, he had a nice year at Syracuse in 1987 — .284 with ten triples and ten homers in a hundred games. He was less successful in Toronto—.188 with one homer in forty-eight at-bats. David "Boomer" Wells had great years in both places. He was the Jays' most effective reliever as they staggered down the stretch, recording a 1.50 ERA with twenty-six strikeouts over twenty-four innings. He dazzled; folks gasped. But Ducey has the car. Wells is bumming a lift home.

Ducey is potentially hot property, and will become genuinely hot property if and when he carves out a spot for himself with the Jays. He is from Cambridge, Ontario, right in the heart of the southwestern Ontario money belt. Homegrown: every Canadian fan's dream—if he plays real good, that is. So we can be nice and proud. 'Cause you know Canadians, eh? If he doesn't play real good, maybe we'll turn and look the other way. Like we don't know him, and who's he playing for now, anyway? And who cares.

> *"You got to catch fi-ire,*
> *To be our dee-sire . . . "*

There is a lot more to Rob Ducey than his smile. The fact that he's young, handsome and gifted gives him that little head start, of course. But he's also warm as a puppy: patient and generous with fans; gentle and affectionate with his brand-new wife, Yanitza; as concerned about and interested in his minor league buddies as he is with his major league friends, proud of his relationship with his parents. This is a nice kid.

Of course, he does strut some.

Watch him go after a fly ball in spring training, handling it with a showy flair rather than the earnest determination the front office likes. And listen to Bobby Mattick, Jays' vice-president for baseball, mutter from his seat next to the dugout: "Don't style it, Rob. Just catch it. Ducey's the style master." Mattick's tone is clear: *Got to knock that out of him.*

But this is more than a preening young rooster. Sit, talk to him about growing up, what hurt him, what thrilled him, what scared him — the vulnerability makes you ache. Oh, what a boy is this!

This is a twenty-three-year-old who certainly—well, almost certainly—has the talent to play in the major leagues. But this is also a complex kid performing under the kind of pressure that Canadian baseball executives have always fretted over. If Rob Ducey were gifted in the way that Eric Davis or Jose Canseco or Kal Daniels is gifted, there'd be no problem: put him on the field and be careful the cash register doesn't melt.

On the other hand, if Ducey weren't quite up to the major-league mark, like Doug Frobel, the Jays could trade him "to give him a chance to play," as they say. Nobody blinked when Dave McKay or Dave Shipanoff disappeared.

But Ducey is a problem. He's got a good chance, but he certainly isn't a sure thing. He's difficult to trade, because the Jays would never be forgiven if he blossomed somewhere else. But it's dicey keeping him, because his skills will have to be honed with precision if he's going to emerge as more than a marginal player.

Is Ducey likely to be any better than Terry Puhl, another left-handed, line-drive hitter with similar outfield capabilities? Possibly, but not probably. Would the pressure on Puhl to live up to expectations have been more onerous if he'd been wearing a Toronto uniform? Probably. Even everybody's Mr. Nice Guy, the dedicated and ever-so-coachable Terry Puhl.

And wouldn't it have been even worse if Puhl had been a touch self-centered, stubborn, difficult to coach? Not that Ducey's like that, is he? Doesn't seem so. In fact the Jays brass were forever crowing about the good work habits and fine attitude that they'd spotted in him right from the start.

"He wasn't average even before the game," Bob Prentice, Jays' chief of Canadian scouting, remembered in a 1987 *Toronto Sun* story. Prentice loved how Ducey would apply himself in an effort to improve."He would do stretching exercises and play long toss before the game started. Not many seventeen-year-olds do that."

So nothing's changed, has it?

Has it?

He was an orphan, a condition which is sometimes romantic, more often tragic. For him, the script worked, although it took a little time. The story line is straight out of a Broadway musical: the right people show up at difficult moments and make the whole stage glow. He is blessed, and he knows it: "God has looked after me all my life."

He was adopted at eighteen months by a Toronto couple with four daughters. His mother, Anita Ducey, settled in Cambridge after her marriage broke up, figuring that Cambridge offered better odds than Toronto did for a single parent to raise five children. Her son was eight when they moved, full of energy and emotions.

"I was probably overly aggressive when I was younger. Even now sometimes I think I have too much energy. It's just too much of something inside. When I was younger I would go, go, go, go, go as long as I wanted. It would be nothing for me to play hockey all day and then go out and play volleyball at night at the Y. I was just going and going. And I was going crazy there for a while. The roof seemed to be caving in. And then I ran away."

When his adoptive parents' marriage broke up, his mother, a counselor working with juvenile delinquents, didn't take long to spot a hole in her son's life. So she hooked him up with Big Brothers. Rob's Big Brother got him involved in softball before he moved away.

Father gone, Big Brother gone, school uninteresting, mother working flat out. That left sports and the prospects of trouble. "It would have been easy for me to get into trouble. My mother had to work all the time, and with no other parents in the house . . .

"I guess I was about thirteen. I was changing a lot—I didn't think people understood me. The sports helped because I had something to go to, something to look forward to. Everything else was . . . well, I was sitting in my chair at school, that was it.

"Then one day—it seems silly now—but my sister wouldn't let me have an apple. That was the last straw. I went out and hitch-hiked, and ended up eighty miles down the 401 in Oshawa. I headed for Oshawa because I knew it was there. We had played a softball tournament there in the summer. I went down to the beach. Then I walked along the main street, and this is why I said God has looked after me all my life. Because I must have passed about fifty restaurants on this street, and there was this old, beat-up shack of a restaurant, and I went in there just to see what time it was. And I asked a a guy where Simcoe Street was, because that's where the hotel was that we had stayed at. I don't know what I would have done when I got there — I had two dollars and fifty cents in my pocket — but that's what I was looking for.

"There was a man in the restaurant. I don't know who he was, but he was sitting there eating. He asked me where I was from and where I was going. I said I was going to Simcoe Street. He asked me if I had any money, and I said sure." Ducey laughs and imitates how the scared, lonely thirteen-year-old quickly hauled his quarters and dimes out of his pocket to prove how well-heeled he was.

"He said, 'I'll tell you what. I know a place you can stay the night, it won't cost you any money.' And he took me to a hostel. He was older, and if I'm remembering right, not really black or white, but similar to my complexion, and kind of balding."

And, for a few minutes, a man to guide Rob Ducey. A few days later he went home. He played hockey. He wrestled. He signed his own report cards unless his mother could track them down. "My mom came to the school two or three times a year, not to get me out of trouble, but to keep me in it. She didn't want me screwing around — she was on their side. It was hard for her. She had to work all day. She wasn't at home as much as she wanted to be."

Just after he turned fifteen a man named Herb Schiel told a man named Ed Heather, who was involved in local baseball, that there was a kid playing softball that might have enough talent to try out for the local Junior Bulldogs baseball team. Heather contacted Ducey and asked him to come out.

Ducey's heroes hadn't been Blue Jays, or any other kind of baseball folk. He was a softball freak. "My idol was a guy named Brian Russell — they called him Mouse. And Marty Myska." Russell and Myska were top-flight Canadian softball players. Ducey aspired to play softball with the Cambridge Gores. But he decided to give baseball a shot.

"I got a letter from the Bulldogs. It was the first time anyone had ever put my name on anything like that. I don't think I would have bothered going out for baseball, but there it was, a photocopied sheet with my name written right in. It was like, 'We're inviting you to attend, and we'd like you to be there.' It meant so much to me that somebody wanted me like that."

In the beginning Ducey played both softball and baseball, but Heather finally convinced him he should choose. It wasn't fair to the teams he was playing for to spread himself thin.

After he started to concentrate on baseball Heather told him he had skills. But he didn't know how far Ducey could go — perhaps a college scholarship. Ducey started working for Heather at his sporting goods store, the Trophy Depot. "I'd do little things here, little things there. I could go in as much as I wanted, and pretty soon I was in there all the time, cleaning shelves and stuff. I used to go there all the time, *all* the time. My mother was worried 'what are you doing, why are you there?' She was asking my sister about him, because my sister had met him before. And my sister was saying he was a forty-year-old bachelor who lived with his mother.

"He was a fatherly figure in my mind. Which I'd never had. I'd had a Big Brother, but that was for two or three hours a week. But Ed was always there. I could always go to the store. He was funny, he'd tell me stories about guys in the Inter-County League and he'd quiz me all the time about baseball: 'What do you do in this situation, what do you do in that situation?' And I'd have to tell him.

"But my mother was worried. She thought something different was going on. She was scared that he might have taken advantage of me, this forty-year-old man who'd never been married. She kinda got on to me about who *is* this bad person. So I said, okay, that's it, I've had enough of this. So I brought him over. There was me and Mom and him and his mother. And they seemed to like each other."

Ed Heather and Anita Ducey were married the week their son turned seventeen. "I felt he was my father before she even met him," says Ducey simply. "I loved him as a father."

Acceptance and rejection have been the poles of Ducey's world for as long as he can remember. Memories of acceptance are imprinted on one

Rob was spending a lot of his time with an unmarried 40-year-old man. His mother got suspicious. (Michael Rafelson)

side of his soul. Rejections are branded in the other. Shortly after his parents' marriage Ducey went off to Seminole Community College in Florida, where he was given a partial scholarship. In the beginning, he remembers, he was just a scrub.

"But Jack Patelias, he was the coach, he saw something in me. But I worried him. I used to be able to sleep anywhere, and I'd sleep on the bus. But he thought I wasn't getting enough sleep at night, so he put me on a curfew. Here I was in college with a nine o'clock curfew! He was all over me all year. I guess he knew that I had something that even some of his better players didn't have. And I guess I responded, because I still go back there." Score one for acceptance.

Bob Prentice signed Ducey for the Jays after he hit a long home run in a Florida tournament. Walter Jeffries, one of Prentice's scouts, had followed him in Canadian tournaments, and the Jays had been watching him closely. "He made things look easy," remembers Jeffries. "He was the best I'd seen."

Ducey signed for $7,500. After his first summer as a pro he wished he'd bargained harder. He won team MVP honors at Medicine Hat over a lot of draft picks who signed for a lot more. A Canadian player with a ready smile and a good bat, he was a fan favorite. "I loved it in Medicine Hat." Acceptance again.

The Jays sent him south to play instructional ball. He has terrible memories of it. "I was put in a category called 'unknown' by most of the other players there. Except for a few friends from Medicine Hat, there were mainly two groups: the whites and the brothers [the blacks]. I was kind of put in the middle somewhere, something like a Latino. The brothers didn't like me because they thought I should talk black if I was black. They thought I was trying to make fun of them the way I talked. And I obviously wasn't white. The white guys didn't know who I was and didn't care much. I got my ghetto blaster and a hundred dollars stolen. It wasn't a nice time." Nobody likes rejection.

Professional sport is a tough arena for a sensitive kid. But Ducey is no wimp. He's hard on himself "I'm never satisfied. If I'm hitting .280 I get up and look at myself in the mirror and say, 'Hey, you, the mimimum is .300. And I think I can hit twenty home runs a year in the majors — I hit twenty-three in Double A in 1966."

He hates to lose. "I'd cheat with my wife at cards to win. I *have* to win." On April 29, 1987, Ducey was called up from Syracuse and put on the major-league roster. What arrived at Exhibition Stadium was a twenty-two-year-old package of contradictions — cocky, sensitive, competitive, brash and vulnerable—sporting a .318 batting average after twelve games with Syracuse (Triple A) in the wake of a .308 average at Knoxville (Double A) the year before. He spent May with the big club, was sent down for June, July and August and was called up when the roster expanded for September. His 1987 major-league totals: forty-eight at-bats, nine hits, a .188 batting average, one double, one home run.

It was the best of years and the worst of years. Playing his first major-league game at Exhibition Stadium was like knocking on the pearly gates. "That was probably the greatest feeling I've ever had in baseball. As I walked up to the plate for my first at-bat, I got a standing ovation. I hit a fly ball to deep center and got another standing ovation. I got a partial standing ovation the next time I walked to the plate, and got a full standing ovation when I got a hit [a single that drove in a run to give the Jays a 2-1 lead over Texas in a game they won]. Then a partial standing ovation when I stole second base. I couldn't have written it any better."

The next day Ducey went had a sacrifice fly in another win. On the Sunday he pinch hit in the ninth with a runner on first. Another single.

"There were two outs. Fred McGriff was on second and I was on first with Tony Fernandez at the plate, and here's the pitch—Tony hits it by the first baseman and I know I'm going to third. The ball is out by the bullpen and [John] McLaren is waving me around. I'm thinking there's no way, and what's going on here, but I'm going hard and I make it—I score!" Ducey takes great relish in reliving his first weekend up, rattling it all off like an announcer.

He takes less relish in talking about the lecture Bobby Mattick gave him when he reported back to Syracuse one month later. An item appeared in Marty York's baseball column in the *Globe and Mail* after Ducey was sent down:

Life as the golden boy of a baseball organization isn't necessarily peaches and cream.

Consider Rob Ducey.

A recent newspaper report in Syracuse suggested the young outfielder was unpopular in the Toronto clubhouse after he was called up by the Blue Jays earlier this season, and the suggestion wasn't far off.

Indeed, many of the Jays were resentful that Ducey was favored by management because, in their opinion, he hadn't paid the kind of minor-league dues they had.

The other day, though, Ducey was the recipient of a private tongue-lashing from Jay management. Club vice-president Bob Mattick had been visiting the Jays' Triple A affiliate in Syracuse, where he chewed out Ducey for "hot dogging" during his stint in Toronto.

And now, Ducey's teammates in Syracuse are irked because of a suspicion that he will be the first position player summoned by the Jays if an opening is created.

"There's no way Ducey should be next in line," says agent Richard Box, who represents the almost-forgotten Lou Thorton, another Syracuse outfielder. "That seems to be the case, but it doesn't seem warranted. There are a number of other players in the organization whose statistics are better than Ducey's."

Box concludes there is only one reason for the fuss over Ducey.

"There's definite favoritism toward him," Box says, "and it's strictly because he's Canadian."

Ducey say he's almost started to resent his Canadian connection. The comments of people like Box have started him thinking about why he's such a special favorite of the fans. It's not that he resents the time spent signing autographs — he's determined to give the kind of attention to kids he wanted when he was younger. But . . .

"I wasn't too impressed with some of the players who I thought were my friends when I went up to the big leagues. After all the time I'd played with them, after hitting .300 almost everywhere I'd been, I didn't make as many errors as a lot of the guys, I'd been consistent all through those years, all of a sudden the only reason I was going to the big leagues was because I was a Canadian.

"There isn't much I can do about it. "But I got to the point in spring training where I started thinking the only reason the people were cheering for me was because I was a Canadian. Not because they liked me as a player. I want to show them I'm a player."

And Mattick?

"I wouldn't call what I did up there hot dogging. I'd call it being happy to be there. I had twenty-eight at-bats in a month. He chewed me out because he said I was spending too much time trying to be showy and not enough time trying to hit the cutoff man. I just couldn't remember the things he said I did being so negative. All of a sudden I went in their eyes from a player ready to play in the big leagues to being not quite the player they thought I was."

He speaks softly when he says these things. There is none of the cocksure swagger that he likes to wear as an outfit. The cheery smile is lost somewhere far away.

The best part of the year was Janitza. Beyond his fine eye at the plate, nice swing, good speed and consistency in the outfield, Ducey has a talent for forging improbable relationships.

Janitza is eighteen, with breathtaking green eyes and a smile the equal of his. She was queen of the Barquisimeto Cardinales, the Venezuelan team he played for over the past two winters.

"I thought she was kind of a spoiled brat. Just one of those snobby kids. One night after a game in Caracas her mother was sitting beside me. We had lost the game in the tenth inning when someone hit a ball into the right-center gap — I'd been playing him in the left-center gap. There's no way I could have caught that ball. And Janitza's mother is sitting right beside me and starts giving me the choke sign. I'd been drinking a little that night and I had had enough. It was close to Christmas, I was getting homesick, I didn't really like the culture because I had nobody there with me, and I didn't like the food.

"So I started saying things to her in English — I didn't know how to argue in Spanish then. But she knew I was mad. And Janitza got between us and made me go off and dance. I didn't even like that, because I didn't know how to dance the way they did. Anyway, I ended up taking her and her mother home. Neither of them spoke much English."

For some reason he doesn't totally understand, Ducey remembered where the house was and went back about a week later. He and Janitza started dating and went to discos—the first five times with her mother as a chaperone. She had abandoned the choke sign.

When he got home to Cambridge he called twice a week. Janitza's English improved. His Spanish improved. They were married on January 22, 1988. He adores her. They joke in Spanish. They joke in English. It has saved a difficult year.

Ducey had a so-so spring training and was sent down to Syracuse. The Jays kept Syl Campusano, Ducey's chief rival for a Toronto outfield spot, instead. Ducey speaks highly of Campusano—"As far as overall ability is concerned he might have an edge on me. I'm talking about speed, power, arm. I might have better instincts, though. I've always been more consistent than him."

Spring training was frustrating. The Jays decided that because Ducey isn't blessed with great power, he'll have to hit for average, and to do that he'll have to learn to take the outside pitch to left field, rather than pulling everything. Ducey grumbled.

"I don't think I'm going to do myself or them any good hitting that way. What got me to the big leagues was my ability to pull the ball. Now [in attempting to use the whole field] I'm having trouble doing that."

Jays' officials, who had spoken so glowingly of Ducey's attitude, began to grumble back. Bob Prentice, director of scouting for Canada, wouldn't specify who he was talking about, but said that while scouts could usually tell a lot about young players' attitudes by watching them carefully on the sandlots, one player in particular had fooled him.

"I found a player who was a good player; he hustled and did everything that was asked of him and worked hard and became a good player. But after a couple of years his true personality emerged, and he became a little conceited, a little bigheaded, and became difficult to talk to, even for me and the scout who recommended him to me. [Ducey was signed by Prentice, on the recommendation of Walter Jeffries.] All I'll say is the young man in question is still playing."

Pat Gillick, who is in charge of the Jays' baseball operations, isn't afraid to talk about Ducey by name. "I think he's got a little bit of a big head," said Gillick, when Ducey was complaining about having to alter his batting stance. "He's moved through the organization pretty quickly, and maybe that's thrown him off. But he's got to get his head back in reality."

One week later Ducey again appeared in Marty York's column in the *Globe and Mail*:

> Syracuse outfielder Rob Ducey, the Jays' Great Canadian Hope, now figures he'll play all season in Triple A.
>
> "I don't think it was necessary for me to be sent back to the minors [in spring training]," Ducey said, "but it's probably turning out to be the best thing. I'm getting a chance to refine some of my skills."

Perhaps the package—cocky, sensitive, competitive, brash and vulnerable —has another component now. There seems to be a new element of maturity in the mix. Maybe, maybe not. But two things are for sure. This is a nice kid. And life as the Canadian golden boy of a Canadian baseball organization isn't always going to be peaches and cream.

24

BOB PRENTICE

Toronto, Ontario
April 27, 1988

There are people talking quietly in the cozy corner office at Toronto Blue Jays headquarters. If you listen carefully you can pick out the ghostly, big-shouldered names of famous Canadian ballplayers who never were.

"Frank Mahovlich — I saw Frank Mahovlich when he was younger. He could have been a heck of a ballplayer," says a wistful voice. "He could run and throw and hit. Carl Brewer, he almost signed as a shortstop with the Cleveland Indians. And Clark Gillies — I think Pat Gillick signed him for Houston as a catcher. He went down and had a good spring, but he was a little further advanced in hockey, so he came back to it."

The man doing the talking is slim, but he doesn't like the word slim. Blue-eyed Bobby Prentice, fifty-nine, has made a good part of his living assessing young men's chances of making a living in professional baseball. It's something you do dispassionately and with candor, or with disservice to all concerned. He finds the word *slim* dishonest. "I was a big, strong guy once," he says softly. "People say I'm slim now, but the truth is I'm skin and bones. I hate what I look like, but I don't have any choice."

Prentice has been the Jays' director of Canadian scouting since the team was founded in 1976. He came out of east Toronto as a big, hard-hitting shortstop in the late forties, toughed out a heartbreaking decade knocking at the big-league door without ever getting in, and later went into scouting — first with the Tigers, then with the Jays. During the 1970s he lobbied relentlessly to bring major-league baseball to Toronto. He even drew up his own plans for adapting Exhibition Stadium to baseball several years before it was converted.

But his forte has been scouting. Prentice knows as much about mining for ballplayers in the northern tundra as anybody who ever lived. Certainly he's had more success at it than anybody else. He discovered John Hiller, Mike Kilkenny and several others who made it onto major-league rosters.

So he knows where the problems are. It's not so much the weather, he

Bob's style as a scout was never to attract a lot of attention. He watched for talent like a shadow. (Michael Rafelson)

says. "Detroit, Boston, Buffalo, Cleveland, St. Paul — their weather is as bad as ours." Hockey, he acknowledges, is a factor. "We've got as good athletes as any other country, but a lot of them go into hockey."

But mostly, he says, it is the coaching. Americans have a proud tradition of knowing how to play ball, and knowing how to play it right. Canadians? "Sometimes I go and watch, and it's embarrassing watching a team take infield. If you're a Canadian kid, you're lucky if you've played with a good coach. Most of our coaches have been parents who've played a little softball. I'm not knocking them. At least they're out there. And there's the odd, isolated good coach around. But on the whole, across the country, our coaches haven't compared with the coaches in the United States. We've played baseball for a long time in Canada, and we've had some fine players. We've had the Terry Puhls. But there were a lot more of the Terry Puhl types who could have been something."

Things are getting a little better, he says. He cites Baseball Canada's coaching clinics, the fact that several provincial baseball associations are bringing in professional people for guidance, the emergence of high-school baseball in Toronto, the Canada Youth Team, the National Baseball Institute . . .

"It's getting better, but it's not going to change overnight." But then, hanging in and working at it has always been something Prentice has been good at. Not that it ever quite paid him the big reward in his playing days. But if anyone is looking for evidence that perseverance is important, it's sitting behind a desk in the cozy corner office at Blue Jays headquarters: Slim Bobby Prentice is alive.

It was in Toronto's east end, a sunny noon hour at Bowmore Road Public School in the spring of 1936. Girls were skipping double dutch and some of the younger boys were shooting marbles around the back. Others, mostly ten- and eleven- and twelve-year-olds, were practicing for the Bowmore Road bantam softball team.

Bobby Prentice, seven, was scuffling his way across the schoolyard, wearing his black baseball cap with white piping, when he heard one of the coaches say the magic words that would still ring clear fifty-two years later. "There he is," said the voice. "That's the Prentice kid, the younger brother. Hey, come here for a second, son. You're young Prentice, aren't you?"

"Yes, I'm Bobby."

"Well, here, let me hit you a few balls."

Young Bobby caught them all—he'd been knocking the ball around with his two older brothers since he'd learned to walk. Before he knew it he was in center field playing with boys five years older than he was, and holding his own. He moved to shortstop the next year and a career was underway.

At Riverdale Collegiate he was an all-star quarterback in each of the four years he played. During the winter he played forward for the Young Rangers, one of Toronto's three Junior A hockey teams. But neither hockey nor football could lure him away from his favorite game.

Just after he turned eighteen he went to a St. Louis Cardinals tryout in Hamilton, along with two hundred other kids. Three were chosen. Prentice signed for no bonus and the promise of $120 a month if he could make a team in the spring.

He could not, playing well below his capabilities at the Cards' minor-league camp in Albany, Georgia, then bouncing around with the Red Sox in Louisiana for several weeks before finally making his way home. That summer the first Canadian all-star team was put together with some of the better Ontario players. They went to Baltimore for a tournament against several other top teams, including a U.S. all-star team. The Canadians didn't win, but by the time the tournament was over Prentice had several scouts knocking on his hotel door. The Philadelphia Phillies lent the Canadian team a coach. He scurried three players, including Prentice and Frank House, the U.S. all-star third baseman, to Shibe Park in Philadelphia for a tryout. The Phillies didn't sign any of them. House later signed with Detroit for $75,000 and a couple of cars.

A scout for the Indians got hold of Prentice and took him to Cleveland, where he was impressive in workouts. The Indians pushed him to sign. He resisted, pointing out that he had promised a Cubs scout he wouldn't commit himself to anybody else before checking back with him. After three days of pressure he succumbed, signing for $2,500. Thus began an unfortunate relationship.

For the next ten years Prentice did everything expected of him. He was six feet tall, big for a middle infielder, and weighed one hundred and eighty pounds. He had an average arm and average range, but all his other skills —hitting, running, fielding with consistency—were above average, particularly hitting. "I was a Bobby Grich type player. I had good power for a middle infielder."

In 1948, in Class D at Batavia, he hit only .257 but led the club with thirteen homers. In 1949 he was bumped up to Class C at Pittsfield, and hit .314, with ten homers. In 1950, playing Class B ball at Cedar Rapids,

Iowa, he hit .280, with twenty homers, third in the league. He was also third with a hundred RBIs, unheard of for a middle infielder. The litany goes on. During his ten-year minor-league career he averaged .273 and fifteen home runs a year, a strong combination for a middle infielder. Three times he led his league in double plays; three times he led in fielding average.

But inching toward the top in the Cleveland organization wasn't easy. The Indians had won the American League pennant in 1948 and would win it again in 1954, with a record 111 victories. The infield was stacked with stars like Al Rosen and Bobby Avila. In 1951 Prentice did get chosen to go to Arizona for a special spring camp with other top prospects, including Herb Score and Rocky Colavito. That's where he first set eyes on Mickey Mantle, who kept paying Prentice visits over at third base on hits that would have been doubles for mortals. Prentice kept progressing, but it was slow going. Class B, Class A, Class A again . . . In 1953 he got lucky when he was traded to the Cincinnati organization, where he played for Tulsa, the Reds' top farm club at Double A. Ed Bailey, who would go on to catch for the slugging Cincinnati team of the mid-fifties, and who would hit 155 major-league home runs, hit 23 that year, second-best on the team. Prentice had 24. The Reds were smart enough to play him at second base, and everything looked rosy: the parent club was a middle-of-the-pack team at the time and there was room at the top.

But it turned out Cleveland still had strings attached to him. At the end of the year he was pulled back and put on the Indians' major-league roster. He went to Venezuela to play winter ball, but got called home when his mother suffered a brain hemorrhage. His father, who had flown Sopwith Camels during the First World War and later sold life insurance in Toronto, was dead. So Prentice went home and did the cooking for his younger brothers, helping his mother out as she struggled back to health. By the time spring training rolled around Prentice was still dickering over his contract. "It came out that only two Indians hadn't signed contracts: Early Wynn and Bob Prentice, the rookie. I wasn't sure I could leave my mother yet. But I didn't tell the Indians that — it was a personal thing."

By the time he finally signed and got to Tucson, spring training had been underway for a week. But heaven seemed finally at hand. He was twenty-three, just the right age to step up to the majors. And what a team to step up with! "Here I'm sitting beside Rosen, and Bob Feller's over here, and Hal Newhouser's over there, and there's Bob Lemon and Early Wynn. I thought, 'This is a long way from Greenwood Park in Toronto.'

"I got dressed and I walked out of the clubhouse toward the field, and who should I run into but Hank Greenberg, the Indians' general manager. He wasn't in uniform, but Greenberg was a big man, about six feet four, and even though I was tall I had to look up at him. He was very imposing, with a strong personality. He said, 'It's about time you got here.' I nodded. What could I say? And he said, 'You're a week behind in training. You could have made this club. But you probably won't get into a ball game all spring.'

"And he turned and walked away. I always wished I had said, 'Wait — there was a reason I was late.' But I was dumbfounded, and I wasn't the type of guy to say anything. Even years later, I would like to have told him. But I never did. And he was right, I didn't get into a game. Oh, I got into one, when Rosen didn't want to play. I went 3-for-5." And then he went to the minors.

Prentice never quit hitting and never quit playing hard, but things had a way of falling just short for him. He should have known that the gods of baseball had sent him a sign in 1951. It was the spring he was sent out to play with the hot prospects. When the instructional sessions were over the prospects were kept around for a few days and got into some games with the regulars against the Yankees, who trained in Arizona that year. Prentice's hero since childhood had been Joe DiMaggio. He was desperate to see the sweet swing he had so vividly imagined all those years, and Joltin' Joe was coming to the end of the line.

Prentice started at third in a game that DiMaggio didn't start. Finally, in about the seventh inning, DiMaggio came to the plate to pinch hit. The Indians' pitcher was a young farm boy named Leroy Wheat. "So Leroy, who could throw, winds up and throws ball one, high. And I says, 'Come on, Leroy, get the ball over.' I badly wanted to see Joe DiMaggio hit. I don't care if he puts it over the lights. I don't care if he hits it to me. I don't care if he hits it *through* me, puts a hole in me. I have been waiting all my life to see him hit. And Leroy throws ball two. And I call time and go over to the mound, and I say, 'Come on, Leroy, he's just another guy. Well, he's really Joe DiMaggio, but just think of him as another guy.' And Leroy throws ball three.

"I like to think I'm a pretty calm guy, but by this time I'm really steamed. I yell, 'Come on Leroy, get the &*#@$%&* ball over. And he throws ball four, and Joe DiMaggio trots down to first, takes the turn and trots into the dugout. It's over. I never saw him again. I didn't talk to Leroy for two days. I saw him in 1985 in Florida when I went down to see Rob Ducey play in a tournament. He coaches college there, and somebody said he was in the stands. I hadn't seen him for twenty-four years, and I went up to

In the beginning signing a prospect in your hospital robe seemed like a cute publicity stunt. But hospitals became less fun. (Toronto *Sun*)

see him, and the first thing he said was, 'Bob, have you ever forgiven me for walking Joe DiMaggio?' I said, 'Leroy . . . uh, no.' And I still haven't.''

By the time he was twenty-six Prentice's major-league dream had started to fade. But it was 1956 and the Toronto Maple Leafs of the International League had the good sense to acquire him from Cleveland. He was a home-town boy with an excellent minor-league record, and the scribes enthused when he hit more than .400 in spring training. The Maple Leafs were a solid, veteran club, with Eddie Stevens at first, Mike Goliat at second, Hec Rodriguez at short and Loren Babe at third. All had had major-league experience, but there shouldn't have been much question that Prentice would get plenty of playing time. Another Leaf infielder, Walter Derucki, had played against Prentice over the years, but had never matched Prentice's numbers. Prentice thinks it might have been because Derucki was a good friend of one of the Leaf coaches. Whatever. The Leafs cut Prentice, who was 2-for-7 at the time. They said Cleveland still had strings attached to him; he'd have to report to Cleveland's Double A team at Mobile. For the first time in his baseball career, Prentice boiled over. His response was in headlines in the *Toronto Star* the next day. "The story quoted me saying, 'I had to come home to my home town to get the worst deal I ever got in baseball.' And that was the truth."

Prentice went to Mobile and hit .301. When he got back to Toronto the Leafs were still in the playoffs, and he went over to visit some of his buddies. Team owner Jack Kent Cooke wandered by, congratulated Prentice on his year and told him he'd go after him again and acquire him for the Leafs.

"Mr. Cooke," said Prentice, "after what this team did to me this year, I wouldn't waste your time. I'll never play for you again."

"But if we got you," countered Cooke, "you'd have to play, or you'd be suspended."

"Fine," replied Prentice. "I'll be suspended."

Cooke got the message, and Prentice finished out his career in Tulsa. He quit at twenty-eight, still shaking his head at the Leafs' stupidity. "They had a local guy who could play. It was dumb." But then Cleveland also had a kid who could play for a decade, and never did anything with him. "I still wonder what would have happened if I'd just said, 'Mr. Greenberg, there was a reason I got here late.'"

He should have been bitter, but Prentice couldn't shake his love for the game. After working briefly in sales with a chemical company, he moved to the new O'Keefe Centre as manager of marketing and promotions. The center bustled with activity as staff worked seven days a week promoting *Camelot* and other show-business hits. There was a new wife, Nancy, and a new son, and a new daughter, and none of this was enough. "I was a big, strong guy then. I could do a lot of things."

Which included running a five-team junior baseball league in Scarborough, scouting part-time for the Detroit Tigers, writing a column on local baseball twice a week for the *Toronto Telegram*, and eventually ending up in a hospital bed on a regular basis. "I guess I'm a medical miracle," he says.

The upper half of Prentice's strike zone, from the letters to the belt, has been riddled with every ailment short of cancer. He has suffered from a hiatus hernia that has never cleared up, been operated on for a ruptured disk, been close to death after contracting tubercular pericarditis (a virus of the heart membrane), had a kidney removed, been hit with a duodenic ulcer and had his stomach simply pack up and quit several times. He emerged from a decade of professional ball as a robust, energetic man.

During the next two decades he lost forty pounds and had to give up curling, golf and tennis. He now weighs 140 and can't gain an ounce, no matter how hard he tries. For an athlete, it's been a humiliating experience.

The irony is that while he was healthy he made virtually no imprint on the Canadian baseball landscape. Since his innards started trying to leave the ballpark early, however, he has made an indelible impression.

Only months after he quit playing he saw a seventeen-year-old left-handed pitcher he thought was pretty good, Marvin Berbeck of Leaside. He alerted the Detroit Tigers, who agreed and signed him. Berbeck never pitched in the majors because he tried to come back too quickly after a kidney ailment. But he was so impressive in his first year of minor-league ball that Atlanta snatched him up in that year's draft, even though it forced them to put the stripling on their major-league roster, which wasn't done often.

Prentice signed John Hiller, of Scarborough, who ranks with the best left-handed relievers in the history of major-league baseball; Mike Kilkenny of Bradford, Ontario, who threw two shutouts in his first two major-league games and nearly threw a third; and Sheldon Burnside, an American-born right-hander from Etobicoke who pitched briefly with Detroit and Cincinnati.

Probably the most breathtaking talent Prentice uncovered was George Korince, of St. Catharine's, Ontario, a six-foot-three-inch 210-pound right-hander who kept getting stronger after he was signed until he had a crackling, ninety-five-miles-an-hour fastball. Korince hurt his arm the year he got to the majors, when Detroit pitching coach Johnny Sain pushed him into working overtime on developing a breaking pitch. He was forced to bow out with a 1-0 lifetime record.

Prentice also uncovered Bernie Beckman, who made Detroit's major league roster and pitched for nine years in the Detroit, Los Angeles and Chicago Cubs' organizations before emerging as one of the most respected pitching coaches in amateur baseball. He is currently with the National Baseball Institute in Vancouver.

There are fans, even passionate fans, who will shrug at Prentice's scouting record and wonder what all the fuss is about. But baseball people know how difficult it is for even the best of scouts to come up with more than a couple of private discoveries over their careers; Prentice's record is extraordinary.

Jack Tighe, the former Tigers manager, acknowledged that one day at spring training in Florida. Cy Williams, then the Tigers' territory scout for much of the northern United States, was Prentice's overseer in the team's scouting hierarchy. "The first time I went down to Florida, Cy and I were in a room full of club people when somebody introduced me to Jack Tighe," Prentice said. "Tighe said, 'Ah, you're the guy who signs all those great Canadian ball players that Cy Williams takes credit for.' He was just needling Cy, but it was a nice thing to say."

Prentice is not your typical scout. "A lot of scouts are very spontaneous, outgoing, fun-loving guys. They spit tobacco and they've got stopwatches around their neck and charts all over and radar guns on their shoulders. I guess my style was a little different. I'd never sit behind the players' bench. I'd always sit a bit off. I didn't want everybody in the ballpark to know I was there.

"A lot of guys would go up to the coaches before and make a big thing of having a look at a kid. I never did any of that. If they knew you were there they might act differently than they normally would have, and I liked to watch how they behaved—with their coaches, their buddies and the girls. I never wanted anyone to know who I was interested in. That's my business.

"We have a rule for our scouts that they're there to be friendly to people from other organizations, but not to give out information. I saw things that maybe other scouts sometimes didn't see because I'd been a player and studied the game when I was a player. I wasn't being paid to share what I saw with other organizations. So if another scout came up to me and said, 'That's a pretty good-looking pitcher there,' I'd say, 'Sure, and the third baseman is okay, too.' I might not be at all interested in the third baseman, but it didn't hurt to divert the guy."

Prentice has been a major actor in the Jays' scouting operation, which was ranked number one in the major leagues by *Baseball America* in 1988. He gives most of the credit for the Jays' success to Pat Gillick, a former scout himself, who as vice-president for baseball operations is directly in charge of scouting. It was Gillick who had the foresight to go after Latin American, Canadian and Korean players when the Jays were desperately trying to catch up to the established clubs, because the Jays didn't have to wait in line for non-U.S. players at the major-league draft.

"Pat's been way ahead of everybody. I've never seen anybody in baseball work at it like he does," Prentice says.

There have been sad parts to Prentice's scouting career, like seeing his organization come up with a great find, outfielder Paul Hodgson of Montreal, and then watch his abilities disintegrate because of injuries. "Paul was like Rob Ducey, only bigger than Ducey, stronger than Ducey, with more power than Ducey. We all loved him, but he hurt one shoulder diving back into first base, and the other hitting a fence, I think. In the end he had both shoulders operated on, and he couldn't throw. He was as good as we've had."

But there have been moments of amusement, as well. In the desk drawer of his cozy corner office, Prentice keeps a folder he calls the Spaceman File. In it are letters from the wild side.

"I get a lot of unusual calls and letters. Some have been from prisons. Some have been from insane asylums. I got one letter from California from a guy who said he was twenty-six, great, and if we didn't give him a chance something terrible would happen to his parents. We had to pass that one on to the police.

"And there was the guy who came to the tryout camp in his suit and tie and went in at shortstop wearing black leather loafers. And the one who called me from Newfoundland and said he was thirty-two, but had a great arm from lifting garbage cans onto the truck. I said he was a little old, that we sent kids to the minors at a far younger age and then hoped they would develop and come up in their twenties. He said he didn't want to go to the minors—'I've watched your guys on television. I know I can pitch better than they can.' "

Don't call Bob Prentice, he'll call you. Unless . . . Unless you've got a big strong kid who's going to the NHL next year and really ought to be playing baseball instead.

25

OSCAR JUDD

Ingersoll, Ontario
April 27, 1988

The question is: Who was smarter, Branch Rickey or Oscar Judd? Judd concedes that as far as school was concerned, Rickey was a hands-down winner. Rickey earned a law degree. Judd didn't make it out of public school, which he attended until he was fifteen. "I didn't learn too quick — we was too busy playin' ball."

Judd had the better arm, no question about that. Rickey caught briefly for the Browns and the Yankees. In one game he allowed opposing base-runners thirteen steals. Judd, a left-handed pitcher, claims he threw a hundred miles an hour even when he was past his prime. Even if that seems a bit out of the realm, Judd could throw. And run. He ran against Jesse Owens three times. But arms and feet aren't the issue here. We're talking foreheads.

When Judd, a native of Rebecca, Ontario, was pitching in the St. Louis farm system in 1934, Cards' general manager Rickey watched him go 4-for-4 in a game at Springfield, Illinois. Rickey — known as "the Mahatma" to those who revered his baseball mind — immediately decreed that Judd should abandon the mound and proceed to the outfield. Not only was Judd a wondrous hitter, but he was also a fleet outfielder.

When the Mahatma instructed, people complied. In this case he had ample precedent: Babe Ruth had been a superb pitcher, but his powerful bat transformed him into an outfielder — and a millionaire. Surely what was good for the Bambino was good for a Canadian farm boy, especially since Judd was walking as many batters as he was striking out.

Wrong, said Judd, right to the Mahatma's face. Not that Judd didn't think he could make the adjustment. There's not much he ever thought he couldn't do. "I was a good outfielder. In fact I could throw with either hand out there. I'd throw right-handed from right field and left-handed from left field.

"But I hated playing the outfield. You were out of the action. I figured

outfielders should pay their way in to the ballpark. They didn't do nothing. I loved to pitch, I loved to challenge the batters. Every batter who came up there, I knew I could beat him.

"So I told Rickey, I said, 'I won't be an outfielder.' And he got mad at me, because he had lots of lefthanded pitchers. So he sent me to Double A at Sacramento. That was the highest minor-league level then. And he left me there, no matter what I did. In three years there I went 19-11, and then 21-10, and then 23-9. As soon as Boston could draft me they did. But I could have been there three years earlier if Rickey hadn't got mad at me."

It may have seemed like three years at Sacramento, but in fact Judd was there for only one year, 1940, when he went 22-13 with a 2.90 ERA. He had been promoted to Sacramento from Decatur, of the old Three-I League, after compiling a 12-6 record with a 2.89 ERA in 1939. Before Decatur Judd had managed only indifferent success as a pitcher, going 6-5 with Rochester with a 4.66 ERA in 1938 and 11-11 with a 5.19 ERA in 1937.

Rickey's point was simple. Judd had hit .351 at Springfield in 1934 and would go on to bat .416, the highest batting average in the Three-I league at Decatur in 1939. The man could hit.

Judd made it to the majors in 1941 at the advanced age of thirty-three. When he got there other players respected his pitching well enough. But they positively marveled at how well he hit, even though he never took batting practice. "They asked me why I hadn't become an outfielder. I told them I didn't want to be an outfielder." Stubborn, stubborn Oscar Judd.

Judd turned eighty this year and, as far as he can see, the world has had eighty years of good value. It's had his pitching: "All you had to do was tell me where you wanted a guy pitched and I could pitch him there. I was the fastest lefthander in the American League."

It's had his hitting: "I could hit — power, average, both. Ted Williams used to come to me when he was having problems hitting a particular pitch."

It's had his running: "I never lost a race to another ballplayer, and I run lots of them."

The world has had his decision-making prowess: "I used to call my own pitches. Once we got a new young catcher, and he went through all the signs and I shook them all off. He came out to the mound and asked me what he should do next, and I said, 'Start over.' "

Lefty was a plain-speaking farm boy who could throw teammates around like wheat sheaves. (Michael Rafelson)

It's had his charisma: "People liked me—they used to get big crowds to watch me pitch, particularly when I came over to Toronto."

It's had his forceful personality: "Once I was helping a guy do some trucking and a particularly mean bull I was trying to load got really cross. I wrestled that thing. Got hold of it by the horns and around the neck and threw it to the ground. After it got up it walked right to the truck with me."

It's had his carpet-laying skills, immediately after he got out of baseball: "I could do two houses a day—that was a thousand dollars. They couldn't build houses fast enough to keep up to me." And after he got out of carpeting it had his skill with machines: "I took a fellow's engine apart yesterday, took all the parts out and cleaned them and put a new diaphragm in. He took a look at it all laid out there and asked me how I was ever going to put it back together. I said, 'I could put it together with my eyes closed.'"

Anyone looking at Oscar (Lefty) Judd's pitching record might think the man would suffer occasional moments of humility. Over eight years he won forty games and lost fifty-one for the Boston Red Sox and the Philadelphia Phillies. He recorded a lifetime ERA of 3.90, gave up 744 hits in 772 innings (good), and walked 397 batters while striking out 304 (not so good). This, you might say, is the record of a journeyman.

Except that there are some imponderables. He didn't get to pitch a full major-league season until he was thirty-four. He made the AL all-star team in 1943—with an 11-6 record and a 2.90 ERA—at the age of thirty-five. That year he finished twenty of the twenty-three games he started, a hearty record even in those days. And not only was he 11-6, he was 11-6 for a Boston team weakened by the wartime absence of Ted Williams, a team that finished seventh with a record of 68-84. In 1944 he injured himself in a freak accident, smashing the bat against his shoulder while he was trying to bunt, and he was never the same pitcher. But he still managed to throw through pain and hang on in the majors until he was forty-one. If he'd quit when he was thirty-nine he would have had a winning record of 36-34, much of it accumulated on a bad arm at an advanced age. It is probably fair to say that if Judd had been brought up to the majors when most pitchers are brought up he would have won a hundred games or more. We'll never know.

But Judd knows. "Everybody thought Branch Rickey was such a smart baseball man, and maybe he was. But he wasn't too smart when it came to managing me, because he could have had me up there with Dizzy and Paul. One time when I was in the minors I dropped in on the ballpark in

St. Louis and Dizzy Dean watched me throw on the sidelines. And he said, 'Get this guy out of here—his stuff is too good.' And that was Dizzy Dean."

Judd cackles at the memory, then his face turns stormy. "People can think what they want about Branch Rickey. I hated his guts."

If Oscar Judd is brash and brazen and opinionated, it might be because there wasn't much call for a sixteen-year-old shrinking violet in 1924 if your father was dead and you'd been left in charge of the family farm. Judd's father, who had been a catcher for the Lucan Irish Nine in the Michigan League in the 1890s, fell off a hay wagon and died of a broken neck.

Judd took over the farm, putting his older brother and sister through school and keeping food in the mouths of his mother and three younger children. He worked hard. "Six in the morning until eight at night, but I'd always find time for ball. When the wheat season was on you used to stook it in the fields and then pile it on the wagon and pitch it over the beams in the barn. I've done seven loads of that, taking it in and pitching it as high as that ceiling, nine feet, anyhow, with the sheaves weighing sixty pounds apiece at the end of the fork, and then pitch nine innings of baseball and think nothing of it." That throaty laugh again. "And today they can't pitch nine innings." His eyes widen with mock disbelief. "I don't call them ballplayers anymore. I call them replacements, substitutes for real ballplayers."

Judd was born in 1908 in Rebecca, Ontario, on the northeast corner of what is now the airport in London, Ontario, and only about fifteen miles from the century-old red brick house he has owned in Ingersoll for the last forty-six years. He played hardball right from the beginning, pitching for the Rebecca public school. His older brother played shortstop and his sister played third. "My sister, she could play as good as I could. We had some pretty good teams. Of course I was throwing.

"We used to make balls out of a rock and cow hair—you'd comb the hair out of the cow and wrap it around the rock and sew some leather around that. I've made hundreds of balls. And I'd paint a target on the garage door—I broke the door down learning to throw a curve. There were boards flying everywhere. But I nailed new ones on. Had to—there was a car in there. And I'd throw apples—we had fruit trees. I'd throw anything, for as long as I can remember.

"We finally sold the farm. Didn't get much for it. Meanwhile I played intermediate ball in Ingersoll. I'd walk as many as I'd strike out, but I wasn't as wild as when I was beating the garage door down. We'd have five thousand for a game here when I was pitching, and there weren't five thousand in the town.

"And then I played senior ball in Guelph, which is where I became a pattern maker for metal designs. A man had come here from Detroit in 1929, when I was twenty-one, and asked me if I'd play pro ball. I said sure. That's when I should have signed. But he asked me what I'd fall back on if I didn't make it in pro. I said I was sure I'd think of something. But I said I had a chance to learn pattern making in Guelph, and he said I should do that first and then sign."

Judd didn't sign for another five years, and then it was with the Cubs. The first train trip of his life turned out to be a long one: first to Chicago, where his first taxi took him on a hundred-mile-an-hour chase to catch a second train, which took him to Los Angeles. In Los Angeles he caught his first boat to Catalina Island, where the California Angels held spring training. Which he didn't like much more than he likes modern-day ball players.

"It was terrible, awful. Nobody down there liked Canadians, not down that far. They wouldn't have nothing to do with you. Why we want to have free trade with them, I don't know. They wouldn't talk to you much, and when they did they asked you how the Queen was. You just had to be about twice as good as they were to play ball there."

He didn't make the team. He was pulled back to Chicago and shipped out to a lesser club in Peoria, which disbanded during the year. Now here might be the first evidence—from Oscar Judd's own mouth—that Branch Rickey may have had a point.

"Phil Cavarretta was on first base at Peoria, and he pitched some. When the team broke up they traded me over to the St. Louis organization, and Cavarretta went up to Chicago! I could field twice as good as him, and pitch twice as good as him, and hit twice as good as him!"

Forget the pitching part. Cavarretta wasn't as emotionally attached to the mound as Judd was, and he never pitched an inning in the majors. But he did play for twenty-two years up there, hitting more than .300 six times, leading the league once with a .355 average and driving in 920 runs. If Judd was twice as good a hitter as that . . .

And even better than a good hitter is a good hitter who can run. Judd ran against Jesse Owens, who won four Olympic gold medals, three times in Buffalo. "Before the games then there was usually something special for the fans. We'd have races, or sometimes they'd have a coon hunt, bring in the dogs, stuff like that. Anyway, I never beat him. The last time we ran I said, 'Let's make him jump three hurdles—maybe then I can beat him.'

They did, but he still beat me. I could go as fast as he could for about seventy-five yards, and then he would seem to take off and go by. I asked him why that was, and he said, 'I train for that last twenty-five yards. You don't.' So I asked him if he'd race me around the bases, but he wouldn't — he wasn't used to turns. I could go around in about 12.6 seconds. Owens was faster than me. But I never was beat by a ballplayer, running.

"Rickey scouted me in Springfield on a day I hit two singles, a triple and a homer. And he said, 'Get that guy — he's an outfielder.' But he didn't do it, did he? Hee, hee, hee."

It is a soft spring day in Ingersoll, and as Oscar Judd talks about the old days, people drift in and out of his kitchen, picking up lawn-mower blades he has sharpened for them or motors he has fixed. He keeps busy, making things out of wood or metal — lamps, squirrel traps, bird feeders, you name it — growing things in his garden, busy, busy, but he always has time for a few droll jokes with anybody who drops in. They all call him "Lefty," which is what he got in his baseball days as well. ("They called me Lefty in Boston until my arm went. Then they called me a lot of things.") How is he thought of here in Ingersoll? "What do we think of him? He's an asshole!" says Jim Arnott, who introduced Judd at his induction into the Canadian Baseball Hall of Fame in 1986. Both men crack up. Crusty, contrary Oscar Judd has been an ornery cuss over the years, but Arnott knows him as an old softy. "He's well-liked here," Arnott says, "and he was well-liked when he played ball. He intimidates some people, but his bark has always been worse than his bite."

Despite having played a sport known for killing marriages, Judd has been married to Helen Judd for fifty-five years.

"I don't know how she put up with it," he says.

"I don't know, either," she replies with a laugh.

But all the bonhomie doesn't mean Judd wasn't a nasty bit of business when he wanted to be, and he doesn't pretend otherwise. For a start, he was never much of an organization man. Once, when he was playing for Columbus, he was suspended for refusing to do what he was told. "They sent a couple of us down to Mississippi to start up a team. I didn't like it there. They gave us peanuts and grits for potatoes. Me and this other guy, we pitched one game each and came home. We were suspended for not staying down there. We sold cars for the other guy's dad, then I pitched for Perth in the old St. Lawrence League for a while. I won nineteen games and lost one, and won three in the playoffs."

Oscar told Branch Rickey where to go when Rickey tried to convert him into an outfielder. Nobody talked back to the Mahatma.
(Toronto *Sun*)

"When I was in the majors I got a manager fired once—Freddie Fitzsimmons. He was managing the Phillies. I threw an 0-2 curve to Mel Ott—it was a real good curve, a strike—and he stuck his bat out and got a little hit over third base. Fitzimmons came out and said, 'That'll cost you $25.' He said he had a rule that you don't throw a strike on 0-2. Seems he lost a World Series game when he did that, so he made this rule. So I said, 'It won't cost *me* that.' He said, 'Yes, it will.' I said, 'I guess I better take my uniform off then.' He said, 'Go ahead.'

"I wasn't going to pay no $25, and I didn't, either. The next day the general manager, Herb Pennock, saw me sitting in the stands out of uniform, and asked me what was going on. I told him, and said the only way I would ever pay Fitszimmons $25 was if he agreed to pay me $25 if I got a guy out on an 0-2 pitch. Because you can get lots of them that way. They expect you to waste a pitch and they leave their bats on their shoulders. So that seemed reasonable to Pennock, and he asked Fitzimmons if he would go for a deal like that. Fitzimmons said no and he fired him.

"The next manager was Ben Chapman. He told us he wanted his coach to call our pitches. I said, 'Look, I'm old enough to call my own pitches, and if I'm not, I'm not gonna pitch.' So he went ahead and did it anyway, but I had a deal with the catcher that I threw the opposite of what they called."

If Judd was rough on managers, he didn't take anything from teammates, either. "Out there in Catalina, they were going to try to cut my hair because I was a rookie. But I was too strong for them. Two of them tried it and I had them down so quick — after the wheat sheaves, they were nothing."

Opponents got it even worse than teammates and managers, especially one, for reasons that were popular enough at the time. "I shouldn't say this, but when what's-his-name came up — Jackie Robinson — I never missed throwing at him. Never. Anytime he come up to the plate, I threw at him. Part of it was I just didn't want him in the league. They had their own league, and it was a good league. And part of it was that I just didn't like Branch Rickey, who was the one who brought Robinson up. You see what I mean?

"Today it don't mean a thing, but it did back then. The day he broke in I was going to pitch against Cincinnati, I think it was. And a guy was supposed to call us from Brooklyn if Robinson played, and we were going to go on strike. I waited to warm up for a long time to see if the call came, but nobody called, and Jackie played, and that let them in.

"It don't matter to me now that they're in. Ballplayers now play in moustaches and beards and don't wear ties, so what does that matter? It doesn't matter at all."

Being a hard-nosed competitor was what mattered to Judd. "You can't be weak and play this game. One day I was pitching against Bobo Newsom of the Athletics. He was a fastball pitcher. I came to bat and hit one right off his forehead, right smack. Around and around he goes. And all the way down to first base I'm watching for him to fall down. I'm not running hard, I'm feeling sorry for him. The ball had gone all the way out to right field. And after that my manager, Joe Cronin, came out and told me that would cost me a hundred bucks. 'You should have been on second base.'" Judd paid that fine. "I liked that kind of thinking."

Which brings us back to thinking. Who was the smartest? Branch Rickey or Oscar Judd? Rickey's thinking seems to have been a little ahead of Judd's on the Jackie Robinson question. But who made the most sense on the question of whether Oscar Judd should have been a pitcher or an outfielder?

Consider the following points. Of the nearly three thousand men who pitched in the major leagues over the preceding half century, the 1982 edition of the *Baseball Encyclopedia* only found thirty to be worthy enough hitters to be listed in its "players" section, where offensive statistics are recorded. Judd is one. In his 317 big-league at-bats—roughly half a season for a regular player—he hit three home runs. No big deal. But he compiled a .262 batting average without playing every day, and without taking batting practice. He hit eleven doubles (which would extrapolate to twenty-two over a full season). Remember, we're talking about a man playing between the ages of thirty-four and forty. Most remarkable, perhaps, is that he hit five triples, which would have doubled to ten during a full season. He hit two of those triples at age thirty-nine, when he was still, incidentally, being used as a pinch hitter. How many players have averaged ten triples a year between the ages of thirty-four and forty? Lou Brock, one of the fastest players in the history of the game, played until he was forty. He averaged five triples a year after he turned thirty-four.

Oscar Judd could hit and he could scamper. Maybe he *should* have been an outfielder. Maybe he would have been a .300 hitter.

"Oh, I'd have been better than that. I hit real good. I'd have made a lot more money than I did pitching. But I didn't like it, that's all. I liked being out there on the mound, challenging. There ain't nothing to playing the outfield. Listen, I enjoyed myself. It was terrific throwing that ball. If I had played the outfield, I don't think I would have had near as much fun. Them hitters, I didn't care who was coming up. I could get him out."

Forget it, Mr. Rickey. He's not gonna give.

26

ROCKY NELSON

Portsmouth, Ohio
May 11, 1988

"Rocky was our Ted Williams."
—David Crombie,
former tiny perfect mayor of Toronto

Everybody who ever saw it remembers *the stance*. Rocky Nelson, a small man for such a big hitter, would crouch with his bat cocked behind his left shoulder, glaring at the pitcher through narrow slits of eyes that hovered above a huge wad of tobacco lodged in his left cheek. His jaw was square, except for the tobacco bulge, and his face was grim. His feet were planted close together, his arms held tight to his body. His front toe was pointed at the pitcher as if to kick the poor slob in the heart, which was the whole idea.

When he stood like that, Rocky Nelson stood with the menace of the ages, for with his feet so close together and his arms in tight and his toe pointed and his dead eyes staring, he looked more like a nineteenth-century ballplayer than Canada's number-one baseball hero of the 1950s. And when he swung! It didn't matter if it was in Montreal, in the early years, or later on in Toronto. Neither Delorimier Downs nor Maple Leaf Stadium was big enough to hold Rocky Nelson.

The whole International League shouldn't have been big enough to hold Rocky Nelson. But somehow, except for a few dramatic years with Pittsburgh, somehow it did. And because it did, no ballplayer — not Rusty Staub, not Gary Carter, not George Bell — ever captured the imagination of Upper and Lower Canadian baseball fans the way Rocky Nelson did.

"For a long time he was a big villain in Toronto," remembers Harvey Trivett, now president of the Blue Jays Fan Club and former president of the Maple Leafs Fan Club. "He used to come to town with the Montreal Royals and just kill us. And then we got him, and to have him on our side seemed to make beating Montreal all the sweeter."

"When I think about Rocky Nelson," says Randall Echlin, secretary of the Canadian Baseball Hall of Fame, to which Nelson was inducted in 1987, "I think about lying awake in Burlington with a radio under my pillow, waiting for him to come to bat. And twice a year traveling to Maple Leaf Stadium with my dad. Rocky Nelson was just a giant of a man to a little kid like me. He was what Frank Mahovlich was to the hockey Leafs."

"Rocky always seemed to me to be a ballplayer's ballplayer," says Senator Keith Davey. "He was hard-bitten, tough as nails. When he tagged a guy out he really tagged him. A lot is made of clutch hitters. Well there aren't many, really. But he was one. He was the real thing."

"He was an absolutely stunning long-ball hitter," remembers David Crombie, a regular at Maple Leaf Stadium. "There was a clutch of houses outside the park over the right-field stands called Little Norway, where they'd housed Norwegian pilots who trained here during the war. Rocky could hit Little Norway. There were very few great baseball heroes in Toronto after the war — you could put them all in one hand. And he'd be the biggest one. Don't even mention he once played for Montreal. I don't remember that and I refuse to think about it."

The object of all this adulation is now a housepainter—"I only do small-ladder, indoors stuff now"— who lives in a smallish bungalow in Portsmouth, Ohio, with his wife of forty years, the perfectly named Alberta. It is the only bungalow in Portsmouth known to harbor a fuctioning spittoon.

Scores of pictures line the walls of the den at Rocky and Alberta Nelson's bungalow. There is a picture of the two of them getting married at home plate in Lynchburg, Virginia, in 1947, making their way through a cathedral of bats hoisted by grinning teammates. "I really didn't want to do that," Alberta says with a sigh and a smile. "Rocky and I have since renewed our vows in a church." Marriage obviously agreed with Rocky: he led the Piedmont League with a .371 average that year, spiced with thirty-eight doubles, eleven triples, eleven home runs and twenty stolen bases. And that was before he shifted his approach at the plate to get more power. At twenty-two, the kid was on his way.

There is a picture of Rocky shaking hands with Fidel Castro: Nelson played for four years with the Havana Sugar Kings and was there when Castro's rebels captured power in 1959. "If I'd have known what he was gonna become I never would have shook hands with him," rasps Nelson.

There was reported to have been a picture of Nelson published in a revolutionary newspaper before Castro took power, showing him holding a machine gun. Nelson says it doesn't exist. "Look," he says, pointing to a picture of Cuban soldiers gathered with players around the Sugar King dugout. Sure enough, at the back you can see Tommy LaSorda, now the manager of the Los Angeles Dodgers, holding a machine gun.

"Tommy nearly got my head blown off. He was kidding one of the *barbudos* that there weren't really any bullets in his gun and the kid pulled the trigger. I was leaning over; nearly took my head off." If anyone's head could have stood up to a machine gun, it was Nelson's. The nickname "Rocky" resulted from Nelson getting hit in the head with a ball during batting practice while kidding around with Enos (Country) Slaughter and George (Whitey) Kurowski. Nelson showed no signs of being aware that the ball had hit him, so Kurowski dubbed him Rocky.

There are photos of many of Nelson's teammates on the 1960 World Championship Pittsburg Pirates. El Roy Face. Dick Groat. Bob Skinner. Roberto Clemente. Bob Friend. There are photos of ballplayers who were both friends and the glory of their times: Willie Mays, Ernie Banks. There is a shot of Nelson with Rocket Richard, and an oil painting done of him after the Pirates won the World Series.

And in the place of honor at the center of this gallery is a portrait of Branch Rickey, general manager of the Pirates when they first owned Nelson in 1951 and still on the board of governors of the team when they brought Rocky up for his final shot in 1959. The portrait is inscribed: "To Glenn Nelson. My brother Frank first told me about you. He was right. You were and are a major leaguer. Best wishes, Branch Rickey." It is strange to see Mr. Rickey sitting in godlike majesty in the middle of Rocky Nelson's world. Because Mr. Rickey presided over one of the most obvious cases of Nelson not being given a chance at the major-league level. Indeed, it is arguable that if Rocky Nelson had never heard of a Rickey — either Frank or Branch — his life might have been showered in the glory his disciples believe he deserved. So Mr. Rickey being there doesn't make sense. But then, if you look at Rocky Nelson's record, what does make sense?

Between 1947 and 1962 Nelson played 1,113 games with five teams in Triple A, the launching pad to the majors. He batted a composite .316, averaging thirty home runs and 108 RBIs a season.

During those years he was given ten "chances" to establish himself as a regular with five major-league clubs: the St. Louis Cardinals, the Pittsburgh Pirates, the Chicago White Sox, the Cleveland Indians and the Brooklyn Dodgers. During his playing days in the big leagues, often competing for jobs against players he had been far superior to at Triple A, he averaged .249, with twelve homers and sixty-eight RBIs a year.

237

"To me, the majors were the easier place to hit," says Nelson. Which is a strange thing to say, on the evidence.

The left-handed Glenn Richard Nelson grew up in Portsmouth playing with a right-hander's glove: "We couldn't afford the proper one. I'd borrow a glove and put my thumb where my little finger should have gone and my little finger where my thumb should have gone and I'd play." He was one of the rarest of creatures on a ball diamond—a left-handed shortstop. "We had a little team of ten players when I was between eleven and fifteen and we beat everybody. Me and my brother and some cousins and the Williams boys. Me and Bill Williams pitched and played short. I don't know how it happened that way, but that's how it happened."

Nelson's father had pitched with both hands at the semipro level, but didn't encourage his boys to play ball because money was scarce and he preferred to have them working. Nevertheless Nelson spent enough time on the diamond to have Frank Rickey, who lived nearby in Portsmouth, keep an eye on him. The Rickeys were still with the Cardinals when Frank signed the seventeen-year-old Nelson at the ninth hole of the local golf course in 1942.

A Brooklyn scout had been looking for Nelson, and was directed to the Portsmouth golf course, where his prospect was out playing the front nine. The scout made the mistake of teeing up for a few holes while he was waiting. Frank Rickey got wind of Brookyln's intention to sign Nelson as soon as he arrived at the eighteenth hole. Rickey slipped over to the ninth and stole the prize.

Nelson spent a couple of months with Johnson City, of the Appalachian League, before going off to serve with the army in 1943. He returned three years later. His unit was gearing up to attempt to clear the island of Saipan, twenty-five miles long by eight miles wide, of eight thousand Japanese soldiers, which would have been a barn burner of a battle. But at that very moment the Second World War ended. "I was lucky." Nelson smiles, preparing a chaw of Red Horse. "I always thought I was lucky, all the way through."

With three years stolen away by the war, it was important to do well and do well quickly when he got home. Nelson hit .319 his first year back, with St. Joseph of the Western Association, then .371 at Lynchburg and .303 at Rochester, his first foray into the soon-to-become-familiar International League. He didn't show a lot of power for a first baseman over

Rocky couldn't pull the ball the way he wanted to until he developed the stance that shook the International League.
(Dan Turner)

those three years—only twenty-three home runs in 1,464 at-bats. But at twenty-four he looked like he might have a future.

In 1949 he was given a fair shot with the Cardinals. In 244 at-bats he hit only .221. He was sent to Columbus, of the American Association, in 1950. He hit .418 in forty-eight games, and the Cards eagerly brought him back up. But he dropped to .247 with the parent club. He was beginning to get a reputation: great minor-league hitter; mediocre major-league hitter.

He can explain. "I hit real well when I got up to St. Louis. I think I played for eleven straight days. I was hitting around .400 and had driven in a number of runs. It was the only time in my life I got *The Sporting News* player-of-the-week award. But the next week Stan Musial turned his ankle in the outfield. They put him on first and me on the bench." Nelson loathed starting once or twice a week and pinch hitting the rest of the time. "Anybody who puts up even half-decent numbers doing that is doing great. You can't get going doing that."

Nelson got into only nine games with St. Louis in 1951 before being traded over to Pittsburgh. He was twenty-six. It was time to prove he could play or get lost in the shuffle. Again, he says, he started out well. "I was hitting about .365 and Bill Howerton, who came over from the Cardinals with me, was hitting .320 and we were in third place. Then the word came down from Mr. Rickey, who had moved to the Pirates, that two other players were going to play instead of us. Jack Phillips replaced me at first base. [Phillips would be given 156 at-bats before it was realized that he was hitting .237 with no homers, and the team had fallen to eighth place.]

"Rickey called me and Howerton in. He says, 'Glenn, you're going great, hitting .345 or something, aren't you?' I says, 'A little higher than that, Mr. Rickey.' I says, 'I don't understand it, I'm hitting well and all of a sudden I can't play.' He said, 'Oh, I don't have anything to do with running the club on the field.' I says, 'Mr. Rickey, who are you trying to fool? Everywhere you ever been, you ran the club from the front office.' "

Howerton ended up getting traded to the New York Giants. In his case Rickey's judgment proved to be sound. Howerton hit only .067 for the Giants in eleven games before disappearing forever. Nelson was sent to the Chicago White Sox, where he went 0-for-5 as a pinch hitter. "Later on people used to count that Chicago thing as one of the chances I was given," he says with disgust, making his way over to the sink to relieve himself of some excess Red Horse.

In 1952 he was traded to Brooklyn, where he hit .256 in thirty-seven games, mainly as a pinch hitter. In 1953, at the age of twenty-eight, he was sent to Montreal. Players sent down at twenty-eight have a way of not resurfacing.

It would be stretching it to argue that any great injustice had been done. While Nelson had hit well in spurts, he had shown no great power. First base is a power position. He had also failed to hit for average as a pinch hitter, which argued against keeping him as a backup player. He was an excellent fielder, but fielding alone won't get anyone regular work at first base, in the majors or the minors. Time was running out. Only something dramatic could turn things around.

And what could have been more dramatic than *the stance?*

"I started the year at Montreal wearing the ball out and getting nowhere. I was hitting three line drives in every four at-bats but they were getting caught, and I was only hitting about .190. So I went to Walt Alston, who was the manager at Montreal then, and I said, 'Get [shortstop Stan] Rojek and a couple of fielders. We're going out for batting practice, and I'm gonna make myself a pull hitter.' He said, 'You think you can do that?' I said, 'I know I can.' So I started messing around with my stance. In hitting you gotta stride, pivot and swing. When I opened up in front I eliminated the need to pivot, so they couldn't get the good fastball in on my hands. In three days I could pull anybody."

That year Nelson played in all 154 of Montreal's games, hit thirty-four home runs with a .308 batting average and drove in a league-leading 136 runs. He was named the International League's Player of the Year. He batted .647 in the Little World Series to lead the Royals to the minor-league championships. Cleveland brought him up for a look, gave him four at-bats and sent him back to Montreal.

In 1954 he hit .311, with thirty-one homers and ninety-four RBIs. In 1955 he recorded his first International League triple crown, leading the league in average (.364), homers (thirty-seven), and RBIs (130). Again he was named the league's Player of the Year. But no major-league team drafted him.

Finally, after he got off to a .394 start in forty-nine games in 1956, the Dodgers couldn't resist. They had the mighty, fine-fielding Gil Hodges at first, but someone decided Hodges could be moved to the outfield, where the club needed a third bat to complement Duke Snider and Carl Furillo. Nelson would replace Hodges at first. Nelson was in Hodges' class as a fielder at first. The only question, crucial to Nelson's chances, was how well Hodges could handle the outfield. "Not too well," remembers Nelson sadly. "And although I started off hitting well, it was always right at somebody." After thirty-one games Nelson was hitting only .208. "They were having attendance problems in Montreal and they decided to try to get me back there. They put me on waivers, but clubs kept trying to claim me, so they'd pull me back. Buzzy Bavazi kept going around telling the other clubs to lay off. But the third time they tried, St. Louis got me anyway."

He hit .232 at St. Louis in thirty-two games. Stan Musial was still in his way at first base, and so was young Wally Moon, who hit .298 that year as the left-handed platoon. The Dodgers ended up going to the World Series after Nelson left them. Dale Mitchell had been picked up to replace Nelson as the club's left-handed pinch hitter. So it was Mitchell and not Nelson who was called in as the last batter to face Don Larsen in Larsen's famous perfect World Series game. Mitchell struck out. But at least he made it to the Series. It looked like Nelson had had his last chance. He turned thirty-two that winter.

Frank (Trader) Lane, the general manager at Cleveland, was a good friend of Jack Kent Cooke, the flamboyant entrepreneur who had turned the Toronto Maple Leafs into a big money-maker in the 1950s after the club had struggled in the early forties. Cooke had always drooled over Nelson, and was willing to pay him a major-league salary. His friend Lane came through, and Nelson became a Leaf. Was Nelson too old? Cooke wasn't worried. When Nelson's acquisition was announced, George Dulmage, sports editor of the *Toronto Telegram* at the time, wrote a story about how Cooke's dream had finally been fulfilled. When Nelson had been with Montreal, Dulmage reported, Cooke was forever muttering, "I gotta have that Nelson. Don't you agree he's the greatest? Wouldn't it be wonderful if we had him?" It was.

But not all that thrilling for Nelson. "This has caught me completely by surprise," he told reporters. "I understand other major league clubs wanted me. But I guess in baseball they can pull a few strings and, presto, the other clubs keep quiet. I hit all those pitchers in the minors, so why couldn't I hit them now? No club ever gave me a chance, that's all. You can't hit in any league by playing once every other week. That doesn't mean I'm sore at Toronto. I like the city and the ball club, and I'll do my best to help win the pennant. But I'll be back up. No one will ever convince me I can't hit in the majors."

Always chattering when he wasn't chewing, Nelson rarely missed a

Rocky and the Rocket give singer Sylvia Murphy some batting tips and terrific smiles. (Graphic Artists Toronto)

chance to mutter about the injustice of it all, often rolling his eyes and grunting Earl Torgeson's name. Torgeson played first base for the punchless Chicago White Sox between 1957 and 1961, usually hitting about .270 with eight or nine home runs. "I could eat that guy. Hell, I could help that club."

But he was as good as his word in putting out for Toronto. The Leafs finished first in 1957 and second in 1958, drawing well both years, although not as well as in the pre-television years of the early fifties. In fact the club was coming to the end of its heyday, which had begun at the end of the war.

But it wasn't over yet. "Under these portals pass the greatest fans in the world," said a sign above an entrance at Maple Leaf Stadium. And the greatest fans loved Nelson. He hit .294 with twenty-four homers and 102 RBIs in 1957. But he was just warming up. In 1958 he captured his second triple crown and third MVP award. He hit .326, with forty-three home runs and 120 RBIs. No other player ever won the International League MVP award more than once. "But then," drawls Nelson with a chuckle, "not many of them who were good enough to win it were around long enough to win it three times. Most of them went to the majors."

Finally, in 1959, Rocky did, too. When it was announced in December 1958 that the Pirates had drafted Nelson, Jack Kent Cooke fell into despair. "I never expected this . . . It's awful. We never thought anyone would claim Nelson. This could ruin us."

In a sense it was ruinous. Maple Leaf attendance plunged from 281,971 in 1958 to 207,505 in 1959, and kept going down every year until the club folded in 1967. But, in another sense, it was a joyful occasion for Toronto fans. Toronto was finally on the brink of proving itself a major-league city. Rocky Nelson, who had signed at seventeen and was now thirty-four, was finally on the brink of proving himself a major-league ball player. Torontonians thought of him as their own, and there was excitement in the air.

Nelson was playing in Cuba when he heard he'd been drafted. "I was really surprised. I didn't really expect to get another chance. LaSorda and some of the others were down waiting for the news to come in, because they expected to get drafted. But I didn't."

The prospects didn't look all that bright — Nelson was up against Dick (Dr. Strangeglove) Stuart and Ted Kluszewski. Stuart had hit sixty-six home runs in one minor-league season and sixteen in half a season in his 1958 major-league debut. Kluszewski had been one of the big boppers on the muscular Cincinnati Redlegs team of the mid-fifties.

And sure enough, during the 1959 season Nelson was confined to his usual role of spot starting and pinch hitting. Kluszewski was traded a third of the way through the year, but Stuart still got most of the playing time, even against right-handers. "Danny Murtaugh would have played me every day if he could have, but he had orders from head office not to. He told Bob Skinner that. The story was that when Joe Brown, who ran the club, went out to Lincoln when Stuart was playing there in the minors, Stuart fixed him up. Who knows? Nobody could figure out why I didn't play more."

Nevertheless, for the first time Nelson turned in a credible performance as an odd-jobs man, hitting .291 with six homers and thirty-two RBIs in a third of a season's at-bats. But 1960 was his year. Nelson hit an even .300 that year, with seven homers and thirty-five RBIs in two hundred at-bats. In a full season he would have accumulated in the neighborhood of a hundred RBIs. The Pirates won the pennant and took on the powerful

Yankees in the World Series. The Yanks were prohibitive favorites.

The Pirates won the first game 6-3, but the Yankees blew them away 16-3 in the second and 10-0 in the third. A horde of reporters, sensing a death rattle, asked Dick Groat to assess the situation. When Groat refused, Nelson blithely commented that with Vernon Law and Harvey Haddix on the mound in the next two games, it shouldn't present much of a problem to build up a 3-2 lead at Yankee Stadium to take home to Pittsburgh. He was the butt of sportscasters' guffaws everywhere, but that's exactly what happened. Then the Yanks crushed the Pirates again in the sixth game, 12-0.

Bill Mazeroski's heroic home run in the ninth inning of the final game is baseball legend: the Pirates won 10-9. But Nelson was very much involved, although he almost wasn't. "Murtaugh made up two lineups, one with me in it and one with Stuart in it. Dick Groat took the wrong one out to the umpire, which put me officially in the game. After it was announced the front office called down to ask why I was playing. Murtaugh said he couldn't take me out now, or I'd be out of the game altogether." Nelson hit a two-run homer into the right-field stands in the first inning to get the Pirates rolling, and horns were honked in Toronto. He would finish the Series 3-for-9 with two RBIS and two runs scored. Stuart was 3-for-20. Three singles, with no RBIS.

Having Nelson in the game also made a difference in the field. Stuart was a notoriously bad fielder. Nelson, even at thirty-five, was superb.

In the top of the ninth the Yankees had closed to within one run. Gil McDougald was aboard at third and Mickey Mantle at first with one out. Yogi Berra hit a liner over the first base bag that Nelson dove for and speared on one hop behind the bag. Stuart wouldn't have gotten it, and Berra would have had a double down the line, scoring two runs and putting the Yankees ahead. As it was they tied the game: shortstop Groat thought the ball had gotten by Nelson, so he moved out to take the relay throw from the right fielder, which cost the Pirates a game-ending double play.

"All I had to do was throw a strike to Groat and he throws one back to me and it's all over." Nelson shrugs. "But he wasn't there." Mantle thought Nelson had caught the ball on a line and dove back into first. Nelson stepped on the bag to get the out on Berra, but didn't get Mantle. So the run scored and the stage was set for Mazeroski's heroics.

"Stuart had a nice sense of humor. He came over to Murtaugh after the game and said, 'Danny, you shoulda had me in the game, I would have ended it in the top of the ninth.' And Danny said, 'Yeah, we would have lost it right there.'

Glory came just in time. In 1961 Nelson hit .197 and was finished forever in the big leagues. He came back to Toronto to play in the International League, which he had lit up during the fifties. (He had actually been inducted into the league's hall of fame in 1960, while still playing.) This time around he hit .217, got cut, played a bit at Denver and was gone.

Maybe Nelson would have been a first-rate major-league regular if he'd been given a shot once he changed his batting stroke. And maybe he wouldn't have: the short right-field fences in both Toronto and Montreal did have something to do with his incredible numbers. Maybe he was one of those guys who froze when he got to the big time, but that seems unlikely. He was the clutch hitter of all clutch hitters in Montreal and Toronto, and clutch hitters don't freeze up.

"Maybe," he says, "it was a bit like getting up on the wrong side of bed." All those maybes, and only one thing for sure. When Rocky Nelson took three days of extra batting practice at Delorimier Downs that day in 1953, he invented something that thousands of middle-aged Canadians in the country's two largest cities will be able to imitate until the day they die.

Ladies and gentlemen — a toast. To two great ballparks. And one great stance.

27

CLAUDE RAYMOND

St-Jean, Quebec
May 9, 1988

Claude Raymond isn't one for cheap tears. "I've never been the kind of guy to let my emotions show," he says, with an ice-blue, matter-of-fact stare. But when five million people gave him a standing ovation, something opened up.

Not that there were five million people there at Jarry Park on the night of May 16, 1969, to watch the Expos take on the Atlanta Braves. There were only 20,872 paid admissions, and only about half were French Canadians.

But when the announcer said, *"Et maintenant, à St-Jean, Québec, Numéro 36 . . . "* those 20,872 represented every Quebecois breathing on that cool spring night. They stood up and roared, and laughed, and cried, and roared some more, without even giving the announcer a chance to say that Numéro 36 was Claude Raymond.

It may have been the biggest round of applause a home crowd has ever given an opposing pitcher coming into a tense, tied, late-inning ball game. But then Raymond was the first French Canadian ever to enter a game on home soil.

When he got to the mound and the ovation just kept swelling, he cried. "I had tears running down my cheek. I even dropped the ball on the mound. This isn't what your teammates are looking for when the game is tied and you're fighting for a pennant.

"So Tito Francona, the first baseman, and Bob Tillman, the catcher, came over and said, 'Hey, what are you doing? You always said you wanted to pitch in front of your people. Let's show them what you can do. Quit crying, let's go, do the job.' "

Which he did. Over the next two innings he held the Expos to two hits, no runs. Francona banged a homer off Elroy Face in the twelfth to win it for the Braves. All Quebec celebrated its new team's loss.

"Quebeckers used to come to me, and it was a very emotional thing," he says, still matter-of-fact, but focusing on some faraway spot. "They'd say, 'Claude, when you're pitching, it's like we're out there on the mound with you.'"

Raymond grew up poor. He didn't speak any English. He was small and wore glasses. Not your typical big-league prospect. But on the other side of the ledger was a great arm, an indomitable attitude and plenty of time to play the game.

There is no false modesty about the arm: "One in ten thousand isn't right," he says, sitting in his expansive home in south-shore St-Jean, half an hour from Olympic Stadium, where he anchors French TV broadcasts of Expos games. "More like one in a million."

There is an aura of physical prowess to Raymond that should be tempered by his *Gentleman's Quarterly* fashions and fastidious grooming, but isn't. He looks completely comfortable in his fine clothes. He also looks like he could stand up and compete in them at a moment's notice, and he gives the impression that being five-foot-ten and wearing glasses and being fifty-one years old and wearing a shirt and tie would have nothing to do with his performance.

"I always thought I was just as good as whoever I played against. That's the kind of attitude you have to have, that you're just as good as the other guy. You can't think negatively. If you think negatively you're in deep stew."

There was no television and not much money in St-Jean when Claude Raymond was a boy. His father, Roland Raymond, worked at the local textile mill. His mother, Rachael, took care of the house. And their son played baseball whenever he could. "I can remember measuring out a field right in front of the church when I was about seven or eight. We cut the grass away with shovels and made base paths. A little later they built a house where our center field was, but we still kept playing.

"We were uppercutters, and we used to hit the ball over the house and church and everything. We'd use any kind of ball we could find, and later on we'd get broken bats from the Provincial League and put them back together with nails and tape and glue. When I first started I hit cross-handed, until my uncle showed me how.

"Today what gets me is you have these leagues that say you can only pitch so many innings a week. When we were kids we pitched all day. The more you throw the stronger you get."

Raymond got very strong very quickly. At eleven he was playing outfield for a local junior team against twenty-one- and twenty-two-year-olds who had wives and children. At twelve he was pitching. "There was this guy named André Petit. He told me to come over that night, that I was going to pitch. It was the second game of a doubleheader. I couldn't come to the first game because my father had ordered some furniture, and I had to go help pick it up. But I ran over for the second game. They had won the first, which put them in a tie for first place.

"The other team had a bunch of sluggers, and some of the veterans on the team said to Petit, 'Hey, you can't let this kid pitch.' And he said, 'Yeah, he's gonna pitch, no matter what.' It was the first time I'd pitched from a mound. The first two batters hit triples off me. Petit was my catcher. He came out and said, 'Don't worry, we'll get them out.' And that was it, they only got one run off me, and we won 2-1. I threw nothing but fastballs."

At fifteen, standing five-foot-nine at 155 pounds, he set out for Montreal. He had earlier gone to Drummondville and assured himself he was ready for the outside world. "I read in the paper that Al Gionfriddo [best known for his great catch in the 1947 World Series] was going to manage the Provincial League team in Drummondville and was holding tryouts. You had to be seventeen. Four of us went and there was snow, but they held the tryouts anyway.

"At the end of a week the others went home. I thought I was going to have to leave, too, because my father didn't have much money, and I think he'd given me almost his whole salary for a week to go to Drummondville. So I told them I had to go home. But they begged me to stay, and I called my dad, and he came over with enough money to live on. At the end of two weeks they wanted to keep me, so I had to tell them I had cheated on my age. But the last game of the camp we played against an all-star team from the Quebec Junior League, and in the three innings I pitched I struck out a bunch of guys, and some people from Montreal asked me if I'd be interested in pitching in Montreal.

"So I hitchhiked to Montreal a couple of weeks later. I got on the field with one team, Plateau Mount Royal, at Parc Lafontaine, but they told me they didn't need pitchers. So I asked where another team, Ville Ray, played, and they told me Parc Jarry, and which way to go. They didn't know I was walking and didn't have any money, and I didn't know it was five miles. I kept walking and asking people, and finally I got there.

"When I got there I asked if they needed any pitching, and the manager told me to go get dressed. I got back, and they were having batting practice, and nobody was paying any attention to me. So I asked if he wanted me to do anything, and he said, 'Yeah, warm up.' But there was nobody to

warm up with, and finally I had to ask for somebody. They gave me a third baseman, Ray Cherier. I threw him about five or six pitches, and he said, 'Whoa, we need a catcher here.' They got me a catcher named Duncan Campbell, and they started to watch me. They signed me right away."

For the next two years Raymond took the bus back and forth from St-Jean, rolling and counting change at the Montreal Transit Authority to support his new lifestyle. He quickly caught the attention of the scouts, and his pitching duels with Ron Piche, from Verdun, Quebec, were crowd favorites. "He was a couple of years older than me," Raymond says of Piche. "I was faster than him, but he could pitch. He had a real good sinker. Whenever we hooked up the score would be 1-0 or 2-1."

In 1954 the Dodgers signed Raymond for $250, but the contract was voided because he hadn't finished high school. The Pirates wanted to sign him and have him play with their St-Jean farm team in the Provincial League. The Braves wanted him, too, but he would have to go away to the southern United States, and he didn't speak any English. "I asked my dad what he thought I should do. He said, 'Do you want to play in St-Jean or do you want to play baseball?' He meant that if I played for St-Jean I would probably end up in St-Jean. I said, 'I want to play baseball.'"

That spring Raymond, Piche and two other prospects, Yvon Dubois and Bobby LaForet, took the train to Wakefield, Georgia. It was a brand new world, in which his name would be Frenchy.

"I loved that name. It meant people knew what I was, and they liked me."

"At Wakefield they told us they were going to release 150 kids in a week, and from what I hear I was supposed to be one of them after I got ripped in one of my games. I was small for a pitcher. I got beat up in that game, and they had decisions to make. But a manager named Bill Steinecke was starting up an independent team at West Palm Beach, and he told them he wanted to take me and another guy with him.

"I was seventeen when I started out in West Palm Beach in 1955. I couldn't speak any English, but I understood some. I knew the words pitch, hit, ball, strike and hot dog. I kept a dictionary with me all the time, and I used to make myself learn ten new words a day. Of course you know the language in baseball: a lot of words I heard I used to look up in my dictionary, but they weren't polite enough to be there. It took me about two or three months to ask a question or say, 'Hi, how are you?' But I'd go to movies, and try to read the newspapers, and listen to conversations.

Frenchy was a little guy with a lot of confidence, which works as well in the broadcast booth as it did on the mound. (Michael Rafelson)

251

"I learned about professional baseball, too. After my first three games I hadn't given up an earned run and I was 0-3. But I finished at 13-12, with an ERA of 2.60. I also learned to throw a curve. Steinecke told me if I was throwing it properly my elbow would hit my knee. So I'd have black and blue bruises on my elbow from where I was following through, but it got so I could depend on my curve as much as my fastball."

In 1956 he was promoted to Class B at Evansville in the Three-I league, where he compiled an 2.57 ERA. His manager was Bob Coleman, who'd spent brief periods with Pittsburgh and Cleveland as a catcher and was in his late sixties. "He'd tell me, 'Keep the ball down, keep the ball down.' He could hardly see any more but he knew if the pitch was high or low, fastball or breaking ball, by the sound. He'd sit on the bench and tell us."

Raymond progressed from Evansville, in 1956, to Jacksonville Class A in 1957 and Wichita Triple A in 1958. On Steinecke's advice he was being developed as a relief pitcher, one of the first to so specialize in the Braves' system. In 1959 the Chicago White Sox claimed him in the draft. The Sox would win the American League pennant that year, and had such an excess of pitching talent that Raymond was returned to the Braves.

But while he was in Chicago Raymond roomed with scrappy second baseman Nellie Fox. Fox compiled a lifetime .288 batting average over an eighteen-year career, but was best known for his grit. "He wasn't afraid to get his uniform dirty, or get hit by a pitch if it would win a ball game. I was bigger than him, but he played without fear, and that made me realize I could, too."

Raymond bounced around from Louisville in Triple A to Atlanta in Double A to Sacramento and Vancouver in Triple A before being promoted briefly to Milwaukee in 1961. He won his first major-league game, but got sent down when the Braves acquired faded veteran Johnny Antonelli from Cleveland. He pitched poorly when he returned to Vancouver, and started to doubt himself. "I was confused and discouraged. For the first time, when I came back to St-Jean, I played hockey in the winter. For the first time I started to wonder if I was really going to do it."

Raymond got off to a good start in 1962 in Toronto, giving up only fourteen hits in twenty-four innings, with six walks and thirty strikeouts. His time had come. When other teams started trying to trade for him, the Braves got the message and brought him up to Milwaukee. Manager Birdie Tebbetts put him right to work, much to the displeasure of Brave heroes Warren Spahn and Lew Burdette. Spahn liked to finish his own ball games:

it wasn't unusual for him to complete two games for every one he'd need help in during a year, and Burdette was almost as strong. "My first game Spahn was pitching, and Birdie called me in, and Spahn was really teed off. I forget what he said to me, but he really wasn't happy. But it didn't bother me. I was there to get people out. I saved the game for him, and after the game he came over to apologize.

"The next day Tebbetts brings me in to relieve Burdette, and he's mad, too. But I saved the game for him, as well. Then we went on the road. Spahn and Burdette would always room together, but their wives wanted to break them up. So Piche [who had joined the Braves in 1960] roomed with Spahn and I went with Burdette, and Ron and I couldn't get away from those guys. The four of us would go everywhere together, and they were great to us. They were making a lot of money and we weren't, so they'd pick up the tab for almost everything. They were just a lot of fun, a lot of laughs.

"Except one time Spahn and Burdette got me between them on a flight from Los Angeles to New York. I'd been beaten by Frank Howard in extra innings in L.A. I knew how I wanted to pitch him: I didn't want to give him anything to hit. On the 3-1 pitch, I put one outside and he swung and missed. So I changed my mind and decided I could put something extra on the ball and strike him out, when my better instincts were to walk him. I put the ball in there, and he beat me.

"Spahn and Burdette gave me hell from Los Angeles to New York. They knew what I'd been thinking out there, and that I'd gone outside myself to try to do something I didn't want to do. I learned a lot about the mental aspect of the game from those guys because they talked baseball all the time. Now, I go in the dressing room before a game and guys are eating or playing cards."

Raymond pitched two good years for the Braves, going 1-0 with a 3.98 ERA in 1961 and 5-5 with a 2.74 ERA and ten saves in 1962. But he fell to 4-6 with a 5.40 ERA in 1963, and was traded to Houston. He had three fine years in Houston, going 5-5 with a 2.82 ERA in 1964, 7-4 with a 2.90 ERA in 1965 and 7-5 with a 3.13 ERA in 1966. He recorded sixteen saves in 1966, the year in which he led the National League in ERA halfway through the season and was named to the All-Star Team, an unusual honor for a reliever at the time.

"I probably had the best stuff of my career that year. Fastball, slider, slow curve, fork ball. You talk about striking out the side, I don't know how many times I did it, but I did it a lot. I'd just go out there and one, two, three . . . . Some days I just felt like nobody could touch me. I'd go

Claude compares grips with fellow flinger Bill Stoneman. Raymond's arm was fading, but his heart never quit. (Montreal Gazette)

out there and throw fastballs and sliders, and they'd all be perfect pitches. Quite a few times I came in with the bases loaded and got out of it without a run scoring. You've got to take those experiences and cherish them, because they're scarce."

He could have had a lot more than sixteen saves, but he volunteered to start the only seven games of his career because of injuries to starters Dick Farrell and Ken Johnson. He completed two of the games and threw like he'd been starting all his life. "I never pitched fewer than seven innings, I never gave up more than three runs and I went 5-2. But when the starters came back Grady Hatton said I was more useful in relief. It didn't surprise me that I did well as a starter, because relief pitchers in those days were a special breed. In those days you had one top short-relief man, and if the game was close after the sixth inning you started warming up. They didn't call you in the bullpen and tell you, it was just automatic. You used up a lot of your arm just throwing in the bullpen. Our endurance was incredible. It didn't matter to us how long we went, because our arms were always hurting anyway."

Raymond split 1967 between Houston and Atlanta, which sent the Astros lefthanded reliever Wade Blasingame to get Raymond back. His ERA for the split year was an excellent 2.89. In 1968 it was 2.83. He recorded ten saves each year. But in 1969, when Raymond was thirty-two, the wear and tear of too many warm-ups and too many appearances was starting to tell. The Braves were on their way to the pennant with twenty-six-year-old righthander Cecil Upshaw as the big man in the bull pen, and Raymond was getting less and less use. When he came in to pitch those two emotional innings on May 16, 1969, he had been called upon only twice in the previous twenty-three days. When he was sold to the Expos later in the year he had an ERA of 5.25. He had noticed himself start to slip.

"Before, I had gotten a lot of strikeouts on high pitches because my ball was moving, it was quick. They used to foul it off sometimes and miss it sometimes. All of a sudden they would foul it off sometimes and hit it sometimes. They could adjust quicker, because I had lost a couple of feet off my fastball."

A proud man with a fine record, Raymond was faced with a dilemma. He had always wanted to pitch in front of his Quebecois, and was elated when Montreal got the franchise and he heard whispers that the Expos would be interested in him. But he had lost his best stuff. Every year between 1962 and 1968 — save one bad year, 1963 — he had come in with an ERA between 2.74 and 3.13. It wasn't going to happen again.

But Raymond was up to the challenge. That winter, while still pitching for the Braves, he had married, and the wedding cake was baked in the shape of Jarry Park. Jarry Park it would be.

In 1970, with a last-place team that went 73-89, Raymond had a 6-7 record with a 4.45 ERA. It wasn't exactly miniscule, but it was the fifth-best ERA recorded by the seventeen pitchers who toiled for Montreal that year. All seventeen of those pitchers worked at least some innings out of the bullpen. Among them they recorded thirty-two saves. Raymond had twenty-three of those.

In 1971 Mike Marshall would take over as the Expos' closer and Raymond would bow out, his arm exhausted. But in 1970 his spirit did the pitching, and Quebec got one last glimpse of the glory. It was a valiant effort. But then Raymond had always been valiant.

One of the most famous lines in baseball history came from Charlie Fox, then in the San Francisco Giants' head office in 1965. It summed up an encounter that year between Raymond and Willie Mays, regarded by many as the finest ballplayer of all time.

It was September and the Giants were fighting for the pennant, which they would eventually lose to the Dodgers by two games. But nobody could blame Mays. He would finish the year at .317 with fifty-two home runs.

"There were two outs and Jesus Alou was on first in the Astrodome," remembers Raymond. "I always liked pitching against Mays. He hit three or four home runs off me, always late in the season, it seemed. And the next year I'd see him, and I'd look him right in the eye, and I'd come sidearm on him. I never hit him, I hit some others, but never him. And I'd strike him out many times.

"Anyway, this time I got ahead of him, and he kept fouling off pitches. The count went to 2-2, then 3-2, and I kept going after him. He fouled off seventeen pitches, sometimes just touching the ball a tiny little bit. And then I got one a little up and in and he hit a home run to beat me. In his book Mays says it was the greatest battle he ever had." *Seventeen* pitches.

After the game Houston general manager Paul Richards called it "the greatest battle I've ever seen anyone give anyone in the major leagues."

But it was Fox's description that would echo through the decades: "It was like challenging God."

28

HELEN CALLAGHAN

Lampoc, California
May 18, 1988

"We got a lot of people who liked to see the legs and have some laughs, but they didn't expect to see us play good baseball. We got them out there maybe because of our uniforms, maybe because of the publicity. We kept them there because we played damned good baseball."

Pepper Paire Davis
Catcher, AAGPBL, 1944–1953

Helen St. Aubin, who used to be Helen Candaele and who was Helen Callaghan before that, has lost it. Not as a mother: she is a notoriously successful mother. Not as a wife: her husband, Ron, treats her with glowing admiration. Not as a breadwinner: she still has her administrative job at the convalescent hospital in Lampoc.

But she can't hit. Her swing stinks. Her son Kelly produced a video documentary, *A League of Their Own*, about the All-American Girls Baseball League, with which his mother starred during the Second World War. Most of the footage was shot at a league reunion held in 1986. Some of the AAGPBL old-timers took part in an exhibition game. Many of the older and wiser girls stayed in the stands, but St. Aubin, who is still slender and sylph-like at sixty-five, was game for a little action.

No good. Instead of snapping her wrists, she pushed the bat through the strike zone. Instead of popping her hips, she swiveled and ended up backward to the pitcher. Oh, she got a base hit, a dinky little thing. But this was the 1945 batting champion, the lady they used to call the female Ted Williams. Washed up.

"I've raised five kids," she struggles to explain. "I didn't play ball after I quit. I'd go to the park to play ball with the kids, but that wasn't the same. Maybe if I were playing in a regular league or something . . ."

Yeah, that's it. And working really, really hard at it. And playing with

the kind of grit and fierce determination she instilled in Casey and her other kids. And . . . Aw, who cares? Helen Callaghan, terror of the Vancouver sandlots and a standout in the only professional women's baseball league ever to play the man's game, discarded baseball for children at twenty-six. For nearly four decades she hardly ever thought about her playing days, much less talked about them. Now she'll talk about baseball, but warily. Baseball has her son.

It's the kind of folksy little story *People* magazine specializes in. Mom never said much about the old days, but it turns out that she used to be a ballplayer, a real slugger. During the Second World War she had played in a long-forgotten professional league for women. She gave birth to five children, and lo and behold, the fifth, Casey, became a ballplayer, too. Not only was Casey personable and lovable, but he looked like he might be pretty good stuff. He hit more than .300 in the first half of his rookie year with the Montreal Expos and finished up at .272. That was good enough for most people to pencil him in as the second baseman on their 1987 all-rookie team.

And get this: his dad didn't teach him to play ball. His mom did! And he uses a smaller bat than she used to. He was the first big-league player whose mother had been a professional player. The ingredients were all there, and on August 17, 1987, *People* came through: "This mother could hit," was the title, a harmless little double entendre. It was all about Casey and Helen, and it was very upbeat. Nothing about growing up poor in Vancouver. Nothing about raising five kids on a shoestring after the baseball cheques stopped coming and things started going wrong.

Helen St. Aubin is driving through the heat between Santa Barbara and Lampoc in her green, once-stylish 1979 Chevrolet Monte Carlo, which she thinks she'll get reupholstered. It is a great long boat of a car, the kind of car that can look shabby in the wrong hands. But with her at the wheel, it looks classy. She is bird-like, only five foot one, with darting brown eyes. And in an era in which it is no longer the fashion to call women girls, and at her age, when it would seem absurd to think of any woman as a girl, she remains girl-like. "That's right," she says. "Lots of people tell me that. When the boys were growing up they kind of treated me as their older sister. That's just me."

She was born Helen Callaghan in the Vancouver suburb of Mount Pleasant on March 13, 1923. She was the fourth of six children and her father, who had emigrated from Ireland and at one point had worked as a cowboy,

Helen stuck an Expos logo on the back of her Monte Carlo,
but her loyalty was wavering even before Casey was traded.
(Dan Turner)

had landed a job as a foreman at a manufacturing company. Just as the Depression hit, her mother was stricken with cancer.

"My father took care of her for over a year. He lost his job. I had a difficult time when my mother died. I had just started kindergarten. I remember us pulling the blinds, and it seemed like forever we were in mourning. My father loved kids, and he opened a little bicycle shop. But he didn't make much money at it, because people didn't have much money. We lost our home."

There were two diversions during the Depression: school and sports. "I always played with the boys, and so did my sisters. I was a quiet kid, and a tomboy. A feminine tomboy, but a tomboy. I used to play lacrosse. You know how tough lacrosse is to play? We used to have to fight like crazy, because we were fifteen, sixteen, and we played against older teams."

What about the rules of feminine deportment?

"They probably did apply, but we never paid any attention to them. That's just the way we were. We were from an athletic family, and there wasn't a lot of money. So we played."

When she was twenty she went with a Vancouver women's all-star softball team to a tournament in Detroit. It was 1943, and P.K. Wrigley, the chewing-gum magnate who owned the Chicago Cubs, had just set up a women's professional league. It was designed to keep morale up in case the major leagues were forced to shut down during the war. There were scouts at the Detroit tournament, looking for young women to play in the AAGPBL. "They just explained what was happening and asked whether we'd like to play for money. Well, I loved to play ball, and the thought of getting paid to play it really excited me. Plus I'd be independent. At that time you were expected to stay in the kitchen and raise kids. It wasn't that I didn't want to do that. But this meant I was going to do something else, too.

"I was going out with my husband-to-be [Robert Candaele] then. He was involved with his father in a taxi company in Vancouver. He never said, 'I don't want you to do it.' But it wouldn't have stopped me if he had. It was just too exciting. I went home and pleaded with my father to let me go. He didn't want me going all that way. But I just kept at him. I wore him down.

"The next thing I knew I was on a plane traveling all the way down to Pascagoula, Mississippi. It was an old army base. There were cockroaches everywhere, but we didn't care. Although quite a few Canadians would end up playing in the AAGPBL, most of the early sign-ups were from California. I was the little girl from Canada. Everybody looked at me like, 'Is *she* a ballplayer?' They didn't figure me for a ballplayer."

Helen St. Aubin isn't much for reminiscing: "I'm just not that nostalgic."

260

But driving through the heat in her big Monte Carlo, the memory of what those California girls didn't figure makes her stick out her tongue and laugh. "I was small and feminine, and a lot of them were pretty big and boisterous. But I wasn't intimidated by any of them."

Female ball teams had barnstormed as early as 1879, but Wrigley's AAGPBL was the first and last professional women's league. It began as a nonprofit operation, with local interests expected to match Wrigley's contribution of $22,500 for each team. The league lasted from 1943 to 1954, when the deadly glow of TV screens began to dot the land.

It featured teams from midsize midwest American cities—the Rockford Peaches, the South Bend Blue Sox, the Racine Belles, the Kenosha Comets, the Fort Wayne Daisies and the like—and usually played a regular-season schedule of about 135 games. Salaries ranged from $55 to $150 a week, at a time the average wage earner took home about $40 a week.

Women's baseball was a dicey concept even during the war, when women were being urged into factories to fill vacancies left by men serving overseas. Wrigley was determined to avoid any suggestion that his "girls" were either (a) butch or (b) easy. So he set up a charm school to make sure they presented themselves as "young ladies of the highest caliber." Not all the players were keen: "It was kind of hard," remembers catcher Pepper Paire Davis, "wearing high heels, with a charlie horse, carrying a book on top of your head, saying bounce the b-a-h-l." But a lot of the players came from rough backgrounds, weren't particularly mannered and appeciated all the tips they could get. One of the categories was how to attract the right kind of man.

Extremely attractive players, such as Mary (Bonnie) Baker, of Regina, Saskatchewan, were selected to adorn as many newspaper features as possible, and in later years appeared on TV shows such as *What's My Line?*

Sharon L. Roepke, a clinical psychologist from Flint, Michigan, has produced a series of AAGPBL baseball cards and a book on the league's history called *Diamond Gals*. She points out that the AAGPBL wasn't exactly bush league: "In 1948, one million fans came out to watch. The expanded ten-team league played a brand of baseball closely resembling the major leagues' dead-ball era, full of hit-and-run fast action plays."

Although the women wore short skirts and satin panties designed by Mrs. Wrigley, there was nothing namby-pamby about their play. Because they wore skirts they were constantly getting bruised, scraped and cut on the base paths: running and sliding were very much part of the league's style. "Hittin' the dirt in a skirt" was part of its lingo. "The sores on some of the girls' legs were terrible," St. Aubin remembers. "They used to make these big doughnuts, made out of tape wrapped around gauze. You'd just pull the doughnuts over your sores and go out and play."

Roepke tells of visiting Olive Little, now seventy-one, at her home in the tiny town of Poplar Point, fifty miles out of Winnipeg. Little, a gray-haired grandmother, gave Roepke a discourse on brushing back opponents:

"It kept them honest. One girl, in a tournament, intended not to be pushed back, and I hit her in the wrist. She was their catcher. I broke two bones in her wrist, and she went around in a cast all through that tournament. I bet she could've killed me." On another occasion Little took herself out of a game when she got carried away and hit her friend Dottie Hunter on the jaw. "This charmingly sweet grandmother," concludes an admiring Roepke, "was a dangerous pitcher."

The AAGPBL started as a slightly altered variety of softball, but within a few years had evolved into full-fledged baseball. Helen Callaghan signed on with the Minneapolis Millerettes in 1944, the last softball year, and hit .287 in the leadoff spot, with 112 stolen bases. Halfway through the season her older sister Marge, who had also been scouted in Detroit, showed up and signed on with the Millerettes. Marge, who still lives in Vancouver, had been reluctant to sign. "My father talked me into it. He wanted me to go down there and look after Helen." Although glad to see her sister, Helen wasn't taken with the motivation: "I figured I could take care of myself."

Although she liked fun, Helen was quieter than her sister and more aggressive on the ball field. Marge was comparatively easygoing. Dottie Collins, one of the league's dominant pitchers, was a friend of both Callaghan girls. She laughingly calls Helen "Queenie" for her indifference to both casual social chit chat and to keeping in touch with old acquaintances. "Marge is more outgoing. Helen is more reserved and quiet, very intense. Both of them were good fielders and both had good arms. Marge was a dandy little third baseman who could play second and was a competent hitter. But Helen was one of the best ballplayers in the league. She was little, but she used the biggest bat. She could hit and she was very fast. Her son Casey reminds me of her because he's such a hustler. When Helen got on the ball field she was there for a purpose, and she was very serious about it."

Not that there weren't light moments, even after the Millerettes folded in the middle of the Callaghans' first season and the team was forced to play full-time on the road under their new name, the Orphans. Helen didn't mind the hardship. "We were on the road all the time, living out of suit-cases, traveling on old buses. We'd sing and play cards. Some of the girls would gamble a bit. And we'd sleep.

"Often we'd play a doubleheader in 110-degree heat and travel to another town and just have time to shower and play another doubleheader. The first year we were with the Orphans, we arrived for a series in South Bend, Indiana, and it was so hot I went up to the hotel room and lay on the floor for an hour. I never did get used to the extreme heat.

"But the guys were fun. Our uniforms were way ahead of their time, and they used to watch us warm up and say things to us to try to get us to talk to them. Sometimes they'd come to our windows at the hotel rooms, just to see if they could get our attention or whatever. And we'd just hang out the window and throw things at them. Like bras, or whatever else. Yeah, it was fun."

The AAGPBL stressed pitching and defence, and Marge's .196 lifetime batting average was good enough to keep her in the league for eight years. Helen hit .299 with the Fort Wayne Daisies in 1945 to win the league batting championship. She stole ninety-two bases and led the league in hits, extra base hits and home runs. She was a star. "I looked feminine, but I played tough. I was real serious about it. Before the game I wouldn't talk to anyone. I wanted to be left alone. That was just my personality. I practiced as hard as I played. I've often said to Casey how important that is. Not all the girls were like that, certainly not. I had more pressure on me, I guess. Maybe because I was small, but I hate that word. It's not your size, it's what's inside that counts. Anyway, after the game started, play ball. That was it. Play ball."

In 1946, her last year as Helen Callaghan, she hit only .213. But she stole 114 bases, a career high. She married Robert Candaele and missed the 1947 season when her first son, Rick, was born. She came back to play for Fort Wayne in 1948, operating out of a revolutionary marriage concept: Robert spent part of his time driving a cab and part of his time taking care of the baby, at first in Vancouver and later in Kenosha, Wisconsin, where Helen played her last season in 1949.

She was only able to play half a season for Fort Wayne in 1948 because of a tubal pregnancy. "I was getting terrible pains that would shoot up and down my right side. I thought it was just a matter of female problems. But one time it was my turn at bat and I just couldn't go up. They took me into the clubhouse and they brought some doctor out of the stands, and he said, 'Aw, take a couple of aspirins and go home.'

Baseball excited her and she played it with skill and ferocity. But when the time came, there were more important things. (Helen Callaghan)

"Well, I took the couple of aspirins, but I just started pacing up and down, the pain was so intense. Later that night the registered nurse I was staying with got another doctor out of a card game, and he told her to take me to the hospital right away. It turned out there was a pregnancy in my tube. It had ruptured and I had all this contagious blood inside me. They couldn't get in touch with Robert, so they finally had to get my sister's permission to operate, because they said I would have been dead by morning if they didn't. I remember going back to the doctor six weeks later. I was cut from here to there, but it had healed and he said I could start to exercise again. And I remember saying to him, 'I've been doing that for quite a while now.' "

She still isn't sure whether she was traded to Kenosha because it was a team that needed players, or because Fort Wayne management figured she was finished. The latter proved to be pretty well true. "It wasn't fun any more. I finally figured out that baseball wasn't everything, and it was time to hang it up and get on with life. A lot of girls played for ten years. Not me. I got out, and I never looked back."

They went to Vancouver, but Robert was restless, and saw opportunity in the States. They moved briefly to Fort Wayne, but found the humidity overbearing. They moved to Lampoc, California, where there was an air-force base and Robert could apprentice as an electrician.

Helen Candaele bore five sons and wrapped them all in love. Rick teaches retarded children less than an hour's drive from Lampoc and is the defensive coordinator for a college football team in Santa Barbara. Rocky, the second-oldest, recently moved to Hawaii to sell real estate. Kelly, one of the twins, is a political organizer for Michael Dukakis in Los Angeles. Kerry, the other twin, teaches Russian history at a private school. And Casey plays ball.

Employment opportunities for electricians at the air-force base proved to be bust and boom, so Helen got a job at a local hospital, working her way up to her current position as an administrator. The way up was paved with the most menial work a hospital can offer. Meanwhile her husband was having serious problems with alcohol, which at times led to a stormy relationship with his family. He left in 1970, when Casey was nine.

Helen Candaele became Helen St. Aubin a couple of years later. For the first five or six years of her new marriage, says Ron St. Aubin, as he putters with some stonework he is adding to the front of their bungalow, she never even told him she had played baseball.

"When I came along she and Casey and I would knock the ball around out here in the front yard, and you could see she really handled the bat well. From what I hear she was always out here with her kids, from the time they were three and four and five. She was a different kind of mother. She loves kids, she'd do anything for her kids. But she didn't baby them, that's for damned sure. Casey would be out there playing football with the older kids, and he'd get knocked down and come to the front door, and she'd say, 'Get the hell out there and take your licking if you want to play.' And that's what he did."

Inside the house there are pictures of all the children, plus the grand-children. Almost a whole wall in the new living room they have added is taken up with photos of Casey. The other kids joke about it, she says, calling it "Casey's Wall."

Casey is the one who was in the house when times were the toughest, and there is obviously a special relationship because of that. She worries about him. She knows enough about baseball to assess his talents, which, while prodigious for normal human beings, are marginal in the major leagues. After a more-than-decent rookie season, he struggled at the plate early in the 1988 season, and was sent down to Triple A. He is fast, but not very fast. He is a good fielder, but his range is limited. To play regularly in the majors he would probably have to hit more than .300 consistently.

"Casey himself would say he's not blessed with all the talent in the world." She sighs. "He got there just from sheer determination. He gave his best all the time, and somebody noticed.

"When he was three or four years old he used to play football with his brothers. They'd get him outside and they'd pounce on him—they weren't too gentle. He'd come to the door after somebody had bounced off his head and want to come in, and I'd say, 'No, if you're going to play with the big guys, you're going to have to learn to take it.' And out he'd go. It wasn't a matter of my being cruel. I just wanted to tell him that nothing comes easy in life. I knew he was going to be small. It would mean he'd have to try harder. When he played quarterback later he could handle himself with the 250-pound linebackers."

She is unhappy with the Expos. They've sent her son down after he has tried so hard and done so much, traveling from town to town during the winter, doing public relations. But she has played pro. She knows the only professional imperative: put the best possible team on the field. No matter what.

"I really think that sports is so psychological, don't you? God, it's mind-boggling. It's not just the talent. You have to be psychologically strong, so it doesn't eat you up. When they sent him down it created all kinds of pressure, because even though he had such a great rookie year last year he knew they didn't have confidence in him, that they thought [Johnny] Paredes was the ballplayer and [Luis] Rivera was the ballplayer and he wasn't. He lost his confidence."

She hesitates, verging on blaming them for ruining him, but teetering on something else. "You know what? I don't know, maybe it's okay. Not okay for Casey, right now, maybe. Underneath all the joking and kidding around he does, Casey is very intense. He felt like he disappointed everybody. But mothers get a different perspective. He's been under pressure for so long, at A ball, at Double A, at Triple A. And sometimes it isn't always that great to be competitive all the time, to always be under pressure from yourself and everybody else to prove what you are.

"I remember that stress. And you know, I'm not sure that baseball is the whole world. You deal with disappointments in your life, sometimes. Whatever he decides will be okay."

When he used to come to the door she'd say no, and send him back outside. Now she isn't sure what she's saying. But it surely isn't no.

It is five weeks later: June 21, 1988. There are only three players in the clubhouse at Olympic Stadium: Casey Candaele is one of them. Candaele has been given a reprieve. He's been brought back to the big team. But after 116 at-bats, he is hitting .172. Yes, says Candaele, he would be glad to talk about his mother while he's putting on his uniform. Although the *People* magazine story has been told.

He laughs when you point out that she's lost her swing. "If it took her this long to lose her swing I think you've got to pat her on the back for that. I've lost mine in less than a year.

"She's a very complex person. She believed strongly in us learning for ourselves, but then she'd worry like crazy when we went out and did it. It was like she was saying: 'Go ahead, go for it! Gosh, I hope everything turns out all right.' It was never, 'You can't do something.' It was always, 'Do things on your own. But if you ever need help, I'll aways be here.'

"She's the one who kept everyone together when we went through some bad times. Being that young, I didn't understand anything that was going on around me. I mean you're sitting in the house and somebody knocks on the door and says, 'We're taking your car away.' And you say, 'Mom, why are they taking our car away? I thought it was ours.' And she says, 'Well, if you can't pay for it they take it back.'

"I remember walking to the store with her, and her pushing the cart home the whole way, and her working in the hospital from five in the morning until four in the afternoon, and coming home dead tired and run-down. She was a maid there, cleaning up most of the time, working for the minimum wage, when the other women were staying at home.

"She'd be so tired, and still she'd always have time for you. She'd go in there and cook you a big meal, and everything was always positive. There was never a negative thing coming out of her mouth during all the hard times, like, 'I can't handle this, I can't stand this anymore.' Instead it was, 'Everything's going to turn out okay if I work hard enough, everything's going to be fine.' That's just the way she was. She was funny. I remember many times just sitting there laughing so hard at her you thought you'd split a gut, laughing until you cried.

"If she's saying things would be okay if baseball doesn't work out, I think I know where she's coming from. She doesn't want anything bad to ever happen to her kids, where they're worried or going through mental turmoil, so she kind of goes a little too far and takes all of that stuff on herself. Which she shouldn't do, but she's just so strong with her kids and loves them so much that every little thing that hurts them hurts her twice as much.

"I just want to get myself in a stable enough position, I hope in baseball, to ask her what she wants for a change, and let her sit back and quit worrying and relax, and just let everything flow out of her and be happy. That's what keeps me battling and going out there every day and trying not to get down on myself. Although it's hard."

It is 3:20, forty minutes until batting practice. Out in the ballpark the orange dome is up, and everything echoes. Down the right-field line there is one yellow seat stuck in among the blue ones, one row from the fence, one seat over from the foul pole, just above the ninety-nine meter mark. The special seat represents two things: the shortest possible distance a home run can travel in this park, and the exact spot Casey Candaele hit the only one of his career.

Out on the bright green carpet Bryn Smith, the Expos' starter, is pitching softly to his six-year-old son, Cody. Cody and a chum run the bases, Smith feigns throws at them, and the boys shriek and double over with laughter. It is Smith's relief from the business of baseball. He has struggled through arm damage, contract disputes and waiting to find out if he will be traded. "The game has changed," he says. "It's like coming to work now."

We talk for awhile, then walk toward the clubhouse, where Rich Griffin, the Expos' publicist, is looking distraught. After several years in his job, Griffin still treats baseball as more than a business. "Casey Candaele and Herm Winningham have been sent out," he says. "Otis Nixon and Rex Hudler replace them on the roster."

In the locker room, Casey is nowhere to be seen. "You have to be psychologically strong," was what she said. "Just so it doesn't eat you up."

29

THE KARN BOYS

Beachville, Ontario
June 4, 1988

We have gathered to be silly. Beachville birds twitter their greetings to the baseballers assembled, recognizing us as brain mates. Blue skies, a few puffy clouds and gentle breezes have been ordered and delivered. Stately Beachville oaks and stately Beachville maples stretch and yawn in the warm sun. The panic over the possibility of rain has evaporated. Being silly on a muddy field, everyone agrees, would have been just plain silly.

We are here to celebrate baseball and, more particularly, Canada's connection to baseball. Granted, baseball has been over-celebrated in the 1980s. At best it is a game, at worst a business, and somewhere in between it has become a cult, attracting more worship than any game deserves. It was Branch Rickey who, nearing the end of his reign, picked up a baseball, pondered it as though it were Yorick's skull and mused: "This ball, this symbol, is it worth a man's life?"

In fairness, baseball hasn't traditionally been over-celebrated in Canada, other than the *Toronto Star*'s annual coverage of the Blue Jays' run for the pennant. In fact it's always been thought a bit awkward to get too nationalistic about Canadian baseball. It's been felt that it couldn't be done with a straight face. Canadian professional teams have been mostly made up of Americans. And as far as Canadians have been concerned, once you got by Fergie Jenkins you were on a very slippery slope. It is not that Goody Rosen, Ron Taylor and Oscar Judd have proven to be lesser men than Babe Ruth, Ted Williams and Hank Aaron. It isn't that at all. And it certainly isn't that they're less *interesting* men. Goodness, no.

It's that baseball achievements tend to be measured in numbers, in the old-fashioned way women's beauty used to be measured in numbers. To be worthy of winning a beauty pageant, a woman either had to be 36-24-36 or have three uncles among the judges. A baseball player worthy of

reverence has always had to hit .300 regularly or win in the neighborhood of twenty games a year.

Never mind. In the early '80s, brave souls gathered around a pot of maple-leaf soup, looked the world in the eye and declared that contributions to Canadian baseball should be celebrated, no matter what the numbers were. Even if it looked a little silly sometimes. That didn't matter as long as it felt good, and everybody agreed that it did. You can feel really fine with someone who isn't 36-24-36, and when you look at it that way we may be talking about the most important emancipation movement in baseball since Jackie Robinson. Or at the very least since free agentry. Freedom from numbers.

So keeping the nobility of the thing in mind, we are here in Beachville to celebrate the induction of twenty-six players into the Canadian Baseball Hall of Fame. Of the twenty-six, three are still alive. They are Reno Bertoia, Ted Bowsfield and Ron Piche. Bertoia batted .244 during an eight-year career. Despite the Hall's repeated assertions that Bowsfield recorded a career mark of 39-39 while pitching with polio, he finished at 37-39 without polio. Mind you, he did have a nasty pain in his arm much of the time. And Piche, who had an exceptional 110-60 record in the minor leagues, was 10-16 with Milwaukee, California and St. Louis during fragments of six years in the majors. In beauty-pageant terms, that's kind of 27-30-27.

But we're talking emancipation. Climb aboard the freedom train.

This year's Hall of Fame festivities are taking place in Beachville and neighboring Ingersoll because (a) Beachville played host to the world's first recorded game of baseball 150 years ago, and (b) Beachville, with only 910 residents, doesn't have the arena and hotel facilities needed for a spectacular of this kind, which is where Ingersoll comes into play. Ingersoll, pop. 8,500, is the Cheese Capital of Canada and has an arena. It also has the Elm Hurst Inn, which is large enough to cope with eighty Reno Bertoia disciples from Windsor and elegant enough to satisfy the Toronto crowd.

Beachville, the Lime Capital of Canada, has limestone quarries, an active community association and a playground at St. Anthony's school large enough to reenact the 1838 game. The community association has been working flat out on the project since Christmas. For instance Al Stacey, who is in glass-chip sales, says, "The phone hasn't stopped ringing for the last three months from eight-thirty in the morning until midnight." It is

The Leatherstockings said they were in Beachville for fun and sportsmanship, but there was perfidy in the air. (Michael Rafelson)

ringing for his wife, Norma, who besides being the mother of three young children is handling the public relations for the event.

The game reenactment will feature a local team, with no special qualification other than enthusiasm, and a visiting team from Cooperstown, New York, home of the other Baseball Hall of Fame. The visiting club is known as the Leatherstockings. They have been around. The home team will be called the Cornhuskers. They have not. The game will be played on Saturday afternoon, followed by induction ceremonies at the Ingersoll arena in the evening. Besides Bowsfield, Bertoia and Piche, the late Jeff Heath and the late Bill Phillips will be inducted.

Bill Phillips was the first Canadian ever to play major-league baseball. Born in St. John, New Brunswick, he hit .266 during ten seasons between 1879 and 1888, and was considered a fine-fielding first baseman.

Jeff Heath was a standout ballplayer between 1936 and 1949, an outfielder who averaged .293 over his career with 102 triples and 194 home runs. In his first full year with the Cleveland Indians he hit .343 with 112 RBIs and led the American League in triples. He finished second to Jimmy Foxx in the batting race. He hit .340 in 1941 and started in the American League All-Star outfield with Joe DiMaggio and Ted Williams. That year he hit the rare "twenties cycle": 20 or more doubles (32), 20 or more triples (20) and 20 or more homers (24). In 1943 he batted .340, with 199 hits, 24 home runs and 123 RBIs. Heath hit more than .300 seven times and might have ended up in Cooperstown, had he not ruined his career with a needless slide into home that broke his ankle on the eve of the 1948 World Series.

Before emancipation, it would have been considered stretching it to call Heath a Canadian. His parents emigrated from England and he was born in Fort William, Ontario, where he lived the first year and a bit of his life. The family then moved to Victoria, British Columbia, and finally to Seattle, Washington, when he was four. Most of his skills, of course, had been deeply embedded by that time, and it remained only for Seattle baseball folk to polish them lightly over the next seventeen years to get him ready for the major leagues.

The Canadian Hall's selection criteria usually limit the number of inductions in a year to five, but because of the 150th anniversary, this year's group has been expanded slightly, to twenty-six.

On April 26, 1886, Dr. Adam E. Ford, a physician who had grown up in Beachville and emigrated to Denver, Colorado, wrote a letter to *Sporting Life* magazine detailing a baseball-like game that had been played in his hometown on June 4, 1838. Plumbing his boyhood memories, Ford gave details of the playing rules and the names of many of the players who had taken the field.

The year 1838 is noteworthy. Mythology once had it that baseball was invented in Cooperstown, New York, by Abner Doubleday in 1839. The Doubleday "immaculate conception" theory has long been discredited: forms of baseball were played in North America well before the Beachville-Cooperstown period. In fact in Ford's letter he refers to "Old Ned" Dolson and Silas Williams, two of the older "gray-headed" players on the field. Both men, says Ford, insisted upon certain rules for the game "for it was the way they used to play it when they were boys."

Ford's gift to history was certainly not the provision of evidence of the first game ever played. Rather it was the first *record* of a game, providing the details of a match between Beachville and the Zorras, a club combining players from the townships of Zorra and North Oxford. The Hall admissions committee decided that players Ford recalled in his letter should be 1988 inductees. Those to be honored for joining in the fun that day in 1838:

Geo. Burdick
Reuben Martin
Adam Karn
Peter Karn
Wm. Hutchinson
I. Van Alstine
"Old Ned" Dolson
Nathaniel McNames
Abel Williams
John Williams
Harry Karn
Daniel Karn
William Ford
William Dodge
Neil McTaggart
Henry Cruttendon
Gordon Cook
Henry Taylor
James Piper
Almon Burch
Wm. Harrington

The ball, "made of double and twisted woolen yarn . . . and covered with good, honest calf skin," was sewed by Edward McNames, a Beachville shoemaker. The game was played on June 4, the birthday of George III, the British monarch who had prompted the American revolution. For the all-American game to have been played in Canada in celebration of George III's birthday the year before the historic Cooperstown game is the kind of thing that occasionally makes the mouse-and-elephant relationship worthwhile. You'll remember that 1838 was the year after the Rebellion of 1837 had been crushed by the government of Upper Canada. The holiday was used for drilling volunteers and playing a little ball.

All of which might leave a late twentieth-century Canadian bored to tears, ready to close this book and wander over to the TV to catch the Jays or Expos game. Well, suit yourself. But if you had been here on June 4, 1988, or better yet, June 4, 1838, you would realize why it wasn't silly to induct the Karn boys and their playmates into the Canadian Baseball Hall of Fame. For this is the simple truth: they played a better brand of ball.

It was all celebrities and townsfolk and chip wagons at the beginning of the 1988 replay, and all townsfolk and chip wagons at the end. Bertoia, Piche, Bowsfield and the Heath women — wife Althea, daughters Peggy and Patricia — arrived by horse and carriage organized by Ye Olde Museum of Beachville. But they had speeches to prepare and tuxedos and fancy dresses to put on, and were only able to catch the early going.

The game was not replayed in the "nice, smooth pasture field" Dr. Ford had described. Shirley Riddick, the local historian, explained that some fool had built houses there about a hundred years ago, not realizing there would be an anniversary this year. But the school playground was smooth enough.

The Leatherstockings were resplendent in red tops and sashes around the waist, the Cornhuskers less flamboyant in their powder blue. The crowd of several hundred people stretched out along what would have been the first and third baselines but weren't, because in 1838, at least in Beachville, there were five "byes" instead of four bases, laid out in a square instead of a diamond. This is not important, except for one thing: getting to first bye was a piece of cake, because it was only eighteen feet away, off to the right. After than it was a little harder working your way around the byes. It was sixty-one and a half feet to get to second, sixty-three feet to third, another sixty-three feet to fourth, and forty-five feet coming home. But, unless the ball you hit with your cedar stick was caught on the fly or the first bounce, you were almost certain to get to first.

Which is where the fun began. Because baserunning was both alarming and exhilarating. Alarming because if you were caught off a bye you could

Dr. Adam Ford transcribed his memories of a Beachville ball-game, and the Karn Boys were history. (Ye Olde Museum of Beachville, Ontario)

be "plugged" by a fielder: hit with the ball, put out. Exhilarating because *you did not have to follow a straight path to the next base.* If you were in danger of getting plugged you could take off into the outfield, and while there was a good chance that the fielders would be deft enough to plug you before you got back in, other runners could advance while you were out there.

This game was made for Tim Raines. Tim Raines loves baseball well enough, but if you talk to him in an unguarded moment he will lament that he didn't get to play professional football, because of the joy of open field running: the fox scampering frantically to avoid the hounds.

The Leatherstockings and the Cornhuskers played a double-header. The first game is hardly worth mentioning because of the perfidity of Leatherstocking field captain William (Old Clothes) Ault. Ault conceded that his Cooperstown side had never played in circumstances of such rapt attention in the two years of its existence. Most often the Leatherstockings have been relegated to performing between minor-league games for a few perfunctory minutes, giving people in the stands a chance to burp and go to the concession booths.

At first Ault seemed like he might rise to the appreciative crowd and play in a way that would leave a good taste for his game, particularly since he billed himself as "the greatest town ball player of the twentieth century, bar none." In truth, he did entertain for a while. He promised to throw his "bamboozle ball" with a curse on it and a "nothing ball" to bore the batters into submission.

But after the visitors had won the first encounter 21-0 — the kind of score bound to dampen the enthusiasm of the best of fans—it was discovered that Ault had been using a mushy calfskin ball when he was throwing, and had provided the Cornstalker thrower, Bill Weatherstone, with a much firmer calfskin ball. The Leatherstockings hit the hard ball for distance, and the Cornhuskers hit the soft ball for porridge.

Granted, the visitors also proved to be more competent fielders.But the treachery involved in the win made a person wonder. How much conniving has been involved in leaving the impression that Babe Ruth and Ted Williams and Walter Johnson were born in the United States? Once you see the mushy-ball trick, you have to question whether some of these stalwarts weren't born a little north of where American folks say they were, like Moose Jaw, for instance, with all records falsified and any chance of putting them into their rightful place in the Canadian Hall thieved away.

The second game was closer: 12-10 for the Leatherstockings in a seemingly honest contest. The crowd must be credited for never turning against the home team, no matter how unflattering the score or how clumsy the play. But the crowd had a palliative: no matter who was winning, Dr. Ford's game was fun. To be sure there were drawbacks. Howard (Tumbler) Deline left his feet to make a spectacular bare-handed catch (bare-handed being the only kind), but fell on his belly as part of the spectacle. So the catch didn't count, because 150 years ago you had to keep your feet for a catch to count. Still, the sound of Gary (Cass) Cassidy getting plugged at first was something to savor, because you knew the embarrassment would leave hardly a bruise.

And that young Bruce (The Kid) Hainey was a sight, running, grinning and free, in the outfield, twisting and dodging while Rodney (Cap Catch) Cornish scored. And Michael (Rabbit) DeGraff, stealing the top hat off the head of Tom Heitz, the Cooperstown librarian, and away he went — you could see why they call him Rabbit.

If you sat along the fourth baseline you could watch Joe Jones of Ingersoll, who works at the Scott's Restaurant on the 401, leading the clapping for the home team. If you listened closely you could hear him say this to a friend: "It looks like they had more fun in those days, don't you think?" And the friend, watching Rabbit run, said yes, it certainly did.

The evening formalities were a great success. Pot roast, baked potatoes and other things Toronto people hadn't eaten for years were served by Beachville ladies to a packed arena. Not a ticket went unsold.

The treat of the evening, for the lucky, was getting a chance to talk to Althea Heath and her daughters Peggy and Patricia. Geoff Heath died of a heart attack in 1975, but thirteen years has not dimmed their affection for him. It was Althea, a high-school junior in Yakima, Washington, who stole Heath away from his northern homeland when he was playing in the Northwest League. Until then, she says, he remained a loyal British subject, despite growing up in Seattle. But after they got married and Peggy was born, he took out U.S. citizenship.

"Still," she says, "he was proud of being born in Canada. He used to go up to Oliver, British Columbia, and help with baseball camps there. He loved to go up. One time he made a trip back on the Canadian Pacific to Fort William, to see his birthplace. He took movies all the way and met people who had known his parents."

The wife and the daughters cherish the memory of what Heath was, both as a ballplayer and as a man who told good jokes and gave good speeches and treated his family like gold. But Peggy didn't always like the ballplayer part. "I was just a tiny girl, going around from stadium to stadium and eating popcorn. Bob Feller was nothing to me. And I remember Dad loved to talk to the man on the street. He would stop and talk and pat them on the back and be very cordial. Well, we were little, and that was very frustrating to us, because we wanted to go on to a movie, or dinner, or whatever. It was only when we got older that we realized he was something special, and we had to share him."

Althea Heath has been brought in by the Canadian Hall of Fame all the way from Clovis, California, to accept Geoff Heath's award, and she is not about to dissolve in tears and ruin the ceremony. "She knows it's her responsibility," says Peggy. "But she's scared stiff." And when the presentation comes, Althea Heath is brave. She takes the stage in her pretty green dress and tells the crowd that Canadians know how to put on a party, and the Beachvillers love her for it. She says how proud she and her daughters are of Geoff. "I'm just sorry Geoff couldn't be here. He would have been so proud." There are tears in her eyes, but she doesn't break down. And right then everyone knew how proud he would have been of her.

There are other moments, some emotional, some funny. Ted Bowsfield says how especially rewarding it is that his membership in the Hall was announced while both his mother and father were still living. His mother, Queen, is very ill and can't be at the ceremony. His father, Frank, died on May fourth. "The one thing he knew, even in his waning days, was that I was going to be inducted into the Canadian Baseball Hall of Fame. And he was very proud."

Ron Piche makes fun of a telegram sent from his employers, the Montreal Expos, citing his place in history as the first French-Canadian coach in the history of major-league baseball, which he became in 1976. "Sure I was the first French-Canadian coach. And at the end of the 1976 season I was the last French-Canadian coach. We lost about 107 ball games that year, and John McHale blamed me."

Reno Bertoia tells a joke for his Windsor entourage, which is well populated with fellow Italians. He says that when the Pope came to Detroit and floated down the river on a barge, the Polish community in Windsor rented the Ambassador Bridge, which passes over the river. Not to be outdone, said Bertoia, the Italians rented the Windsor tunnel. (Get it? The tunnel runs *under* the river.) The whole arena liked the joke, and liked it even more when Bertoia said that not many history teachers, like himself, could say that they belonged to the same organization as the late prime minister, Lester B. Pearson, another Hall of Famer.

Some of it was corny, some of it was sad, and of course—of course—it was silly. But Chris Karn liked it. Chris, who is a baby-faced twenty-six, a machinist in Woodstock, sported some sun on his face from watching the day's activities at the playing field. He had a particular interest: four Karns, all his forefathers, played in the 1838 match, Adam and Peter on one side, Daniel and Harry on the other.

On Sunday many of the Toronto people departed, but a number of others stayed to watch another calf-ball game between people from the Beachville and Zorra township area. Young Karn played for Beachville, which lost something like 23-17.

Karn popped up the first time up: they got him on the hop. Later he hit a dumper into center field, but somebody plugged him coming home. "It doesn't hurt at all. There's nothing to it. It was fun.

"You know, it's a lot more action-packed than the game is today. And all the time, during the game, I kept thinking back to what it must have been like then, with all the trees, and just a few guys gathering around to play."

Gathering to be silly: just like us.

FINAL POSTSCRIPT

—*Casey Candaele* was traded to Houston in July for Mark Bailey, a minor league catcher hitting .172. Candaele hit .170 with the Astros.

—*Doug Frobel* signed with the Expos again, who sent him to the Mexican League. Transferred to Jacksonville Double A in July, he hit .216 with three homers. He went to Triple A at Indianapolis late in the season, batting .176 in eight games.

—*Larry Walker* was touted to play with the Expos in 1988, but tore the cartilage in his knee during winter ball and sat out the 1988 season.

—*Andy Lawrence* played with Jacksonville again until June 30, but hit only .242 with three home runs in 45 games. He was unconditionally released.

—*Scott Mann* was demoted to Class A, Rockford. After a poor start he was transferred to West Palm Beach, where he hit .256 with a homer before being sold to the Cardinals.

—*Queen Bowsfield's* cancer forced her out of the family home in early September. She entered Penticton General Hospital, where she died 16 October, 1988.

—*Rob Ducey* struggled through early 1988 at Syracuse, but he moved up to the Jays in early August and averaged .315 in 54 at-bats.

—*Denis Boucher* made an impressive debut with the Myrtle Beach Blue Jays. He was 13-12 with a 2.84 ERA, striking out 169 batters in 197 innings, giving up only 161 hits and 63 walks.

— *Fergie Jenkins* sold his farm in Blenheim and took a job as a minor league pitching instructor with the Texas Rangers.

— *Terry Puhl* played more than expected with the Astros. He hit .303 in 234 at-bats, with 22 stolen bases in 25 attempts.

— *The Canadian Olympic Team* was eliminated early in Seoul, but not before beating the Americans, the eventual winners.

—*John Hiller's* aching leg proved to be a severe circulatory problem, and forced him out of coaching. Doctors were considering amputation in October.

—*Bill Lee* left the Moncton Mets following a fight with his manager in late 1987. In 1988 the Sydney Sooners flew him in for weekend games. The team went into a prolonged losing streak when its catcher ran down a black cat with the team van.

DAVE STIEB
Dave Stieb
BLUE JAYS

Reno Bertoia

3rd BASE

AAGBL

OLIVE LITTLE

FLEER

DAVE SHIPANOFF
PITCHER

PITCHER   BILL ATKINSON

William Atkinson

EXPOS

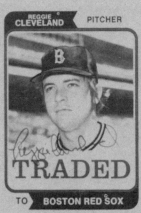

PIRATES

Topps

★★★ 1987 ★★★
ALL-STAR

Larry Walker OF
Jacksonville

RON
TAYLOR

PITCHER
METS

GLEN GORBOUS
Buffalo PHILADELPHIA PHILLIES

REGGIE
CLEVELAND   PITCHER

TRADED

TO   BOSTON RED SOX

AAGBL

PETE WARD • 3B

Pete Ward

WHITE SOX

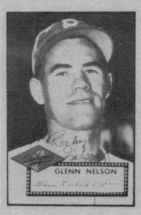

GLENN NELSON

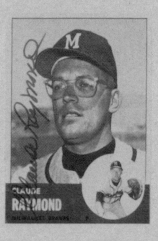

CLAUDE
RAYMOND
MILWAUKEE BRAVES

ROB DUCEY
Ventura OF

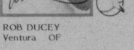

DICK FOWLER
Dick Fowler